# Ronald Wright - Sir Gay

Ronald Wright was born in Hertfordshire, England in 1928. A spiritualist writer, gay magazine illustrator, celebrity portrait artist, author, artist's model and psychic medium, Ronald Wright's life has been filled with strange encounters and extraordinary experiences. Seduced by the sparkle of cinema's entertainers the young Ronald Wright was drawn to London's West End in the early 1950's. With youthful determination Wright found ways to meet the stars he idolized, and more importantly stumbled upon the secret world of London's homosexual scene. First gaining a reputation drawing the likeness of 'Theatreland' stars like Marlene Dietrich, Mae West and Vivien Leigh, Wright eventually turned his graphic skills to the burgeoning 'Physique' and 'Men's Interest' magazine industry. Wright's artwork featured in many of the internationally renowned publications including Fizeek, Adonis, Sir Gay, Male Classics, Modern Man and Body Beautiful. Imprisoned for being gay in 1959, he was released a year later and began a successful career as artist model, most notably posing as 'the body' of Rudolf Nureyev for a Madam Tussaud's waxwork. Wright himself became entertainer, model and muse, performing at private parties and clubs throughout the 1960's. The 1970's and 80's saw Wright's interest in the spiritual world taking centre stage. After a visitation from 'The Spirit of Light' during a séance in Belgrave Square, he became a man with a mission to channel, write and distribute the message of Hafed Prince of Persia, leader of the legendary 'Three Magi' of biblical fame. He also became a well-known healer. These are Ronald Wright's memoirs of a very unconventional life, which may shock many even in today's more enlightened times.

D1742344

# RONALD WRIGHT

# SIR GAY

### An Autobiography

To Leon —
With all best wishes.

Ronald Wright

Revelation Press

Published in 2012 by Revelation Press.

Cover portrait by David Edwards for OUT THERE magazine
Design / Production by www.permafrost.org.uk


ISBN 978 1478 1787 29

**www.ronaldwright.co.uk**

# RONALD WRIGHT - SIR GAY

## CONTENTS

# Introduction

How do you condense more than eighty years of memories and experiences into a book of a few hundred pages? The simple answer is that you cannot, especially if your life has been as eventful as my own. In the early stages of writing this book I made the mistake or trying to include literally everything. But I soon realised that, if I was to avoid producing a volume which resembled the ENCYCLOPAEDIA BRITANNICA in size, then it was not so much what I put into the book that mattered, as what I left out. Something people invariably ask when aware that you are writing your life story, is 'Why?' A good question. I cannot of course speak for others, but personally I had several reasons. First I wanted to write not so much about myself, as about the fascinating variety of characters I have been fortunate to encounter from all walks of life and from a wide range of professions. Just what makes people tick has never ceased to intrigue me.

Secondly I wanted to expose so much of the hypocrisy and intolerance that exists in our society. All my life I have had strong inclination to stand up for oppressed minorities, be they sexual, racial, or religious. It has been this overwhelming concern for humanity in general which has driven me on to seek knowledge beyond the confines of this material planet to gain an awareness of the spiritual reality which unfortunately all too few posses or are even conscious of.

No doubt some readers will wonder why I have included a number of rather raw sexual descriptions in the book. I would point out that sex plays a very important part in the lives or most people, and it certainly was no exception in my own. Indeed it would not be possible for readers to form a proper impression of the environment in which I lived and worked for many years, had I hidden the facts.

At the age of eighty-four I have seen enormous changes take place in the life of the nation since the 1930s. In those days everyone was much more nationalistic, and the images of 'Britannia' and 'John Bull' were much more in evidence. Britain had the largest Empire the world had ever seen. The largest and most powerful navy, and London was the largest city and port in the world. King George V and Queen Mary were on the throne. Horse-drawn vans and carts were a common sight on our streets, delivering bread, milk, coal, to peoples' homes, and beer to public houses. There were few cars to be seen outside the big towns, and trams were the most popular transport in London. There were 240 pennies to £1 sterling, and you could buy an ice cream cornet or a bar of Nestle's chocolate for just one penny. Farthings were still in circulation- 960 to £1. You could buy a two-piece suit for fifty shillings (£2.50), and an Austen car cost £100. A Ford cost £107. You could also buy a two-bedroomed house for £100, but few people could afford such luxuries. The average wage for a workman being about £2.50 a week. My first wage at the age of 14 was £1.50 (thirty shillings). The old age pension in those days was ten shillings a week (50 pence in today's money). As a child I was only allowed one Christmas present and it had to cost no more than a half-crown (12.5 pence today).

Only the wealthy had bathrooms and indoor toilets. Most people had to make do with a tin bath in front of the fire once a week and a bucket (pail) for a toilet in a shed at the bottom of the garden. In the countryside, where there were no main services, people collected rainwater in barrels to wash in, and pumped water to drink. Food was cooked on open coal fires, and lighting was supplied by oil lamps or candles. There was no street lighting. There was so little crime, most people did not bother to lock their doors at night. In most cases no-one had anything worth stealing anyway Television did not exist. Radios were large and powered by 120 volt batteries and acid accumulators which had to be regularly replaced or recharged. My grandparents only had a crystal set, or 'Cat's Whisker' as it was known. This could only be listened to with a pair of earphones. The public's main entertainment was sports of all kinds, and black and white movies. Every small town had at least one cinema, and the larger towns also had music halls with live performers.

By far the biggest change I have seen however, has been the increase in population. When I was at school the population of England was 36 million. Today I understand it is over 50 million. What an enormous increase in my lifetime. As in my childhood, the country is again facing an economic crisis and resulting poverty. However there is still a long way to go before we can say things have really gone full-circle, and on the whole people still have a better standard of living than we did when I was a child in the 1930s.

At some time in all our lives we ask the questions, 'What IS the purpose of life? What ARE we all doing here?', and over the years I have discovered the answers. I only hope they will give YOU food for thought.

Ronald Wright, 2012

# The Transfiguration Medium

Conscripted into the army for two years National Service at the age of eighteen, I was thankful when my spell in the services drew to a close. Not that I really had much to complain about for, after the initial six weeks basic training everyone was obliged to undergo, I had been drafted to a particularly cushy unit - The Royal Army Corps in Manchester. Nevertheless I still couldn't escape the feeling that these two compulsory years of service had been an awful intrusion and a complete waste of valuable time, despite the fact that I had done very little with my life so far. Leaving school in 1942 at the age of fourteen I had simply spent the next four years in a drawing office. But I was young and filled with the zest of youth and eager to achieve something, although as yet I knew not what.

Now with just a couple of months to go before I was due to be demobbed, I was suddenly invited to participate in an experience that would be so amazing, so dramatic, the memory of it would remain with me for the rest of my life, although at the time I was too young to appreciate the opportunities and possibilities it presented me with.

It all began one afternoon at the pay office when I was approached by a fellow serviceman in the canteen, enquiring whether or not I would like to attend a seance. Although he and I had frequently discussed a great variety or subjects, Spiritualism had never been one of them, and it was something I knew little about. However, the lad explained that he was trying to organise a party of eight interested people for a visit to a well-known medium the following Friday night, would I like to go? Noting my hesitation - although the medium only charged half-a-crown per person, he remarked, 'You don't have to decide right away. Think it over and give me your answer tomorrow'.

Well I did, and although at first I felt inclined to turn down the offer - a fear of the unknown I suppose - the more I considered it the more I felt I should take advantage or this opportunity, since I might never have the chance again. Gordon was delighted next day when I told him I would go, for now he had the full quota of people required.

Having all assembled outside the pay office building the following Friday night, our party of eight boarded a tram and headed for one of the city's outer suburbs where the medium lived. To my surprise Gordon and I were the only two service personnel, the rest or the group consisting of his landlady and her daughter, plus four of her neighbours and friends.

I also discovered that apart from Gordon and one other person, all of whom were total strangers to me, none had ever attended a séance previously.

Arriving at the medium's small but attractive semi-detached house, Gordon rang the doorbell and we were greeted by a middle-aged woman wearing a simple black dress, who gave us a warm smile and bade us enter.

Once in the hall we were invited to follow the lady upstairs and into what I suppose was the largest bedroom in the house. Here we were told we could deposit our hats and coats on the big double bed if we so wished.

'That's a nice golliwog' Gordon suddenly remarked to the medium, indicating the black rag doll propped up against the headboard or the bed.

'Yes, isn't it', she agreed. 'It was a gift to Mimi from one of my regular clients.'

Turning to Gordon I whispered, 'Who is Mimi - funny name for an English child.'

'Mimi is a spirit child,' Gordon replied in hushed tones, adding, 'She is one of the medium's helpers.' At the thought of a ghost coming to play with a golliwog I started to giggle and Gordon dug me in the ribs, whispering, 'You must not laugh, she will be offended.' I tried hard to look serious, but still could not help wondering just what kind of mad house I had come to.

We left the bedroom and followed the medium across the landing and into a small room at the back of the house. Immediately we entered this I began to feel most uncomfortable, for the room had no window and the walls, ceiling, and the woodwork had all been painted black. There was even a heavy black curtain to draw across the door once it had been closed so that light could not penetrate around the edges of the door.

The furniture of the room consisted or eight chairs arranged in two rows of four, facing a ninth which was placed behind a small table on which stood what I at first mistakenly thought was a fortune-teller's crystal ball, but which I later discovered was merely a powerful electric light, used when the medium was in trance.

Once we were all assembled in the room, the door closed, and the curtain drawn, the medium requested we be seated. I made certain I was in the back row - as far away from her as possible, although in a room as tiny as this one I was in fact no more than six or seven feet distant from her. Enquiring how many of us had ever attended a materialisation before (for that is what this séance turned out to be), the medium turned her attention to me and remarked that I was emitting very strong waves of psychic power. She also asked if I was aware that I had a Chinese guide, adding that if I was lucky I might possibly meet him that night. The thought quite terrified me, and more than ever I wished that I had not come.

Addressing herself to the whole group, the medium proceeded to explain that she used the services of two spirit guides to make contact with those on 'the other side', one being a little negro girl called Mimi, the other a North American Indian whose name I have since forgotten, but for the purposes of this book I will refer to as Flying Cloud.

Now that we were all ready to start, the medium seated herself behind the small table. The ceiling light was extinguished but instantly replaced by the one on the table. Immediately I was to appreciate just why the medium had chosen to wear a black dress, and the whole room decorated in the same colour, for the effect was quite stunning - a sea of inky darkness in which only the brilliantly lit face of the medium was visible. It was so dark that I could not even see Gordon seated beside me, and pressed closer to him just to make sure he WAS still there. Once more I regretted coming, but it was too late now.

For some minutes the medium simply sat there with her eyes closed, then suddenly she asked, 'Mimi, Flying Cloud, are you there?'. Instantly a childish peel of laughter burst upon the room, and a small girl's voice answered, 'Yes I'm here'. I was absolutely shattered, and had to pinch myself to make sure I was awake and not imagining the whole thing.

Moments later I got the impression that my spectacles were misting up, so took them off and wiped them on my handkerchief. When I put them on again I was to find the medium was looking mistier than ever. Thinking that perhaps someone in the front row must be smoking, although I could not smell tobacco, I whispered to Gordon for confirmation that he too could see the smoke, as I had begun to wonder if I was experiencing some kind of illusion.

Gordon whispered back that what I could see was 'ectoplasm', a substance spirits draw from the body of the medium in order to materialise. Slowly it obscured the whole face of the medium, then just as suddenly as it had made its appearance, so it began to dissolve, and there to my utter astonishment, instead of medium's face, was clearly visible the face of a little black girl. Not wispy or semi-transparent as one would expect a ghost to be, but as solid as the medium's face had looked only moments before. Mimi then began to relate a few facts about her earthly life and I became aware that the feelings of fear, which I had earlier experienced, had now been replaced by one of utter peace and well-being. Mimi's little introduction over, she declared that Flying Cloud would now have a few words with us. Again the 'smoke' appeared and, after blanketing out Mimi's face for a few moments, it dissolved to reveal the rugged weather-beaten features of the Red Indian, complete with huge feathered headdress, which gave the appearance of being illuminated from behind.

Quite fearsome in appearance, and speaking in a booming voice which rocked the room, he announced that he and Mimi were now ready to assist the various spirits of our various friends and relations, who were gathered around waiting to speak to us.

The spirit of an old man, father of a lady in the front row was the next to materialise. She recognised him immediately and talked with considerable emotion since apparently he had only died recently.

When all four people in the front row had each seen one or more of their friends and relations, it was the turn of those seated at the back. As my own turn drew nearer, so my feeling of uneasiness temporarily returned.

At last, when only Gordon and myself were left, Mimi announced that a young airman named Brian wished to speak to Gordon. His response was that he knew of no airman of that name, whereupon Mimi asked, 'Is it not true that you once lived in Bournemouth when you were a little boy? Don't you remember Brian the boy who lived next door?'

Suddenly Gordon realised just who she was talking about. Of course he remembered Brian. This established, Mimi went on to explain that in the intervening years since they had last seen each other, Brian had served in the Royal Air Force and had been killed in a raid over Germany during the war - he was a few years older than Gordon.

Another swirling veil of ectoplasm, and a few moments later we were all gazing at the clean-cut features of an attractive young man wearing a Royal Air Force hat, and in no time at all the two of them were chatting away and laughing about their boyhood escapades in the same way two living people might. I say 'living' but it was perfectly clear that this young man most certainly WASN'T 'dead'.

At last there came the moment I had been dreading when Flying Cloud appeared and said in his deep booming voice, 'Young man sitting on end seat of back row, I have a lady here who wishes to speak with you'. Dumbfounded, I tingled with a strange kind of excitement. The lady in question turned out to be my aunt Elsie, father's youngest sister who had been killed by a land-mine in Hertford during the war.

When Elsie's face appeared, although I was to recognise that it WAS her, I could not help feeling that something was different about her appearance. Perhaps noting my puzzled expression, Elsie smiled and said, 'I see you can't quite decide what is different about me now? Isn't it my eyes?'. Yes, of course that was it. Elsie had been born with a lazy eye, but now both eyes appeared to be quite normal. Elsie then went on to explain, 'No matter what defect we may suffer on earth, be it blindness, lameness etc., when we pass on to spirit we are made whole, and when next you go home Ron, I want you to tell your father this. He will understand why.' Then Elsie went on to tell me something which, although it made no sense to me at the time, later when I repeated it to my father was significant enough to convince him that I really HAD spoken to his sister, for it had been a secret known only to the two of them and not another living soul.

Father also explained the reason Elsie was so eager for him to know that both her eyes were now normal, saying that when he had pulled her from the ruins of her home on the night she had died, one of her eyes - the lazy one - had been knocked completely out of her head, and poor father had been having nightmares about it ever since. The news that she had now regained her eye, set his tormented mind at rest.

Next Mimi appeared and asked if I would like to see my grandfather? He had died in the same air-raid as Elsie. Once again the temporary veil of ectoplasm, and then we were all gazing at my

8

grandfather. He looked just as I always remembered him - big walrus moustache, and wearing the flat cloth cap that always seemed to be a permanent fixture on his head, indoors or out.

'Hello, Granddad', I blurted out. But to my surprise there was no response, and after only a few moments more he was to disappear and be replaced by Flying Cloud.

He apologised for the fact that grandfather had been unable to speak to me and explained, 'You must realise that not only has this been YOUR first experience of this kind of thing, it has also been the first time your grandfather has attempted to materialise, and it is a VERY difficult state to achieve, requiring much time and a great deal of patience. However the more frequently you attend this kind of séance, the stronger will grow the power between you, and in consequence the better contact established.'

Next Flying Cloud asked if I would like to meet my own guardian spirit (we all have one) and moments later I was looking into the face of a Chinaman wearing a pill-box type hat, and long black moustaches. He did not speak himself, perhaps because the power was now failing fast, but Flying Cloud's voice could be heard explaining that my guide's name was Fu Ming, that he had died two centuries earlier, and during his lifetime had been an artist. Then he predicted that I would have to endure many years of hardship in the future, and much unhappiness, but the time would come when I would achieve my heart's desire.

When the face of Fu Ming had finally dissolved, it was replaced by that of Mimi expressing her sorrow that they must now say goodnight to us all, although it was hoped that everyone had enjoyed this evening of reunion.

Following one final veil of ectoplasm, the face of the medium returned looking extremely pale, her eyes still closed. After a few moments she shook slightly, and her eyes opened as if waking from deep sleep. The ceiling light went on, the table light went out, and the medium enquired if we had all enjoyed a satisfactory evening, then rising from her chair, she led us into the big bedroom to collect our belongings before seeing us to the front door and bidding us all goodnight.

I myself had found the events of the evening quite devastating, and had been astonished by all that I had seen and heard. I was absolutely convinced that what we had witnessed had been completely genuine, and that trickery had played no part in it. With the exception of Gordon everyone present had been complete strangers to me, and at no time had I ever discussed Elsie or my grandfather with Gordon. How could the medium have known about Elsie's eye for example or better still, the secret shared only between Elsie and my father?

Certainly my curiosity concerning Spiritualism had been more than satisfied, and in the face of all the evidence that had been presented, life after 'death' proved a fact. This revelation that there actually existed TWO worlds, two universes alongside each other, was fascinating indeed, and the possibilities it opened up for those sensitive enough to bridge the gap between these two plains of existence, seemed quite fantastic. However at my age of only twenty, I was not prepared to devote the time needed and necessary, if one wished to delve deeper into the subject, and another thirty years would have to elapse before the spirit world would consider that I was sufficiently prepared to do the work they had in mind for me to carry out.

*My mother with her parents and
her brother, 1912*

*Aged about 7, 1935*

# The Early Years

I was born on the 20th of April 1928, in the tiny cottage of my mother's parents at 10 Ashton Gardens, Puckeridge, a small village set amid the gently rolling hills of East Hertfordshire.

Grandfather Lodge was known to the people over a very wide area of the countryside, because he was the local postman, although he had spent the greater part of his life in the army, carving a distinguished career for himself as a company sergeant major in the Duke of Wellington's West Riding Regiment. He fought Boers, Matabili and Zulus in Africa, served in India and Burma, and during the first World War, on the battlefields of France and Belgium. In 1917 King George V had decorated him with the 'Military Cross for Gallantry'. A very proud old man, he was even prouder when my mother presented him with his first, and indeed, only grandson. Mother too had been born in Puckeridge. Educated at the local village school, and later privately at the Rectory, she eventually went into service as a housemaid to a middle-class family living in Hertford, some eight miles away.

Here it was that pretty little Ada had attracted the attention of 'Scottie' Wright, a young butcher's delivery boy who called at the house regularly with meat supplies. After a brief courtship they had married, renting furnished rooms at a house in Currie Street, Hertford, but six months later they managed to rent a small house in Byde Street (No 26), which would remain their home for the next ten years.

Receiving only an elementary education at various schools in the town, I was never a brilliant pupil, usually coming fifth or sixth in a class of about forty. I hated arithmetic, English grammar, and sports of all kinds, but excelled in history, geography and the arts. Never a good mixer at school I made very few friends, and the gentle passive nature or my character was revealed by the fact that on one school report the headmaster wrote, 'A good sound boy in every respect, but lacks a certain robustness'...

The fact that I loathed all sports must have come as a great disappointment to my father, a strong and beautifully built man who played football for Hertford Town, was a star player for a local bowls team, and won many prizes for running when young. Unfortunately father was also a compulsive gambler, with the result that money which would have been better spent on the home all too often found its way into the pockets of local bookies. Matters were not helped by the fact that shortly after our arrival in Byde Street, Britain was plunged into a period of acute economic depression, and my father found himself numbered amongst the millions of unemployed.

The future looked bleak indeed as mother found herself having to cope on a total unemployment benefit of twenty-one shillings a week (£1.05p), half of which had to be set aside for the rent, there being no such thing as supplementary benefit in those days. However circumstances improved a few months later when mother secured a job as a cleaner in one of our three local cinemas ('The Regent'), and since one of the perks or the job was that the family was allowed to visit the cinema twice a week free of charge, I soon became an ardent film fan.

1936 saw the birth of my sister Shirley, and although there was an age gap of eight years between us, we soon became quite inseparable despite the fact that temperamentally we were complete opposites, Shirley being very strong-willed and displaying a fearful temper if she could not get her own way.

1936 was also to see a change in our family fortunes when after nearly seven years of total unemployment, father at last managed to get permanent work as a fitter with the local gas company, and we moved into a larger house near the town centre, which although unfortunately placed in the middle of the industrial area, did have some lovely stretches of countryside and waterways nearby.

Following this move mother gave up her job at the cinema and became a cleaner at a nearby infants and junior school which my sister was later to attend. Small, dark and attractive, mother really was a remarkable little woman. A tireless worker, both inside and outside the home, never once do I ever remember her losing her temper or uttering the mildest of swear words, quite unlike my father whose every other word was blasphemous. Kind and considerate at all times, selfishness and thoughtlessness were quite alien to her, and she quickly gained the admiration and respect of all who came into contact with her.

Quite religious in her own way, she made certain I went to Sunday school every Sunday morning and to Church with her every Sunday evening. Dad stayed at home.

Sadly father was one of those macho men who seem to have little or no interest in their homes or families, and as I grew older and the bond between my mother and I increased, he seemed jealous of the place I occupied in her affections, and in consequence the gulf between him and myself grew ever wider with the passing years.


I was eleven years old when the Second World War started, bringing with it a very different way of life for everyone - the blackout, food-, sweet- and clothes-rationing for instance, and rationing did not simply mean less of some commodities either, but the complete disappearance of some items like fruit which came from abroad, for our shipping needed to carry more vital things now. Soon too, fewer young men were to be seen walking the streets, and most of the older ones were in uniforms of one kind or another, home guard, air raid workers, emergency medical or fire services.

As the young men and women left their homes to go and serve in the forces, so thousands of evacuee children from London and the big cities fled into the countryside for safety. Although my own parents were not asked to accommodate any of these children, we were asked to house two middle-aged factory workers who had been bombed out in London and transferred to a new plant in Hertford.

Whenever the local sirens wailed their warning of approaching enemy aircraft, mother, Shirley and I would go and sit under the stairs, father having told us this was the safest place in any house. At night we all slept together in the basement.

By now the gas company had promoted father, and he was the foreman of a gang of men whose job it was to go out and inspect any gas mains in the area which may have been damaged by enemy bombs, and since this meant that he was on call twenty-four hours a day, we saw very little of him. His job being considered one of national importance, he was exempt from military service. Sometimes the sirens wailed their warning and nothing more would be heard until the 'all clear' thankfully sounded some time later, but at other times the air would be filled with the noise of gunfire, the dreadful whistle of descending bombs, and violent explosions. When poor old London was taking a particularly bad battering at night, a dim red glow would be visible on the horizon although the city was some twenty miles distant, and in the stillness of the night the London blitz could be quite clearly heard. Fortunately, although so close to London, Hertford suffered very little real enemy damage during the war, and the death toll of civilians was mercifully small, although amongst those who did indeed perish were two members of my father's family, his father and youngest sister. They had been killed when a land-mine had silently floated down by parachute, landed in their garden, and devastated all the surrounding area. A large portion of the school I attended was also destroyed by bombs, although thankfully this had occurred at night when the school was closed.

With the ending of the war, flags and decorations went up, bonfires were lit, and the people made merry in the streets. Some rejoiced that they would soon be reunited with their loved ones who had been away on active service. Others, in sorrow, thought of loved ones who had perished during those terrible six years.

Of course although the war was over, the country's way of life did not return to normality overnight, and it took several more years for things to get back to something approaching pre-war standards.

*With mother and my sister Shirley, 1945*

# My First Gay Encounter - Mixed Emotions

With today's liberal attitudes to nudity and sexual matters, children grow up aware of the facts of life from a very early age, but in the 1930s and 40s sex was still a subject that many people did not care to talk about openly, and the only information most schoolboys like myself obtained, was what we picked up from older boys.

In the first instance of course the interest centred on our own and each others bodies. We would for example compare penises to see who had the largest - I always won hands, or rather pants down! Incredible as it may seem, I was actually the ripe old age of twenty-five before I knew exactly what a homosexual was, although I was only thirteen when I had my first encounter with one.

A sturdy, well-built lad with very broad shoulders and fine limbs, I was out walking in the countryside near my home one fine summer's day, when I stopped on a bridge to watch a group of boys swimming in the river beneath. Several other people were gathered on the bridge, and soon I became aware that one of them, a large middle-aged man, was interestedly eyeing me up and down.

As our eyes met he gave me the kind of smile which for some reason made me feel uneasy, and I quickly returned my gaze to the swimmers. Minutes later however, I felt the urge to look at the man again, only to find him still intently studying me. Puzzled by his interest, but now feeling distinctly uncomfortable, I walked off down a pathway leading to some meadows where I wanted to sit and do some homework I had brought with me. I had been writing notes for about half an hour, when suddenly, I heard a movement in the long grass behind me. I turned, and there standing just a few feet away, was the man from the bridge, still smiling. For a moment I panicked. Why had he followed me? Remarking what a lovely day it was, he came forward and asked if he might sit down beside me for a moment. Too scared to refuse, my heart was now pounding so loudly I felt sure he must hear it. However I was sensible enough to realise that the worst thing I could do was make my alarm apparent, so I tried to behave as calmly as possible, deciding that at a suitable moment, I would make an excuse to get up and walk away. Seated beside me the man explained that he was an evacuee from London, but hated the countryside, and was hoping to return to London shortly. Then placing a hand on my nearest knee, he said, 'I like to have fun with young boys. Do you ever go into the nearby woods? You can have a lot of fun in there.'

I was wondering what HIS interpretation of fun might be, when he continued: 'There is a young lad in the house where I am staying - he brings me a cup of tea in bed each morning. He is a nice boy, but he starts to shout if I do anything to him. I don't like boys who shout!'

By now I had heard enough, and decided it was time for me to depart, but I knew I must exercise caution, otherwise he might attack me. I therefore remarked how much I had enjoyed his company, but stressed that I really HAD got to go now. I was already late for tea, and my father would be looking for me. I added that since I always came to this particular spot to do my homework, father knew exactly where to look for me too! Gathering up my books and papers, I slowly got to my feet. The man rose too, saying he would accompany me part of the way. 'I am sorry if I said anything to alarm you. I like you very much, and would like to see you again,' he said. He continued talking, and the nearer we got to home, the happier I felt. But, when we finally reached the turning that led to my house, the man suddenly grabbed my nearest arm and threatened he would not release me until I promised to meet him on the bridge the following night at eight. As much afraid that a neighbour would see me in the grip of this total stranger as I was of the man himself, I agreed. 'Good', said the man. 'Then we will go to the woods and have SUCH an exciting time.'

I did not tell my parents what had occurred, but all next day at school, the man's conversation kept flowing through my mind. Of course I had no intention of keeping my appointment with him, but that evening as I sat in the kitchen watching the clock tick away the hours to 8pm, I could not help wondering just what WOULD have happened had I gone to meet him. WOULD I have experienced some forbidden delight? I even began to have slight regrets for being such a coward.

Although I was never to set eyes on the man again, many times in the years that followed, men would look deep into my eyes, smile and sometimes wink knowingly at me, and although I really did not understand the reason, I had to admit I found it all rather flattering.

As I approached the school-leaving age of fourteen, father suggested I go to work with him at the gas company and was most disappointed when I raised objections. For years my ambition was to become an artist, and being an ardent film fan, I had frequently made drawings of the glamourous actresses whose photographs lavishly illustrated the pages of the film magazines I bought weekly. But I had to be realistic. I knew that without proper training, I had no hope of fulfilling my dream. Anything even remotely artistic was quite out of the question in a small town like Hertford in those days. However, since I did not want to work in a shop or factory, office work was the only alternative, and so when Hertford County Hall advertised for a map tracer, I quickly applied for, and got the job.

My bitterly class-conscious father was so certain I would fail the interview. 'A boy from a working-class background like you, won't be posh enough for the likes of them,' he commented, and instead of congratulating me on my success, he merely called me a little snob. 'I suppose you are afraid to do a proper job and get your hands dirty?' This attitude was typical of my father.

Since all my work consisted of was tracing large areas of

agricultural land from ordinance survey maps onto sheets of paper, the only requirements were neatness and a steady hand. Although I quickly became bored with the job, I did find my fellow workers stimulating company, particularly the boss' secretary, Dorothy. She was five years older than me, but I quickly developed a crush on her, despite the fact that she had a boyfriend in the Royal Air Force. Dorothy it was, more than anyone else, who was responsible for my growing interest in music, pacifism, vegetarianism, spiritualism, and all the other 'isms'. I made a lot of new friends at County Hall especially amongst the girls with whom I seemed very popular. However only on one occasion did I ever take one of them on a date, and that proved to be such a disaster that I swore never to repeat the experience again.

Nevertheless a few months later mother persuaded me to start corresponding with a cousin named Barbara who lived in Somerset. She was quite a pretty girl, and having received her photograph I quickly forgot my reservations about the fair sex, and later when mother suggested we invite Barbara to spend a short holiday with us, I was delighted.

I met Barbara in London and escorted her to Hertford, and she settled down comfortably at home. Next day I took her on a sightseeing tour of London, and she seemed quite happy in my company, but by the third day I sensed that all was not well. She was quite friendly, but I was aware of a distinct cooling. The whole thing came to a climax the following day when I invited her to go to a local cinema with me. She complained that she had a headache and would prefer to sit quietly in the garden. In the garden however, she soon got into conversation with the boy next door and, a short time later, gaily bounced into the house to announce that she WAS going to the cinema after all - with the boy next door!

Humiliated and insulted I avoided Barbara for the remainder of her stay with us and when the time came for her to return to Somerset, I only escorted her as far as the local railway station, leaving her rather ungallantly to find her own way across London to Paddington station. WOMEN! They were a complete mystery to me. A mystery that did not intrigue me in the least, I decided. In future I would stick to male companions. At least I knew how THEIR minds worked.

A few weeks later a new tracer joined our staff at the office. Shy, sensitive, and handsome, Dennis was only a few months older than myself and we became instant friends, visiting local cinemas and making regular trips to London together. Dennis also became a regular visitor to my home, and on Sundays mother would always invite him to stay and have tea with us.

One winter's night when the family had all gone off to a local cinema for the evening leaving the two of us sitting alone in the darkened living room, lit only by the flickering flames that danced among the coals in the grate, we started to discuss sex, and in no time at all I had developed an erection.

Dennis, highly amused by the sight of the rigid form straining against the restriction or my trouser leg, leaned forward and suggested he release it before it burst through the material, and since I offered no objection, with trembling fingers he proceeded to unbutton the front or my trousers.

It was the first time in my life that I had ever allowed anyone to touch this most private part of me, and a great wave of excitement flooded through me as Dennis slid his hand inside my pants and closed his cool fingers around my hot throbbing cock.

Following his instructions I lay back in my armchair and allowed him to bring me to a shuddering climax. The satisfaction being clearly mutual, and more fun than a solitary wank. So it was that whenever we were left alone in the house after that, we took the opportunity to indulge in a little harmless repetition of this innocent pleasure. It had all happened so naturally, with none of the hang-ups I had experienced with females.

It was also around this time that my father saw me naked for the first time since I was an infant, and just for once showed a little pride in me. At the time I was taking a bath, standing in a small tin tub that mother used for the weekly wash. None of the local houses had bathrooms in those days, and for privacy I had taken the tub into the utility room. As I was in the process of rinsing soap off myself, dad walked in saying he needed a hammer from his tool kit. I was aware that he was looking me over as he passed, and it seems with approval, because as he returned to my mother in the kitchen and was closing the door behind him, I heard him remark, 'The boy's bigger than I am!' After that he seemed to find regular excuses for coming into the utility room whenever I bathed, and a few weeks later he told me he had spoken to the man in charge of the bath-house at the gas works, and I was welcome to go along and use their communal showers any time I wanted to. Dad clearly wanted to show me off to his mates. The idea of seeing a group of hunky, naked men showering got me excited, but I was also scared that the sight of them might give me an erection - but I decided to risk it.

I only went a few times however because my 'audience' grew larger with each visit, and I was never short of someone offering to wash my back when dad wasn't around, and as their hands began to stray towards my arse, there would be broad smiles all round when I DID start to get hard, no matter how much I fought to stop this happening. The visits to the bath-house however had given the chance to see that I HAD got more between my legs than most of them.

*Pencil drawing of Mae West, 1940*

# The Army and Mae West

In 1946 soon after my eighteenth birthday in accordance with the national service regulations of the time, I was drafted into the army for two years, and underwent six weeks basic training at Warley Barracks in Essex, loathing every minute of it.

How repugnant and futile it all seemed. Were there to be another war I could not start killing other young men simply because a bunch of politicians had agreed it was now legal to go out and commit mass murder. Taking this moral view I suppose at heart I was a conscientious objector, but it takes courage to be one of a minority, ANY minority, and for the moment I chose the easy way out, that of getting on with the job in hand, and hoping that the situation would never arise where I might have to face the reality of it all.

Something I found particularly objectionable was bayonet practise. On a large piece or waste ground a rag dummy representing an enemy soldier, would be suspended from a wooden frame by a rope. Then with bayonets fixed to our rifles we had to run screaming and yelling at the 'enemy' and kill him with several sharp thrusts. We were told that the louder and more blood-curdling our screams, the better, for it helped to demoralise your enemy before you killed him!

Having worked in the sophisticated environment, of County Hall, I had come to believe that we were living in a highly intelligent society, however this current experience seriously made me wonder. I felt disgusted with mankind that a situation could possibly exist in the 20th century where this kind of thing WAS necessary.

Apart from receiving instruction on the use of rifles and machine guns etc., there was plenty of crawling about under barbed wire, long cross-country runs, endurance marches, PT and good old square-bashing, and as distasteful as the training had been, I had to admit that at the end of six weeks I felt fitter and healthier than at any other time in my life.

Towards the end of the training period, all recruits underwent an intelligence test to determine which branch of the army they were best suited for, and for some strange reason, I was selected for the Royal Army Pay Corps, and sent to Manchester.

The pay office was located in the suburb of Longsight, in what had originally been a vast cotton mill (the Daisy Pownall Works), and staffed by some three thousand soldiers and ATS personnel plus another thousand civilians. The Manchester office had the distinction of being the only one to deal exclusively with the pay and accounts of officers from 2nd Lieutenants to Field Marshalls, and I soon found myself handling accounts, which included those of Field Marshalls Alexander and Montgomery.

However figures had never been my strong point and in no time at all I had the accounts of everyone in such a mess, that I was quickly transferred to where I could do less damage, although oddly enough they put me in a position which was far more prestigious - general 'dogsbody' to the the officer in command of the entire unit, a Lt. Colonel Herbert Buckmaster, founder of 'Bucks' club in London and creator of the beverage Bucks Fizz.

An ATS Sergeant Major Batty was his secretary and main confident, a stern but pleasant enough woman, and I became her assistant, passing on the Colonel's various messages and instructions to all the other officers throughout the unit, and since my position gave me direct access to the Colonel at all times, I was envied by the 'other ranks', and treated with particular courtesy by all the officers.

The Colonel was a pleasant man, but by no stretch of the imagination could he be described as attractive, indeed the poor man was quite ugly. I was therefore more than a little surprised to learn from Sergeant Major Batty that he had once been married to actress Gladys Cooper, although this did explain why a number of personal letters I had posted for him had been addressed to Sally Cooper, actress daughter of Gladys.

No doubt because of his former wife's show business connections, the Colonel knew a lot of the film and stage personalities who came to Manchester to appear in plays or attend premiers etc., and Sergeant Major Batty having seen some sketches I had made of various pay office personnel, suggested I show them to the Colonel - he might just introduce me to some of his show business friends and get me to sketch THEM? Although I had my doubts about this, Batty took it upon herself to show the Colonel some of my work, and he was most impressed with it, particularly when told I had never had any art instruction or training. Even so, I thought that would be the end of it.

However, the Colonel resided permanently at the Midland, a plush hotel in the city centre, which was a great favourite with visiting stars as it was so conveniently close to most theatres and cinemas, and a few weeks later the Colonel asked me if I would like to meet Hollywood star Marjorie Reynolds who was staying at the Midland and starring in BURLESQUE at the Opera House.

Of course I was absolutely thrilled, and it occurred to me that this might be a opportunity to start a unique collection of autographed drawings - perhaps one day I might even have enough to form an exhibition, and so I always made it a rule to make two drawings: the original, which I gave the star in the Colonel's suite, and which they were always happy to pay me for, and a copy I made for myself which I got them to autograph as a souvenir.

My second 'sitter' was the very beautiful Vivien Leigh. I thought her the most beautiful woman I had ever seen, and she had a pet Siamese cat called Mr. Jones who accompanied her everywhere, even to the theatre where she vas appearing nightly. World-famous for her role as

Scarlett O'Hara in 'GONE WITH THE WIND', she had just completed the film 'CAESAR AND CLEOPATRA'.

In quite quick succession I also met Anna Neagle (with her husband Herbert Wilcox), Michael Wilding, Glynis Johns, Kay Kendall, Phyllis Calvert, Valerie Hobson and Eric Portman.

I also started using my own initiative by making friends with the stage door keepers at the theatres, and this got me backstage. Jessie Mathews, starring in 'MAID TO MEASURE' at the Opera House, looked at the sketch I had just made and remarked that I had made her look more like Claudette Colbert adding, 'I wish I DID look as good as that!' A very outspoken woman she also voiced the opinion I was much too quiet personality-wise. 'You have to shout and let them know you are alive,' she said. Well, she certainly knew how to herself.

In most cases I found the stars charming and polite, rarely were they ever rude, the one exception being Stan Laurel, the 'thin' man of the famous Laurel and Hardy team. In sharp contrast to the loveable idiot he always portrayed on screen, I found him very off-handed. Stern-faced and wearing a beret instead of the more familiar bowler, he was not easily recognisable, and stage hands at the Palace Theatre where he and Oliver Hardy were appearing, told me the famous partnership now seemed little more than a business arrangement, both men leaving the theatre separately with their respective wives after each performance. Oliver Hardy was quite different. A very charming man indeed, I was amazed just how agile this big man really was on his feet. His facial expressions, dainty hand-gestures and mannerisms being in every way identical to his behaviour in the many films I had seen and loved over the years.

However of all the celebrities I met in Manchester, the one who really made the biggest impact on me was the legendary Mae West who arrived in the city for a six-week run of her play DIAMOND LILL.

Mae believed in doing everything in style, and travelling between the Midland, where she was staying, and the theatre, she rode in a large and very old-fashioned American chauffeur-driven limousine, which newspapers had declared was bullet-proof, a relic from the days when Chicago gangsters had once threatened to throw acid in her face unless she paid them 'protection' money. Three huge bodyguards also accompanied her everywhere. They were built like wrestlers, and indeed that is what they were. Mae loved to be surrounded by men with muscles.

My first meeting with her took place at the hotel, and when she looked at my finished sketch she drawled in her broad New York accent, 'Gee, now ain't that pretty', and immediately invited me to visit her backstage at the theatre the following evening to sketch her in one of her favourite show-gowns. I felt so flattered to have had her personal invitation to 'Come up and see me sometime'.

# A Fresh Start

When I finally did return home to Hertford once more, I began my search for a job. Since I did not want to work in an office again, I became a sales assistant in a small menswear store at Puckeridge, the village where I was born. Working in the village I was able to pop along to my grandfather's cottage each lunch hour to make sure he was alright, grandmother having died of cancer some months earlier.

My position at the store lasted exactly a year, and then I was sacked! Unjustly in truth, because when I had first joined the staff my employer had promised that at the end or twelve months, I would be entitled to a two weeks holiday, and having booked a two week trip to Paris, a few days prior to my departure, my employer suddenly announced that he was going to have a sale and could only spare me for one week. Furious that my employer had gone back on his word, I went ahead with my holiday as planned, only to find on my return that I had been fired for doing so. I was not particularly upset, the two weeks in Paris, my first trip abroad, having proved to be a most enjoyable experience, and I had in any case found myself bored to tears working in a small village shop.

That same week a very large departmental store at Welwyn Garden City, seven miles from Hertford, advertised in our local newspaper for a 'Window Display Assistant' and I applied for the job. I was told that unfortunately they were only prepared to take on someone with experience in one of the big London stores, although they COULD offer me an assistant's job in their ironmongery department, which I decided to take.

The store, which had over one hundred departments, was an exciting place to work because it was always staging various exhibitions and promotions, and had quite a lot of famous people as regular clientele. In just my first week at the store I found myself serving the Queen Mother's sister-in-law, and the Woolworth's millionairess Barbara Hutton (once married to Cary Grant). Ex-King Carol of Romania was said to be a regular visitor to the Store's book department, and George Bernard Shaw always had his hair cut in our barber's shop- I was told that tufts of his hair changed hands for half-a-crown a time!

One day in the staff canteen talking to a couple of friends about the collection of autographed star portraits I had accumulated during my two years in Manchester, my conversation was overheard by the manager of the store's art department, who asked me if I would bring in half a dozen of the drawings to show him. He said sales of art materials had slumped rather badly recently- perhaps I would allow him to exhibit a couple of my drawings to encourage members of the public to buy art materials and 'have a go' themselves!

The following day the manager of the art department was so

delighted by the half dozen drawings I took along, he asked if I had more? Eventually two dozen of my pictures were put on show, and all bore autographs with one exception - a portrait of Dinah Sheridan, a star I admired very much but who to date I had never met. My drawing had been copied from a photograph I had seen in a film magazine a few months earlier.

A few days after my pictures had gone on show, a lady came to the ironmongery department asking to speak to 'The young man responsible for the drawings on display at the art department.'

Having introduced myself to her, the very elegant and aristocratic old lady then said, 'It is a really excellent drawing you have made of my daughter. I must tell her to come in and see it for herself.'

I thanked her for her kind remarks, and she walked away leaving me to wonder who on earth her daughter was. When I asked another assistant, if he knew who she was, he replied, 'That was Lisa Sheridan, the royal photographer. Her daughter is Dinah Sheridan and her son-in-law is Jimmy Hanley. You HAVE been honoured - normally she only speaks to department managers.'

A few days later Dinah arrived to see the portrait of herself, and afterwards came to tell me how delighted she was with it. She was so sweet and charming, I asked her if she would allow me to present her with a larger, framed portrait to hang in her home? She said she would be absolutely thrilled, and if I would like to telephone her when the work was completed, then perhaps I would like to take it round to her home personally.

Dinah had recently separated from her husband, and when I called at her home the following week to deliver the portrait, I found that the house she now shared with her two children, Jenny aged three, Jeremy aged five, and their pet Corgi Tina, had the accent on homely comfort rather than the ostentation one normally associated with film folk.

Little did I dream that day in 1949 that I was about to embark on a friendship with Dinah that would span the years right up to this present day, and as I came to know Dinah better, so she would confide in me things which were not common knowledge to the press or general public, and I was to learn something of the heartache as well as the glamour that go to make up the life of a film star.

The sketch I had made for Dinah normally hung in her sitting-room, but between films she would sometimes appear in stage plays, and on such occasions would often hang the portrait in the foyer of whatever theatre she might be playing, and in later years when I had made several other portraits for her, she would sometimes hang her favourite right on the stage itself, where it would form part of the set furnishings.

Working at the store, naturally I also made friends amongst the staff, and chief of these was a young man about my own age named Jim. A nice-looking lad, slim, with shiny black hair and a neat moustache, he was married to a Welsh girl several years older than himself called Olwen, and they lived in a tiny flat in St. Albans. To begin with the relationship between Jim and myself was restricted to chats in the store's canteen during coffee breaks, and lunchtime visits to a nearby pub, the 'Cherry Tree', where we would wash down our sandwiches with a couple of beers. But gradually as I got to know him better, so he would invite me to stay at his flat for weekends, and since there was only one bedroom in the apartment, this always necessitated making up a bed for me on the floor in front of the fire in their living room, but it was quite comfortable, and I always looked forward to my visits.

One day I made the acquaintance of another person working at the store, whose name was Charles. Tall, fair-haired, and always immaculate in appearance, he greatly impressed me with his sophisticated conversation, and his very gay manners - gay was the right word too, although I did not know it at the time!

When Jim noticed I was talking to Charles one day, he advised me not to do so again. 'Why not?' I asked. He simply replied, 'He is not nice to know,' and would not explain further, which only intrigued me all the more.

A couple of days later as I sat in the canteen alone - Jim had some business in the store to attend to - I noticed Charles sitting alone at another table, so decided to join him. As I sat down he looked up with surprise. 'YOU are being very brave, aren't you? You really should not sit with me you know. You will have people talk about you.'

Although his remark quite puzzled me, I did not wish to appear ignorant in the presence or someone so worldly, and so said I did not care what others thought. We fell into conversation, and learning that I was interested in art and antiques, he mentioned that he had a rather nice bronze statue I might like to see, and I agreed to go round to his flat later in the week to see it.

At that point in our conversation Jim entered the canteen, and I went over to join him. He asked what I had been talking to Charles about, and when I told him, laughed and remarked, 'Well if you do go round to his flat he will show you more than his bronze!' Jim then went on the say that most people in the store were aware that Charles was 'queer', and strange as it may seem, I had not the faintest idea what a 'queer' was. Having briefly explained, Jim quickly changed the subject, but curious to know just how two males COULD have sex together, I decided to keep my appointment with Charles and see what happened.

Arriving at his flat a few nights later, he first seated me in his beautifully furnished lounge, and then went into the kitchen to make some coffee. Later as we sat drinking this, he talked about life at the store and our common interest in art. At this point he suggested we go and look at his bronze, which apparently was in his bedroom.

The statuette stood on a small bedside table. It was a beautiful thing some fifteen inches high depicting a male nude in very great detail.

Picking it up, Charles handed it to me for my inspection. Then having replaced it to its original position, he suggested we stay in the bedroom and make ourselves more comfortable. Starting to unbutton his shirt, he said, 'Why don't you take off your clothes and relax?'

Feeling both embarrassed and far from relaxed, I hastened to say I must be going as I had another appointment to keep. I hadn't of course, but it was the only excuse I could think of. Charles looked furious, and seeing me to the front door, slammed it unceremoniously after me! He passed by me without speaking the next day in the store, and Jim curled up with laughter when I told him what had happened.

A few weeks later another member of the staff took an interest in me. Manager of the glass and china department, I was aware that he was a great friend of Charles, so wondered if I had been a topic of conversation between them.

The fellow's name was Horace, and remarking that he liked to cycle in his spare time, mentioned that he often went to Hertford and would call and see me next time he was passing through, so that he could see some of my drawings which had heard so much about.

About the same age as myself, Horace was tall and very thin, with gaunt features in which were set two fiercely staring eyes. The day he called to see me he was wearing an open-necked shirt and the briefest pair of shorts I had ever seen. These did not suit him at all, his legs being much too thin.

Alone in the house at the time, I invited him into the lounge where, seated on a divan we proceeded to look through a pile of my drawings. Then, suddenly grabbing my nearest wrist and twisting it a little, he said, 'You have a lovely body. I am very strong, you know. I could easily rape you if I wanted to.'

Shocked and surprised by this sudden outburst, I wrenched my hand free, at the same time punching him so hard with the other, that I sent him sprawling onto the floor. Then leaping to my feet I positioned myself behind a heavy table in the centre of the room, waiting to see what his next move would be. However as luck would have it, at that very moment, I heard my mother unlocking the front door, and advised him to leave, and without saying another word he quickly departed via the back door.

Our paths did not cross at the store for the next few days, perhaps he was at pains to avoid me. But a week later while I was on a visit to Jim in St. Albans, Horace called at my home again leaving a small package with my mother, saying, 'Would you please give this to Ron. It's just a little present.' It turned out to be a beautiful bone china cup and saucer; a collector's item.

Naturally my mother was curious to know who Horace was, and why he should want to give me an expensive present. I could hardly tell her what had happened the previous week, and that this must be a peace offering for the way he had behaved. I explained that since he was manager of the glass and china department, he would be able to buy the china at a considerable discount.

In the box with the china had been a sealed envelope, which I took the precaution of opening in the privacy of my own room, and I was so thankful that I did, for it contained a selection of photographs of Horace and another young man naked, and having sex in a variety of positions which left nothing to the imagination.

My first reaction was one of utter shock and disgust, however I have to be honest and say that after the initial shock, I was a little fascinated. I had never seen anything like these before. So THAT was what 'queers' did together!

I decided to return the photos to Horace without delay, telling him I wanted nothing to do with him, and if he pestered me any more, then I would go to the police.

He was very upset, but the threat worked, and he never bothered me again. As a matter of fact he left the store a few months later end moved away from the Garden City. I only ever saw him once after that. Many years later as I was strolling down London's Regent Street I suddenly spotted him on the other side of the road. He did not see me, but I recognised him immediately, despite the fact that he was now wearing a SCOUT MASTER'S UNIFORM!

Whilst on the subject of sex, I should mention another little incident, this time with Jim. At the time Olwen had gone into hospital to have their first child and Jim wanted to decorate the kitchen for her while she was away. I had gone over to give him a hand, and when the job was finished we went to a nearby pub for a couple of pints. On our return, Jim said there seemed little point in making up my bed on the floor of the living room. I might as well share the double bed with him. It was a warm summer's night, and although I had climbed into bed naked as was my usual custom, Jim kept his underpants on.

Once in bed he had switched off the light and I settled down to sleep. However a few moments later there was a lot of movement on Jim's side of the bed and I asked him what he was doing? He said removing his underpants to be more comfortable.

We lay flat on our backs talking for a while, then when the conversation ceased, I began to speculate what might have happened by now had Charles or Horace been lying beside me instead of Jim. Time passed, and since all was quiet on his side of the bed I resigned myself to the fact that I had best get some sleep.

I was just about to drift off, when suddenly I was aware that Jim was whispering my name, and something about the way that he whispered it, gave me the impression he hoped I was asleep. Deciding not to answer, I waited to see what would happen. Once more he whispered my name, then pausing for a few moments, he slowly raised the sheet, and ever-so-gently put a hand on my tummy. It remained there perfectly still for several minutes, presumably to see if I would waken.

Fighting hard to control my breathing for fear he would realise I was not asleep, although I had developed a throbbing erection, I waited with tingling suspense. Then very slowly his hand moved lower and I became aware of his fingers slowly creeping through my pubic hair, moments later his fingers were encircling my rigid cock, and he began to gently masturbate me.

Gradually becoming more and more excited himself, he worked harder and harder to bring me to a shuddering climax as I lay groaning and moaning with pleasure. Afterwards however, Jim seemed overcome with guilt, murmuring, 'Olwen, Olwen', and moving away he gently cried himself to sleep, leaving me to lie for what seemed like hours, wondering what to make of it all. The incident was not mentioned next morning and I realised he just wanted to forget it had ever happened.

For four years we had a very close relationship, but then one day towards the end of 1953 Jim arrived at the store with news that he had been offered the management of a small confection and tobacco business in Luton, which also had a spacious apartment above the premises, all ready for immediate occupation, and he was intending to hand in two weeks notice at the store. I was shattered.

Only days earlier Dinah had broken the news to me that she too was leaving Garden City to get married. Feeling extremely depressed, I decided to hand in my notice too. The store had too many memories for me to want to remain there anymore. I must also break away and make a fresh start.

My parents thought me quite mad giving up a perfectly good job simply on emotional grounds, especially as I did not have another job to go to.

Jim tried to cheer me up by remarking that Luton wasn't SO far away, and I was still welcome to visit him and Olwen whenever I wanted to, but when I did call a month later I found he was so involved with the business, I felt distinctly in the way, especially when I discovered that since leaving Welwyn he had also acquired a new male friend locally. Once again I felt it was time to make a clean break - this time from Jim and Olwen, and I never saw them again.

*Dinah Sheridan*

# Dinah's Golden Years

Luckily Dinah's departure from Welwyn did not herald the end of our friendship. I was disappointed to think I would see much less of her, although of course we could still correspond and telephone each other.
During the four years I had come to know her, Dinah's career had made great advances. In 1950 she had gone to Kenya to make a film called WHERE NO VULTURES FLY with Anthony Steel, and in 1951 this had been chosen as the Royal Command Performance Film for that year.

In those days the event was far more important and glamorous than it is today, the stars of the big screen being THE idols of the day. The premier took place at the Odeon cinema in Leicester Square in November, thousands of fans flocking to the Square to witness the arrival of the Royal Family and a host of stars that included Fred MacMurray, Lisbeth Scott, Van Johnson, Merle Oberon, Jane Russell, Richard Todd, Googie Withers and Phyllis Calvert, although Dinah was the real star of the evening wearing a gown of shimmering cream silk brocade, embroidered all over with golden birds of paradise.

Later Dinah had to attend a gala premier of the film in Johannesburg, and the evening before she flew out to South Africa, I called at her home to wish her bon voyage and give her a Saint Christopher medallion to wear on the flight.

A week later I received a postcard from Johannesburg. On one side was a photo of the hotel she was staying in, an 'X' marked against windows on the seventh floor, and on the reverse she had written:

'X' marks the balcony of my suite. It is very hot, and at present there is a violent storm. Swam all day yesterday, am very brown. Fly to Durban on Thursday, then on to the Cape on Friday. I have an ADORABLE lion cub I'm bringing with me.
Love,<br/>Dinah.

When Dinah returned to England a short time later, her children wanted to keep the cub at home as a pet, but of course animals have a habit of growing up, so this was not practical and Dinah presented it to the London Zoo.

Following the general release of the film in Britain, Dinah made a series of personal appearances up and down the country and received an enormous amount of publicity. I myself took on the job of sorting out all the press clippings and pasting them into large scrap books for her future reference, something I carried on doing for many years.

1952 saw Dinah appearing in David Lean's THE SOUND BARRIER, and shortly after this she was starring opposite Dirk Bogarde in AN APPOINTMENT IN LONDON. At the same time she was also working on THE GILBERT AND SULLIVAN STORY, which gave her the opportunity to wear some really gorgeous period gowns and look quite ravishing.

1952 was certainly a very busy year for her, for quite apart from the films mentioned, in the autumn she was to commence yet another, the now famous GENEVIEVE.

A few days before Christmas 1952, I went to see Dinah taking presents for her and the children. We had sat down in front of a blazing log fire, and I was just about to taste a large glass of wine she had handed me, when suddenly she said, 'Ron, I have something to tell you that I think will come as a bit of a shock. I am getting married again, AND I am giving up my film career.' I was absolutely stunned.

She went on to explain that since her 'intended' was the most powerful man in British films (John Davis, managing director of the giant J Arthur Rank Organisation - he also held more than 150 directorships in other companies), she would be called upon to do a great deal of entertaining and simply would not have time for a film career as well. Dinah continued, 'I suppose a lot or people will think me quite mad retiring just now, and had GENEVIEVE looked like being a flop then I might have been tempted to stay on, however it looks like being the most successful film I have ever made, a real box-office winner, and so I shall be quite content to put my feet up. Surely that is the best time to finish, when you have reached the peak of success? But actually, as the wife of JD I shall be able to enjoy all the pleasures that the film world has to offer, premiers and film festivals all over the world, without having to endure all the chores and tensions of actually working in the industry itself.'

I did not like to voice my real opinions, but could not help feeling that Dinah was making a dreadful mistake. She was only thirty-two at the time. I had grown very fond of her, and the thought of gentle Dinah marrying a hard-headed tycoon like Davis, filled me with secret dread, especially when a few days later her mother mentioned to me that JD had already been divorced three times. 'How long will it be before Dinah becomes redundant wife No 4?' Lisa asked me with great concern.

Dinah's news had been given to me in the strictest confidence, and when some time later the national press announced 'Jimmy Hanley and Dinah Sheridan Divorce', they had no idea that plans of her remarriage were already well in hand, nor did they know she was intending to give up her career.

Dinah's departure from Welwyn Garden City to take up residence in new homes in both London and Kent, plus Jim's move to Luton, made my own prospects for 1953 seem very bleak indeed, and I felt that the bottom had dropped right out of my own little world.

*Pencil drawing of Marlene Dietrich, Elstree Studios, 1958*

*With Marlene Dietrich, Elstree Studios, 1958*

*My staircase of drawings, 1956*

*Julia Arnall and myself at exhibition of my work, 1956*

# The Sweet Taste of Success

When I became sales assistant in a Hertford menswear shop, a small family concern centred in Hertford with branches in three neighbouring towns, I began the job full of enthusiasm. But this was quickly quenched by the senior assistant who liked to set the pace of everything. Such limitations plus the fact that there was so little to do for most of the time, soon bored me to tears. However the pay was reasonable, the job was stable (too steady), and I was able to walk home in less than ten minutes at midday for a hot meal, which made a nice change.

Occasionally I was asked to help out at one or the branches, and one day when I was at the Hatfield shop, I chanced to meet pretty Pauline Stroud who a few years earlier, amid a great deal of publicity had won a nation-wide campaign to discover an unknown girl to star in the film LADY GODIVA RIDES AGAIN. The winner was also to receive a five-year film contract, but little or nothing had been heard of Pauline since, and I was curious to know why?

She was flattered that I had recognised her, and pleased to accept my invitation to visit my home and see my collection of drawings, and naturally I wanted to add one of her to it. During her visit I heard how after making the Godiva film, on the insistence of her boyfriend, she had turned down the 5-year film contract because he was afraid of losing her, but only a few months later cruelly deserted her for someone else, leaving her without both a boyfriend and a promising career.

Another glamorous blonde I met a few months later was the legendary beauty Marlene Dietrich. I had always been a great fan of Dietrich, and when I discovered she was to appear in cabaret at London's Cafe de Paris, I was determined to fulfil a lifelong ambition to meet her.

Marlene was staying at the Dorchester Hotel, and I wrote to her public relations officer, Major Neville-Willing for an appointment. I was told to be at the hotel at 11pm before she left for her nightly cabaret performance.

Armed with a sample sketch of Marlene off I went to the Dorchester. I was shown to her suite, but still had to wait half-an-hour before she appeared, but suddenly, there she was, blonde hair piled high on her head, diamonds sparkling in her ears and around her throat, her body wrapped in a three-quarter length white fur coat, and the famous million-dollar legs encased in tight white silk toreador trousers. I had known she was short, but now as she stood there in a pair of heelless white satin slippers, she looked positively tiny.

Coming over to look at my drawing, she studied it, asked a few questions, and agreed to sit for me one afternoon the following week. Then turning briskly away, she swept out of the room, Major Neville-Willing and her hairdresser following in her wake. I followed, too, and on reaching the hotel entrance was surprised to see a huge crowd gathered even at that late hour, to see her depart. Dietrich, always the perfect artiste, strode over to her waiting Rolls Royce, put one foot on the running-board, then to the delight of the crowd, flung back her fur coat to treat them to a glimpse of the famous silken-clad legs.

In the years that followed I was to meet her several times, once down at Elstree Studios where she was making WITNESS FOR THE PROSECUTION, and on another occasion when she was in the company of Burt Bacharach, her musical director.

With more time on my hands now, when I was not working at the shop, I was hanging around West End theatres and adding an ever increasing number of new portraits to my 'Gallery of Fame'. I met Bob Hope surrounded by a horde of hangers-on, and when I asked him to write some comment on my copy of his portrait, wrote, 'I may sue', his followers all doubled-up with laughter!

I met Gloria De Haven the same day, and later Diana Lynn, Guy Mitchell, Vivien Leigh (again), Sir Laurence Olivier, and Vivian Blaine, in London to star in GUYS AND DOLLS, in a role she had created in the film.

With enough drawings now to stage a small exhibition in my parents home, I arranged some one hundred and twenty drawings around the walls of our sitting-room and staircase. I made no charge for admission, but accepted donations in aid of the Spastic Society, and later when I took the proceeds to the secretary of the local group, so pleased was she with the result, she suggested the Society help me stage a second, proper show, in the town's largest public hall. Naturally I was thrilled when the chairman agreed to this.

I had hoped that Dinah might open the exhibition, but when I telephoned her, she already had other commitments. However she got the Rank publicity chief, Theo Cowan, to provide me with lovely starlet Susan Beaumont.

When the young actress arrived, she looked very glamorous in a coolie hat of black glossy feathers, black silk two-piece suit, black court shoes and sparkling jewellery. We posed for the local press and gave interviews, then she moved on to her next engagement while I returned to the shop - my brief spell in the limelight quickly over. I had only been given the morning off on the understanding that I returned to work in the afternoon.

The exhibition was only a one day affair, but as brief as it had been it stimulated local interest and raised a nice sum of money for the charity.
Glowing with satisfaction I immediately set to work planning another exhibition. Obviously it was too soon to hold another in Hertford, but what about the big departmental store in Welwyn Garden City? This time I wanted to raise money for cancer research, my dear grandmother having died of that cursed disease.

When I first put the idea to the store's general manager he

hesitated, but when I remarked that a film star would be opening the exhibition thereby attracting large crowds to the store, he not only agreed to stage the show for a period of one week, but told me I would have the full co-operation of the store's display team, and see that the event was well publicised.

All I needed now was the film star I had promised! I decided to obtain the services of not one star but two. This I achieved by pitting two rival film companies against each other. The Rank Organisation offered me lovely Julia Arnall, and ABC Jill Adams .

Unfortunately right in the middle of my preparations I received a telephone call from ABC studios regretting that Jill Adams would not be available after all as she was needed for a new film in Australia. They also regretted that they had no one to replace her.

Thankful that I still had Julia Arnall to fall back on, but fearing something might cancel her visit too, I thought it best to look for someone else, and remembering that Hollywood star Edmund Purdom was currently staying with his parents in Welwyn Garden City, I telephoned and made an appointment to see him.

Arriving at his home the following day armed with a portrait of him, which I intended to include in the exhibition, I asked him if he would oblige with a personal appearance at the show. Not only did he come along himself but brought with him the beautiful Linda Christian his lover and ex-wife of Tyrone Power.

The store's display team did a magnificent job of staging the exhibition, and my visiting stars attracted large crowds. Reports of the show appeared in several local newspapers and one national magazine the following week, and as a result I was asked to speak at a dinner given by Hertford's 'Inner Wheel Club.' Incidentally also at the dinner was actor Brian Wilde best known for his performances as Mr. Barraclough the comic warder in the TV series PORRIDGE and 'Foggy' in THE LAST OF THE SUMMER WINE. Brian and I had been at school together in our junior days.

A few weeks later I was approached by a London photo agency who said that having just read an article about me in the LONDON EVENING NEWS, they would like to do a photo-story about me and my drawings. Would I be willing?

The agency said they wanted a story with 'human interest', showing both sides of my life - shop assistant one moment, rubbing shoulders with stars the next. Having agreed to co-operate, they sent a photographer down to Hertford the following day. My employer thinking the publicity would be good for his business allowed pictures to be taken of me in the shop, and later I posed at home with some examples of my work.

Before leaving Hertford, the photographer said he would also like to take some photos of me in the company of a couple of stars, could I arrange this? I telephoned Julia Arnall who agreed to give us an hour of her time the following Wednesday, and later the agency rang me to say that they had arranged for Elizabeth Sellars to pose with me. At the time she was appearing on the West End stage in the play TEA AND SYMPATHY, and said we could have half an hour of her time before she went on stage Thursday afternoon. I made a sketch of her while I was there.

The photographs all taken, it was six months before WEEKEND REVIELLE bought them and sent down their own reporter to interview me for a suitable article to put alongside the pictures. Her name was Betty Boxall, one of London's best known female correspondents.

During the interview Miss Boxall asked if I had ever experienced any embarrassing moments with the stars? She seemed disappointed when I said no. Afterwards I escorted her to the station to catch her train, but as we reached the station she suddenly realised she had left all her notes at my home. I told her not to worry I would mail them to her. To my surprise she told me not to bother, she could remember all that I had told her. Nevertheless I did mail the notes to her next day.

When her newspaper finally published my feature, I was furious, as parts of the write-up were quite untrue. It stated for example, 'Occasionally the stars have put Ronald on the spot. One top flight Hollywood glamour girl volunteered to pose for him in the nude, then threw him out in a rage when he told her he only wanted to sketch her face.' Another piece read: 'One ageing glamour girl threatened to have him beaten-up, if he did not remove the true-to-likeness lines on her face.'

Both these statements were complete figments of Miss Boxall's over-developed imagination and clearly intended to inject the story with some sex-appeal which she felt it lacked. I was blazing with anger. I consulted a solicitor to see what action I might take, but he said that since newspapers had far more money to throw into any legal battle than I might have, he could only suggest that on this occasion I should swallow my pride and put the whole matter down to experience. He did however suggest that if anyone ever wanted to interview me again, I should ask for a typed copy of what was actually to appear in print, and get them to sign it. Without this I would not have a leg to stand on.

At the time I felt very bitter, but a couple of months later when Betty Boxall interviewed Hollywood star Jayne Mansfield and gave her the same verbal treatment, Miss Mansfield sued both Miss Boxall and her newspaper, and to my delight won her case. The newspaper sacked Betty Boxall!

Many years later (1988) radio presenter Nick Ross asked listeners who had suffered humiliation or slander at the hands of the press to get in touch with him. I did, and featured in a program which concerned itself with the proposed 'Right to Reply' bill, which many people were trying to push through Parliament. I was delighted to have this opportunity to air my views.

On a pleasanter note, two handsome young men turned up on my doorstep one day asking if they might be allowed to see some of my drawings which they had read about. I invited them in and could not help feeling that the face of one of them was very familiar, which prompted me to ask if we had ever met before? 'No', replied the young man, 'but you may have seen me on cinema screens.' Only then did I realise he was James Kenney, star of COSH BOY, (opposite Joan Collins), and many other British films at that time. Currently he was starring on the West End stage in the musical EXPRESSO BONGO. Cliff Richards would later play his role in the film version.

Kenney was very impressed with my drawings and an idea suddenly struck him. He had been planning to sink some of his savings into a coffee bar, why not open one in Hertford and decorate the walls with my work, a kind of permanent exhibition? I said I thought it a marvellous idea, whereupon he said he would return to Hertford the following day and perhaps we could visit a few estate agents to see what suitable premises might be available. True to his word Kenney came down again next day, but sadly there were no suitable premises available for conversion, and with that Kenney lost interest in the project.

*My sister Shirley, 1953*

# Roy Enters My Life

By 1950 my sister Shirley had completed her education and gone to work in the offices of a local glove-making factory. She had her own group of friends of course, and chief among these was Joyce, who had been an evacuee during the war.

During those years Joyce had lived with an aunt who lived close to us, and she attended the same school as my sister. When hostilities had ceased, Joyce had returned to live with her parents in Finsbury Park, North London, but frequently came to visit both her aunt and Shirley.

By 1953 Joyce had acquired a boyfriend named Roy, who in turn introduced Shirley to one of his pals named Ron, so that they might make up a foursome to visit cinemas and dance halls etc.

One day Joyce suggested to my sister that it would be nice if the boys could accompany them back to Hertford one Saturday night after they had been dancing, so that they could all spend Sunday together. Joyce got her aunt's permission for Roy to sleep on a settee in her living-room, and Shirley asked if Ron might be permitted to share my bed, which was a double. I agreed.

Having travelled from London by Greenline coach, all four of them came to our house for supper. Both lads were very likeable, especially Roy who was a handsome, well-built young man with a head of thick black curly hair, and a very mischievous smile. A really rough, tough, little character, his gruff voice, breezy manner and cheeky self-confidence, made an immediate impact on me, as he was so very different from anybody I had ever met before.

Introductions and supper over, Joyce took Roy to her aunt's house for the night, returning soon after breakfast next morning to spend the day with us. Poor Roy having spent the most uncomfortable night cramped up on the settee, said that rather than endure another such night of torture he would not stay overnight in Hertford again. Joyce was extremely disappointed, until I mentioned that I thought my bed might be large enough to accommodate three, and Roy agreed to give it a try next time he came down.

When the lads visited Hertford again a few weeks later, both young men shared my bed as suggested. It was a bit of a squeeze really, but Roy said it was decidedly better than sleeping on the settee, and after that the lads began to visit us quite regularly. However as the summer approached and the weather grew warmer, I suggested that it might be better, more comfortable, if the lads took it in turn to stay overnight.

As can be imagined my sister did not take too kindly to this idea, being of the opinion that HER boyfriend was more entitled to the hospitality of my bed than Joyce's. The new arrangement however made no difference to their Saturday night excursions, and soon indeed Roy was inviting me to join them, too.

The better I got to know Roy, the more obvious it became that he was a young man with very broad sexual tastes, and he confessed to me one night that he had enjoyed sex with countless girls, and even a few married women. When Roy went out with a girl he clearly had only one purpose in mind.

One Saturday night as Roy lay beside me relating some of his sexual experiences, he declared that he had often wondered what it would be like to have sex with a MAN. At first I was astonished and could not believe my ears, but since the remark had been made in such a matter-of-fact tone, knew he was thinking of it purely as a fresh experiment in sex. Then in his typically blunt manner he said, 'Why don't we try it?'

I must confess I had often wondered myself just what it would be like, but now that I was being invited point-blank to make the discovery, I hesitated and wondered what role Roy was expecting me to adopt in the exercise. However taking my acceptance for granted, he soon left me in no doubt as to the role HE intended to play, for throwing back the covers from our naked bodies he commanded in his gruff voice, 'Right, roll over.'

Not wishing to appear squeamish, I did as he asked, tightly gripping the mattress as he lowered himself down onto my back and began first a steady, then a frenzied assault on my arse. I tried hard to relax, but was all too conscious of the pain I was experiencing. Then just when I felt I could endure no more, he collapsed exhausted and satisfied onto my back, exclaiming, 'Oh boy, that was wonderful. Even better than fucking a girl - so much tighter! But next time I will get you a jar of Vaseline so that it will be more comfortable for you.'

Clearly determined that there was to be a 'next time', Roy did indeed buy a jar - a large one, for having enjoyed the experience so much, he was eager to have a repeat performance as often as possible. At first I did not share his enthusiasm, but gradually as the discomfort wore off, I actually began to enjoy it myself and was happy to oblige.

Actually I had become a substitute for Joyce, because her aunt had recently discovered that she was having sex with Roy, and forbidden Joyce ever to see Roy again.

At that time Roy was employed as a labourer working with a gang whose job it was to take up tram lines all over North London. His parents, two younger brothers and little sister, all lived in a small, shabby house in Finsbury Park, and whenever I was in the neighbourhood I would go and visit them. I liked them enormously, and they in turn seemed genuinely fond of me. In fact later when they moved to a nice new apartment in Highbury, I was invited to spend every weekend with them.

Most Saturday nights Roy and I would go to a cinema or play cards with the family. Sundays were spent in a like manner, except that in the mornings Roy and I would spend an hour wrestling or boxing in our bedroom. I was not keen on the boxing, especially after he accidentally knocked me out cold!

For the first three years our relationship was perfect, then Roy began courting a girl from Crouch End. Her name was June, and jealous of Roy's affection for me she attempted to split us up, telephoning me at the shop one day to say that Roy did not wish the see me anymore. Stunned, I refused to believe her, and calling her a liar retorted that were this true, he would be man enough to tell me himself, not leave it to her.

Later when I confronted Roy with what June had said, he flew into a rage and said he would go round to her house and settle it once and for all, 'No fucking bint is going to tell me who I can and who I can't see', he declared, 'and if she doesn't like it she can get fucking stuffed. I am not giving you up for her or anyone else!'

These words as crude as they might be, were music to my ears. Now I had the assurance I needed, and never again did June ever dare to interfere between Roy and myself.

# Bitter Disappointment

Soon after Roy's family had moved to their new apartment, Roy suggested that he and I go 'shares' hiring a car to take his family to visit relatives in South Wales, as his mother was Welsh.

Deciding to make a long weekend of it, I took a couple of days off from the shop. June was angry when she discovered that there simply was not room in the car for her to come along, too.

We set off on the Friday morning, our destination a small village in the Rhonda Valley called Tir-a-beth. Our first call was to see Roy's grandparents, who, with several young uncles, all lived in a tiny house, part of a row that backed onto a river aptly named the 'black river' since it's waters were thick with coal-dust. All the family worked in the mines, including several other uncles who lived in the vicinity, whom I was to meet later.

By contrast with the sombre surroundings, the warmth and simple friendliness that radiated from absolutely everyone I came into contact with was truly wonderful, and I have never forgotten it.

Roy's aunts and uncles were fascinated by what they considered my sophisticated appearance and manners, and they were continually apologizing for their humble surroundings and lifestyle, I could not make them understand that I only came from a working-class family myself, and when I showed a genuine eagerness to throw myself into their ways and customs, they took me to their hearts completely. Especially when on the first night of our arrival I went off on a drinking spree with Roy's granddad and got blind drunk, much to the annoyance of Roy who said he would beat me up if I ever drank like that again.

Naturally there was not sufficient accommodation for all of us at the grandparents' house and so Roy and I stayed with relatives a short distance away.

The following evening with Roy keeping a strict eye on how much I drank, we accompanied all the male members of the family to a nearby dance hall. One of the uncles and I settled down with a drink, while the others all found themselves girls to dance with on the crowded floor.

Roy, always attractive to London girls, was even more so here in Wales with his slick good looks and fashionable clothes, and soon he was dancing with the prettiest girl in the place. Unfortunately however, she had been escorted to the dance by a local boy who obviously resented the intrusion of this 'foreigner' from London trying to dazzle the local girls with his smooth ways, and in no time at all a fight had broken out between them.

Roy's uncles, all with reputations as fighters, also waded in, and soon the place was just like a battlefield, with chairs and tables being thrown about, bottles and glasses smashed and girls screaming.

Suddenly, above all the noise and confusion, there came the

sharp, shrill notes of a whistle. Someone shouted 'the police are here!' and one of Roy's uncles grabbed hold of my nearest arm and bundled me out through a side door. Roy and the rest of the family followed hot on our heels, and down through the valley we ran, across the bridge spanning the black river, not pausing for breath until we were all safely indoors. Then we all rocked with laughter.

All too soon it was time for us to return to London. It would be a weekend I would never forget. I had seen something of the way these people lived, which impressed me far more than any books I had read, or films I had seen about Wales.

They pleaded with Roy and I to return again the following summer and a couple of the younger uncles said they would try to visit us in London soon.

It was shortly after this happy weekend, that another memory was to leave itself firmly implanted in my mind, though this time it was not a happy one. It occurred one Saturday night as Roy and I lay side by side in bed, having our usual chat before going to sleep. Suddenly Roy started to discuss a visit I had made earlier in the week to where he had been working with members of his road gang. 'After you had gone...', said Roy, 'one of my mates who had not seen you before, asked how long I had known you. "I shouldn't have any more to do with him any more. He is one of those."

I lay there struck completely dumb as he continued, 'I told him he didn't know what he was fucking talking about. I had known you for years and you were not like that at all. But my mate insisted he was right, saying he could always spot one a mile off'.

I was terribly upset. Why should Roy tell me this? What did he expect me to say? It is true that we had indulged in homosexuality at one time, but it had been Roy who had made the original suggestion, and nothing like that had taken place for nearly three years now. We horsed around like most guys do, and I had to admit that I derived great pleasure from seeing Roy naked in the bath and bedroom. I also had to admit I had yearned many times for him to fuck me again, but I knew that since he had met June his attitude to that sort of thing had changed now. I knew Roy was far too interested in females to resume that kind of a relationship again, but it nevertheless gave me a great satisfaction to know that as far as I knew, I had been the only male who had ever shared this unique experience with him, and it HAD forged a special bond between us. But now, something that had once seemed so fine and beautiful, suddenly seemed sordid and crude. I was confused and bewildered, and I was heartbroken.

I recalled how repulsive Horace had appeared to me that day long ago when he had threatened to rape me, a wild-eyed sex maniac. Now I was being classed as one of THOSE. My head spun and ached, and I felt the loneliest person in the world. I wished I was dead and out of my misery. So I was not NORMAL any more, I was a FREAK, I was one of

THOSE. Oh how that awful word kept spinning in my head until I thought it would burst. Yet if I was guilty, surely Roy was too. He had encouraged it.

Thankful for the darkness, as quietly as I could, I was sobbing into my pillow, although I should have realised that no matter how hard I tried to stifle the noise my convulsive movements betrayed what was happening.

Through the darkness I heard him say, 'Ron, what's the matter? Are you crying? Speak to me.'

I opened my mouth to speak, but no sound would come. What was there to say anyway?

Again his voice came through the darkness and in unusually tender tones he said, 'Ron, please don't cry. Come on. Talk to me, please,' and reaching out, he gently placed a hand on my shoulder.

Reassured slightly, I said, 'we had better stop seeing each other. You ought not to be seen around with one of THOSE.'

Gripping my shoulder tightly, Roy suddenly laughed and said, 'Don't be silly Ron. Why should I stop seeing you? I know what you are REALLY like, my workmate doesn't. We've been mates for over three and a half years now, and there is no reason we should not be pals for the rest of our lives.'

I told Roy that if his workmate had such thoughts about me, others must have too. What about his parents for instance?

In a deeply serious mood now, Roy replied, 'You know very well you are an accepted member of the family. Mum and dad both think the world of you, and so do the kids. If THEY like you, does it really matter what others think? If the family had thought you an odd sort of guy they would soon have said so.'

By now I had ceased trembling and gained control of my emotions. What DID it matter what others thought so long as I still had Roy, although I had no wish to be an embarrassment to him.

Then as if to drown any lingering doubts I still might have, Roy said, 'Ron, I have never had a friend like you. I could not love you more if you were my own brother. I have never felt the way I do about any other guy. Now do you feel better? Don't think any more about it. Have a good night's sleep and things will seem different in the morning, and remember, no matter what anyone else may think, I will always be your friend.' Well, I did get to sleep eventually, and things did seem a little better next day, but for months afterwards I felt uneasy.

The following summer Roy developed an interest in photography and bought a 35mm camera, the idea being to take wedding pictures for friends and relations, and make a little spare cash. He suggested I buy a camera too, and next suggested we develop and print all our own films. I thought this a good idea, but since this required, amongst other things, the purchase of an enlarger, quite an expensive item, Roy wanted me to advance full payment, and allow him to pay for a half-share out of the profits he hoped to make from the wedding photographs.

The photographic equipment was kept in a spare room at Roy's home, and he demonstrated a couple of times how to use it, however I never got the chance to and Roy failed to reimburse me financially although I knew he was earning quite a lot of cash taking pictures. Just what he was doing with all of this I could not imagine, but I never liked to question him, for fear he would think I was pressing him.

However the time came when I myself wanted to print and enlarge some prints, only to discover that all the photographic equipment seemed to have disappeared. When I went into the kitchen and asked Roy's mother if she knew what had happened to it, she looked a little guilty and said, 'Oh Roy sold it all to buy June a ring, they are getting married in three months time. He's been waiting to tell you himself, but was worried you would get upset by the news.'

Trying to disguise how I really felt, I said, 'Well it I was inevitable, wasn't it.' She agreed. To my question where they would live, I was told that an uncle in Finsbury Park had agreed to rent them a couple of rooms in his house for the time being.

When Roy came home that night and brought up the subject of his engagement, he remarked that marriage or no marriage, he still intended to see me each week. He also said he wanted me to be his best man.

As the weeks sped quickly by I noticed a new name creeping into the family's conversations, a boy's name, and it became clear that this guy, who owned a car, frequently made up a threesome with Roy and June when they went out together.

Roy had never mentioned him to me at all, and this only made me suspicious. Then one morning in the early hours I was awakened by the sound of a car drawing up outside the apartment and jumping out of bed I went to the window and looked down into the street below. There I saw Roy getting out of a very smart saloon car. Knowing that this must be the new friend that Roy was being so secretive about, pangs of white-hot jealousy flooded through me, for I could not compete with a car.

Leaping back into bed, I pretended to be asleep when Roy entered our room, then slowly 'waking up' I asked him what the time was and what transport had brought him home? 'Oh... A taxi,' he said, then quickly changed the subject.

I decided to bring up the matter of the missing photographic equipment and he admitted selling it to pay for June's engagement ring, but he added that June's father was the union boss at Smithfield and had promised him a well-paid job in the market. Once he had got this, he would be able to pay me back. He never did however.

The final crushing blow came a week later. Roy took a bath, and having asked me to scrub his back as usual, asked me to lay his clothes out on the bed ready for him to put on, he was going out with June.

As I took his suit from the wardrobe, the jacket slid from the hanger onto the floor, and as I went to pick it up a slim bank book slipped from an inside pocket. Before returning it to the pocket, I could not resist looking inside to see how much Roy had got, and to my utter amazement saw that he was worth over £500 - perhaps not a lot of money by today's standards, but a lot in the 1950s. I felt so angry and so duped, and by Roy of all people. I had known him for four years, yet did I really know him at all? I felt I would never be able to trust him again.

At first I considered confronting him over the matter - it would be interesting to hear what excuse he would concoct. However I decided I longer CARED what he might say. If he had lied to me over this, what other things had he lied about also? Maybe our whole relationship had been one of convenience as far as he was concerned. I'd had enough: It was all over now as far as I was concerned. My love for him was utterly dead. I decided I would see him through the wedding as promised, but once it was over, I never wanted to see him again. I said nothing to him as he got dressed, and behaved as though I had discovered nothing.

Shortly before the wedding Roy told me that one of his cousins was apparently expecting to play the role of best man and rather than cause any friction between his relatives, Roy had consented. He asked if I minded? At one time I WOULD have been disappointed, but now I was really rather thankful, and I think Roy was a little surprised how ready I was to relinquish the 'honour'.

The wedding and the reception all went according to plan, but I was too tired and too bitter to join much in the festivities that followed and I left early without saying goodbye to anyone. Incidentally my sister and Ron, who had married six months earlier, were also there as Roy's guests. The occasion over, I made no further attempts to see Roy again, but a few months later I received a telephone call from him to say that he was in Hertford with a 'friend', could I meet him somewhere in the town for a drink?

My curiosity aroused, I suggested we meet in the bar of the Salisbury Hotel, and when I arrived twenty minutes later, found him in the company of a very brassy blonde girl who had all the hallmarks of a prostitute, although she claimed to be a hostess at the 'Nell Gwyne' night club in Soho.

It appeared that having secured the job he wanted in Smithfield Market, Roy had already tired of June sexually. During the evening he asked why I had not been to see him since the wedding? I made my excuses, and when it was time for us to part, said I would call next time I was in London, although I had no intention of doing anything of the kind.

I never saw Roy again, although he did call at my home some months later and spent a couple of hours talking to my parents. I was away at the time.

More than twenty years later, in the summer of 1983 Roy's name was splashed across the headlines of all the national newspapers with the claims that he was now the 'Mr Big' of London's criminal underworld. There were claims that he was also the brains and finance behind many of the biggest armed robberies taking place all over the country, and he was said to be a millionaire night club owner who had links with crime even in the United States. There were also pictures of him with various show business personalities. He had lost a lot of his hair now, and he had put on a lot of weight.

Later still, in 1984, his name was all over the front pages of national newspapers again, this time it seemed he had been sent to prison for four years for trying to evade paying tax on fourteen million pounds-worth of gold Krugerrands he had imported into this country, then resold. It was reported that Scotland Yard had been trying for twenty years to nail him, now at last they had succeeded. Television too was to devote a whole programme to his criminal exploits.

Incredible as it may seem however, even in prison Roy was able to mastermind an operation to smuggle ONE HUNDRED MILLION POUNDS worth of cocaine into Britain, for in March, 1989, all the national press carried front page and even double-page stories about how the customs and excise people had thwarted the attempt, and Roy had been sentenced at the Old Bailey to a further TWENTY years in prison! It was claimed to be the biggest drugs haul ever.

At last it looked as if Roy had finally bitten of more than he could chew, and the man the press and television had been referring to as 'The Godfather' and 'The Untouchable' because of his ability to evade prosecution, looked like being out of circulation for a VERY long time.

This latest news made me feel terribly sad, for I could not help but remember the handsome, vital and confident young man who had once played such a very important part in my own life and affections more than thirty years earlier. Roy had certainly come a long way sine the 1950s, but sadly he had chosen to take the wrong pathway, and my heart bled for his parents and other members of his family.

# Boys or Girls?

A few weeks after ending my relationship with Roy, I was travelling into London on a Greenline coach, when an attractive blonde-haired young man who had also boarded the coach in Hertford, came and sat next to me. We engaged in conversation and he mentioned that he had read all about my artwork in the local newspaper, but had not had the opportunity to see any of my work for himself. Named Ray, like me he worked in a Hertford menswear store and asked if he might call round to see my drawings some time, adding that perhaps I would allow him to bring a friend as well? I agreed and we made a date for the following week.

When Ray and his friend Ian did call, we all got along famously together and as the evening proceeded they confessed that they were both homosexual. Ray told me that he had been raped by a man when he was only twelve years old, but had enjoyed the experience so much, that he had since been to bed with more men than he could possibly count. Ian on the other hand, was looking for a more enduring relationship, but had had more than his fair share of men, too.

I liked both lads but found Ray the most shocking. He was so fearless and blatant about his homosexuality, and he asked how many men I had been to bed with. When I told him only one, he remarked that life was too short to waste it being virginal.

In conversation the boys used all kinds of expressions I had never heard before, and spoke of places I never knew existed. Their world was so foreign to me, but the more they talked about it, the more wonderfully exciting it sounded.

Ray said one of the most notorious places in London's West End was a large public house called 'The Standard' (since closed) in Piccadilly Circus, and he asked if I would like to visit it? 'But you will have to wear the right gear', he added quickly. My curiosity aroused, I agreed, and during the next few days Ray set about selecting the kind or clothing I would need. He said that since I had a good figure and fine legs I should make the most of them.

On the night chosen for my 'debut' I hardly dared set foot outside my house, and we certainly caused a few eyebrows to rise before we reached London. Ray wearing a black leather jacket open to the waist to reveal that he was bare-chested underneath, a scarlet handkerchief round his neck, pale blue jeans and no underwear, plus black leather boots.

My own outfit consisted of a scarlet shirt with a stand-up collar, a black handkerchief round the neck, black skintight jeans and no underwear, with black suede shoes. By today's standards NOT very bold, but in 1957 when men's clothing was still extremely sombre and sober, we must have looked like something from another planet. At first I was terribly embarrassed, but Ray was enjoying all the stares and whispers we generated, and pretty soon I found I enjoyed being a rebel too.

Arriving in London we headed straight for 'The Standard'. Crowded with servicemen and civilians of all nationalities, it was exclusively male, although Ray told me there was a 'normal' bar downstairs.

We ploughed our way through a sea of grinning faces, unseen hands groping and fondling us as we passed. Reaching the bar at last, we ordered a couple or drinks and leaned on the counter to take in the smoke-filled scene. A short distance away Ray saw some friends, and we endeavoured to reach them. They were four in number, and the face of one looked very familiar.

After introducing me to them, and chatting for only a few minutes, Ray suggested we go back to the bar again and I asked Ray who the owner of the familiar face was?

'Why, he is Daniel Farson, the television presenter', he replied, and in answer to my next question 'What is doing in a place like this? Looking for talent to put in his shows?' Ray burst out laughing and said, 'Looking for talent to put in his bed would be nearer the truth!'

A few moments later a handsome Italian-looking man just a few feet along the bar, smiled at me and moved closer, then he offered to buy me a drink. Thanking him I declined, while under his breath Ray called me a fool, but I told him I had only come along as an observer - I had no wish to get involved. A moment later seeing someone else he knew at the other end of the room, Ray said he must go and have a few words with him - alone, if I did not mind? Then reassuring me that he would not be long, he slipped away.

Feeling very conspicuous and vulnerable as the minutes ticked by and Ray did not return, I felt very uncomfortable, especially when I noticed that Ray's friend was moving towards the door, Ray following.

Shifting my gaze along the bar once more, I was aware that two men just a few feet away were very interested in me, and overheard one say, 'I really fancy that in the red shirt.' Horrified, and filled with sudden panic, I pushed my way out of the bar as if the devil himself were after me, and made my way out into the street.

Outside there was no sign of Ray or his friend, and I was angry that he had left me alone in a place like that. It was nearly half-an-hour later that he returned on his own, grinning all aver his face. He said he was sorry for leaving me, but explained that since his friend only lived in a flat 'just round the corner', they had gone there for a 'quickie'. He roared with laughter when I told him what the fellow at the bar had said, and that three other men had offered to take me inside for a drink while I had been waiting outside for him to return! He remarked I was lucky I was attracting so much attention.

Calming me down, Ray suggested we go to another bar not far away called 'The Captain's Cabin', promising that this would be quieter. It was in a basement and there were a few odd characters standing and sitting about, but here they were less bold and obvious. We stayed for a couple of drinks, then Ray wanted to move to another bar in Piccadilly before closing time.

Called 'The White Bear' it was actually a large restaurant, but it had a small bar discreetly screened off from general view, because the clientele were mostly heterosexual. Ray led me to a group of rather smartly dressed, but effeminate-looking men wearing lounge suits, all of whom seemed pleased to see Ray. He introduced me, and at once they made me feel they had all known me for years. One, who turned out to be Frankie Howard, kept everyone in fits of laughter with his funny remarks, and seemed to take a particular fancy to me when I made a few remarks with a rather masculine flavour. Turning to his companions, he announced, 'Darlings, this one is mine. He is the only REAL man among us!' Then digging me in the ribs he said, 'You WILL come back to my place for the night, won't you?' Not wishing to hurt his feelings, I told him I had already made my plans, but perhaps another time.

Soon the barman was calling for last orders and everyone made preparations to leave. Ray and I joined a few who were making for an all-night cafe for coffee and sandwiches, while others began to hunt around the streets of Soho looking for a suitable bed-mate.

Later, on a homeward bound train with Ian who had arrived at the all-night cafe at the same time as Ray and myself, I started turning over in my mind all the events of the evening, and expressed my fascination at seeing smart sophisticated men mixing so freely and so unselfconsciously with rougher, courser types.

Ian said there were no class barriers in the gay world, nor racial ones either. He said the gay world was full of contrasts - you could be surrounded with friends one night, and quite alone another. The vast majority of men who visited the pubs and clubs were very promiscuous in their lovemaking, and friendships were usually very short-lived. Everyone was looking for the impossible, the ideal partner.

When I remarked that a lot of servicemen seemed to flock to the bars, Ray explained that when they were short of money and a bed for the night, they always knew that both could be found in these places. He said that sailors, for obvious reasons, were more inclined to indulge in gay sex, and had a particularly tolerant attitude to queers.

Having enjoyed my introduction into London's 'gay scene', I made regular trips to London with Ray every Saturday night, although usually I returned to Hertford alone, Ray having found himself a 'bed for the night' with some attractive young man. I met lots of amusing people, and became very popular among Ray's friends who were continually trying to seduce me, but at that point I was cautious about going to bed with any of them.

Something I forgot to mention is that although Ray and Ian were friends and both gay, their relationship was purely platonic. Originally they had met while both serving in the RAF, Ray had come from Newcastle, Ian from the small Scottish island of Rassay, a few miles east of Skye. When demobbed, they decided to stick together and move south. Ray had taken a job with Burtons the big chain of tailoring stores and been sent to Hertford, and Ian took a job in a big pharmaceutical company in Ware, just a couple of miles away, and they had both taken lodgings with a Hertford widow.

But to return to the story. Occasionally Ray mentioned two handsome young men who lived in the same street as he and Ian. Their names were John and Don, and since John owned a little three-wheeled car, and Ray owned a scooter, Ray frequently used the topic of mechanics to get into conversation with John. Ray knew that both John and Don were straight, but that only encouraged him all the more - he said it was a greater challenge to attempt to seduce a 'normal' guy.

One day as I was leaving my shop to go home, I saw Ray talking to two handsome boys on the opposite side of the street. Seeing me, Ray called me over to meet John and Don. We got onto the subject of my artwork, and both lads expressed the desire to call around and see it sometime, and so I invited them round the following week. So impressed were they with the sketches, they asked if they might bring their respective girlfriends round also. I said I would be delighted, and the girls were brought round a couple of days later.

John's girl, Diana, was particularly sweet, and after that John and Diana became regular callers, all three of us often squeezing into their little two-seater car for drives into the countryside and visits to local pubs. This meant that I saw much less of Ray and Ian, but they had their own lives to lead.

About this time I also met a very attractive young woman named Patricia Thompson. A receptionist with a firm of local opticians, I had first met her when taking a pair of my spectacles in for repair. She had asked if I was the artist who had held an exhibition in the town some time ago and said she was sorry she had missed it, so I promptly invited her to come round to my home one evening for a private viewing, and she accepted.

When she called a few evenings later, she explained that she and her widowed mother lived in a large twelve-roomed 16th century house, close to the town centre. I also learned that her father, who had been a test pilot for De Havilland's, had been killed trying out a new plane, while her eldest brother had been killed in the army during the war, but that she had a younger brother serving as a Frogman in the Royal Navy.

Pat was a very educated girl who spoke seven languages. She had hoped to be an Air Stewardess, but had failed the medical with an ear problem. She was also a very vivacious girl, and I liked her enormously. At the end of the evening I walked her home, and before parting she invited me to meet her mother and take tea with them later that week.

Pat's house was a large double-fronted place, part of a long row of ancient buildings, it had once been an inn, and had white plaster walls and lots of sombre black woodwork both outside and in. I gathered that because of its size, most of the rooms were never used.

Pat's mother was a rather mannish type of woman, with grey severely cropped hair, who wore equally severely-cut Harris Tweed two-piece suits. After tea we sat round a huge open fireplace in which some logs were burning, and talked. I was fascinated to discover that the house was haunted by a ghost they called 'George'. They had never actually seen him, but said he could frequently be heard walking in the large stone-paved hall, which ran right through the middle or the house. Mrs. Thompson said that far from being frightened of George, they found it a great comfort to have him around, and asked if I had not noticed the peculiarly 'friendly' atmosphere the house seemed to possess.

The house had no electricity or gas, and consequently when one wished to use the bathroom at night, it was necessary to take e torch or candle to light one's way. Despite Mrs. Thompson's assurance that George was friendly, I never liked to linger in the hall or on the stairs at night.

Before long I too was to hear the ghostly footsteps. They approached the room we were all sitting in, and instinctively we all turned our heads as if expecting the door to open and someone enter, but then Mrs. Thompson relaxed and said, 'Oh its only George again.'

As my friendship with Pat blossomed, John suggested that we make up a foursome since he had now acquired a larger car. However having spent a couple of evenings in this fashion, it soon became apparent that the two girls did not get on too well together. Pat considered Diana scatter-brained, and Diana thought Pat a snob. Eventually Pat announced that she wanted to make up a foursome with two friends of her own set, her best friend Carol, and Carol's boyfriend Mike. I had met the couple a few times, and quite liked them, but since neither Mike nor I owned a car, we had to do all our travelling by public transport.

During the winter of that year, Pat gave a party at her house for about twenty people, and to please me invited John and Diana. The party was a great success, but a few days later tragedy struck when Pat's youngest brother drowned in Portland harbour during a naval exercise. It seemed so sad that all the male members or her family were now dead. Christmas was only a few weeks away, so my parents invited Pat and her mother to spend Christmas with us.

After a respectable period had passed, I decided to hold a party to cheer Pat up. It was the first big party I had ever given, and I devoted a considerable amount of time and money to make it a success. However it was to be the last evening that Pat and I would ever spend together.

Carol was one of the guests, and when she arrived alone, she explained that Mike had urgent business in London but would be putting in an appearance later. Pat seemed unusually concerned by his absence, and I thought this very odd.

Eventually when Mike did turn up around 10pm, he was driving a brand new car he had just collected from London showrooms, and we all trooped outside to admire it, a new car in those days of severe austerity being really quite something. We were all most impressed, particularly Pat who remarked, 'Lovely, now we can REALLY go out in style.'

The party over, Pat, Carol and Mike all stayed behind to help with the clearing-up. Then I was just about to fetch my overcoat to take Pat home, when Mike said, 'No need for that Ron, I can drop Pat off on the way back from Carol's place.'

A couple or evenings later when I called at Pat's home to take her to a cinema, Mrs. Thompson came to the door looking distinctively uncomfortable and told me that Pat was not at home. Puzzled, I said surely she had not forgotten our date? I asked where Pat had gone, but Mrs. Thompson was evasive. I said I would call again the following evening. When I did however, I was again informed that Pat was 'not at home'. Very annoyed by now, I asked Mrs Thompson what kind of game Pat was playing? Stating that I would not call again, I said Pat knew where to find me if she wished to see me.

Well, Pat did not call to see me, but a few nights later Carol did. In tears she told me that Mike had given her the brush-off in favour of Pat.

'Have you seen her since your party, Ron?'

'No.'

'And you are not likely to either. The little bitch. This is not the first time she has taken a boyfriend away from me, but it WILL be the last. I am absolutely finished with her this time!'

It was several weeks later that I caught a glimpse of Pat coming towards me down one of the streets of the town, but having seen me, she quickly ducked into a side turning. Six months later I heard that she had married Mike.

When I got over the initial shock of being jilted, I vowed never to get involved with females again. John and Diana were surprised when I gave them the news, and Diana declared, 'I never did like her, and anyway, she was not the kind of girl for you, Ron'.

Ray and Ian, who still called occasionally, said they had known from the start that my romance would not work. 'How could it? You should accept the fact that you are gay, and realise that the only happiness you are likely to find is amongst members of your own sex.'

They were right of course, and so to boost my flagging self-esteem and make myself more attractive to other gays, I went out and bought some weight-lifting equipment to give my body a little more bulk and definition. I also bought a sunlamp to give myself an all over tan in the winter months. During the summer months I went to the nearby common and sunbathed naked at every opportunity. I would liked have joined a nudist club, but the nearest ones were all between Watford and St. Albans on the other side of the county. I loved being naked.

*A selection of my Physique drawings*

# International Success

For years now, because of my interest in body-building and nudism, I had regularly bought copies of HEALTH & STRENGTH and HEALTH & EFFICIENCY magazines. The former magazine was always well illustrated with photographs of splendidly-built young men wearing only swim-slips, and posing in appropriate manner to display their muscles to full advantage.

Inspired by these photos I made drawings of a similar nature, and these hung side by side with the film star portraits at my public exhibitions, but later Ray and Ian introduced me to another type of 'physique' magazine, which daringly showed young men posing naked except for a tiny G-string.

In this type of magazine the models often did not have exaggerated muscles, but were more slender and natural. The poses too were not of a 'strained' variety, but showed the models doing simple things like showering, bathing, or simply lounging, draped over a settee. It was perfectly obvious that although these magazines might carry some form of literature to give the impression that they were intended for body-building enthusiasts, in truth they were simply pin-up books aimed at a mainly gay public.

Frequently these magazines also contained drawings of a similar nature, showing young, men nude or semi-nude in erotic situations which gave ample excuse to flatter the male anatomy. Technically these drawings were usually very poorly executed, and both Ray and Ian had often remarked that my own standard of work was far superior. Why not try to get my work published?

Having made enquiries, I discovered that although there were a number of brilliant British photographers operating in this field, there was only one British artist of any consequence. His name was Marc Angelo, and his work was so dreadful I decided I WOULD try my luck. All the real competition came from the United States and one lone artist in Scandinavia - Tom of Finland.

The first person I approached was a man calling himself 'Lon of London' with an office in New Oxford Street. A very seedy-looking man he published a magazine called PHYSIQUE ARTISTRY. He liked my work and did publish one of my drawings, a duo, but when I discovered that he dealt in pornography as a sideline, I did not return to him.

Next I went to see a very well known photographer, John Barrington, who also used the name John Paignton, he had an office above a shop on Richmond Hill. He made it clear that he also dealt in pornography, but liked my work and would be happy to publish it, on one condition - he put HIS name on all of it! Clearly I was not prepared to have him do that, and was amazed that he should suggest such a thing, so I promptly left.

Next I decided to write to a photographer calling himself 'Scott', and was asked to go along to his home in Bayswater Road with samples of my work. The door to his top-floor apartment was opened by a handsome, dark-haired young man aged about thirty, who invited me into a very tastefully furnished lounge, and looking through my work said it was extremely good.

'I shall be pleased to act as your agent' he declared. 'However to make the work more appealing to my clients I would like you to make them as provocative as possible, without breaking any laws. Do this, and you could do very well for yourself. I suggest we go fifty-fifty with the profits- are you agreeable to this?'

Well, of course I was delighted, and during the next few weeks I spent all my leisure time producing the desired drawings and mailing them to Scott. However as months passed and none of my work was published, I began to wonder what was wrong. Then one day I arrived at his apartment unexpected, and found a party in progress. Scott smiled as he opened the door to me, and led me into the lounge where a crowd of good-looking young men were all drinking and talking. I was briefly introduced to them, before Scott suggested we go into his bedroom so that he could look at my latest work in peace.

He spread my drawings over the surface of the bed, and was just about to comment on them when the door opened and a young man looked in and asked, 'May I come in?' The new arrival was introduced to me as Marc Angelo. Quickly I recalled all those terrible physique drawings I had seen in various magazines.

So THIS was Angelo.

'Is this the fellow whose work you intend to market?', Angelo asked. 'Very wooden and lifeless, isn't it! You are taking a bit of a risk, aren't you?'

'Personally I think its excellent', said Scott.

'Oh well, that's up to you I suppose!', retorted Angelo, and promptly left the room ignoring me completely. I felt utterly humiliated.

Gathering up my work Scott invited me to join the party in the other room, but I was in no mood for parties, and made an excuse to leave, Scott escorting me down to the entrance hall of the apartment building.

As we were descending in the elevator he remarked, 'You aren't really worried by the bitchy remarks Marc made, are you?' I replied that naturally I was. It was alright for Angelo, he was already established, adding that what made the insult worse, was that his own work was so atrocious. Scott gave a little laugh and said, 'You must not mind Marc, the very fact that he was so spiteful only confirms how good you ARE. He is afraid of the competition. Instead or being miserable, you should be rejoicing.'

Scott was right of course, and I became more than ever determined to succeed. I would show Angelo who was the better artist! When another couple of months passed without my work appearing in print however, I felt I really must do something about it, find someone else to represent me. I therefore wrote to another well-known photographer whose work I greatly admired, known as 'Royale'.

I wrote explaining what had happened with Scott and a few days later I received a reply that he was not at all surprised to hear I had come to a full stop with Scott, for he happened to know that Scott was financially indebted to Angelo, and so clearly the artist was stifling any efforts made on my behalf.

Royale went on to assure me that if HE liked my work, then I would definitely see results for my labours, and he invited me to go along to his home in Pimlico provided that I could retrieve all my drawings from Scott, saying he would want to handle my work exclusively.

Arriving at Royale's elegant white-painted Georgian house a few days later, I rang the bell and the door was opened by an elderly housekeeper dressed all in black, who asked me to make myself comfortable in a sitting-room on the first floor until Mr. Clavering (Royale's real name), could join me.

As I waited I admired the sumptuous surroundings. Walls covered in green damask and hung with oil paintings in large gilt frames, the furniture all antique, Persian rugs on the highly polished floor. Antique bronze statues and gilt candelabra gleamed everywhere under the light of a huge crystal chandelier which hung from the centre of the ceiling. 'The physique business must be extremely profitable,' I thought to myself.

A few minutes later Mr. Clavering entered the room. A tall, slim man in his early fifties, with dark hair having traces of grey at the temples. He was not particularly attractive, but clearly a man of taste and style. We shook hands, he looked through the work I had brought with me, and he expressed his pleasure with it.

'I shall be happy to act as your agent,' he said.

Delighted, I remarked, 'Judging by your beautiful home, the physique market must be very profitable one?'

He laughed and replied, 'Physique photography is merely my hobby. My real interests are in film business. I own a chain of cinemas, a film distributing company, and I sometimes put money into film production. I went into the physique business quite by chance. I had always been interested in photography and the male nude, and one day decided to try my hand at some physique shots. I submitted the results to a couple of magazines and to my surprise they immediately asked for more, in no time at all I was doing very well. Because of my wealth, I was able to equip myself with the best studio in London, and offer double the normal fee to get the best models. All of which made me very unpopular with all the other physique photographers of course, but I am wealthy enough not to care what they think, and they know it!'

Pouring us both drinks, he told me to call him Basil, and sat down beside me. Then gazing down at my tight-fitting trousers he edged closer, but the next moment the door opened, and a very handsome young man, dark and in his early twenties, entered the room. There was something familiar about his face and then I remembered where I had seen it, on the pages of numerous gay magazines, for this ruggedly good-looking young man was a model whose naked beauty I had admired many times.

Basil introduced him to me as Don (Avard), his 'private secretary', and I stood up to shake hands with him. Don said he was on his way to meet his girlfriend, and asked Basil if he might borrow the car for the evening. Basil agreed and the young man left the room. Later I discovered that Basil owned a Bentley Continental, and when on business trips, Don wore a smart chauffeur's uniform to drive him around.

With Don gone, Basil asked if I would like to see his studio and took me down to the basement. It was a huge room with batteries of lights everywhere. Apart from a large assortment of props, there were also racks of every kind of clothing imaginable, military, naval, Roman, leather, as well as boots, helmets, and other equipment, all used for semi-nude shots. I was most impressed.

Suddenly Basil pulled a large and beautiful leather-bound book from a shelf saying, 'These are the type of photographs I am MOST interested in.' Holding it so that I could see, he flicked quickly through the pages, remarking that I could have a proper look at it next time I came to visit him.

The book was a collection of fantastic pornographic photos, heterosexual as well as gay, with couples and groups indulging in every kind or sexual act imaginable. Basil said he had collected them from every continent in the world. Having replaced the book on the shelf, he suggested we return upstairs, and as we climbed the stairs he followed behind me, gently probing his fingers into the cleft between my buttocks.

It was about 7pm now, and Basil invited me to stay and meet two guests he was expecting to arrive for dinner. I asked if I might use the bathroom and he gave me directions. WHAT a bathroom! I had never seen anything like it. Larger than my sitting-room at home, it had three walls of black marble, and the fourth made entirely of mirror. The floor was white marble, and the bath itself was a solid block of black marble placed directly in front of the mirrored wall. The hand basin and the toilet, which was concealed behind a frosted glass partition, were also black, and all the fittings were of gold. A large crystal chandelier hung from the centre of the ceiling.

Returning to the sitting-room, I was just in time to hear the doorbell ring, and Basil said his guests must have arrived, Mr Josh Joshua and his wife. Basil explained that Mr. Joshua owned three of the world's most important physique magazines and was the country's main distributor for such materials from abroad. He also said that Mr. Joshua's wife, Jackie (Verne), was one of London's top fashion models.

The next moment into the room walked a very beautiful red-haired woman in her late twenties, and an attractive dark-skinned man with thick black wavy hair, who was short and powerfully built. The woman wore a white silk trouser suit and gold sandals, the man a dark lounge suit. They smiled and shook hands with Basil, then with me as Basil introduced us to each other. Basil offered us all drinks, and while he discussed some business with Joshua, I chatted to the beautiful Jackie. A little later the housekeeper announced that dinner was ready, and we made our way into another splendid room. Here we ate a delicious meal, washed down with champagne, under the light of yet another huge crystal chandelier and candles, which gave an extra sparkle to all the glass and silverware on the grey marble table.

During dinner Joshua asked questions concerning my work and myself, and although his manner was brisk and business-like, he had a keen sense of humour. I learned that although he had been born in India, he was now an American citizen. He had been living in London for the past four years, and married to Jackie for just one. His powerful build he explained, was due to the fact that he had once won the title 'Mr. India' and been a runner-up in the Mr. Universe contest.

After the meal we all retired to the sitting-room again where Joshua asked to see examples of my work. He was most impressed, and asked if he might take some away that night for use in the latest issues of his magazines.

Basil was delighted, and an hour later when the couple had gone, he said, 'Well you are off to a good start. If Joshua likes your work, you can't fail.'

I was delighted too. In just a single evening I had obtained as allies and friends, two of the most powerful men in the business. Now I would show Marc Angelo!

In the weeks that followed I worked hard to produce more and more drawings, and what a thrill it was to see all my work appearing in print. Not only did they appear in the magazines, Basil was producing prints, which gay men could buy to hang on the walls of their bedrooms or dens. Once a month I would go along to Basil's opulent home to deliver a fresh batch of drawings, and within a year I had become the most popular gay artist in Britain, with a big following in the USA as well. I was on my way.

On my visits to Basil's home I often met some of the young men who modelled for him, and was surprised to discover that among these were not only wrestlers and weight-lifters, Basil liked more muscular models, but quite a lot of guardsmen from Wellington Barracks who were keen to drop their pants if the price was right. For his military-type photos, he adopted the professional name of 'Hussar'.

Basil loved to entertain in his beautiful home and many famous people were his guests. In recent weeks I knew both Brigitte Bardot and the Duke of Bedford had dined with him.

On one occasion when he was going to Cambridge, he broke his journey to visit me in Hertford. I was surprised when I opened my front door to find Don Avard standing there in his smart chauffeur's uniform and Basil sitting in the back of the Bentley.

I invited Basil to meet my family and take a cup of tea with us, and when he met my sister who happened to be visiting us, he was so impressed with her glamorous face and fabulous figure, he immediately offered her a five-year film contract, but to his surprise and my own, she turned it down saying she had no wish to take up an acting career. How many girls would have turned down an opportunity like THAT! Basil only stayed about twenty minutes, then continued on his way.

By now with the help of Basil and Josh Joshua I had become an international name in the world of gay magazines, my work appearing regularly in Adonis, Body Beautiful, Male Classics, Fizeek and AMG (Athletic Model Guild) of California, to name just a few.

Being an era when it was illegal to draw or photograph frontal nudes, I would first draw a naked figure, then sketch seams down the sides of the legs, adding wrinkles around the knees and across the genitals, add a fly and waistband, then some shading to give the appearance of skin-tight jeans. In some cases they looked as if they were tattoos! Very sexy and erotic. As Mae West once shrewdly said, 'It's not what you show, it's the way that you show it.'

I also drew groups of men in situations that were either suggestive or told a little story. Often I made them very humorous. The titles I gave my drawings would give a little idea of what I wanted to achieve: 'Cool Cats on a Hot Night', 'The Old Water Hole', 'Men About The House', 'No Business Like Show Business' etcetera, etcetera.

Gay magazines never paid fees to photographers or artists for their contributions, instead they gave them free space in the magazines to advertise their wares. Photographers sold sets of photos of hunky men wearing just G-strings, and artists sold prints of their drawings in a variety of sizes suitable for large pockets or hanging on bedroom walls. At my peak I was selling prints to clients in 37 different countries throughout the world.

As can be imagined, many customers were eager to get their hands on pornography, and I knew that quite a lot of photographers were happy to secretly oblige. Artists too got the same request in form of 'private commissions.' One of the perks of being a gay photographer or artist was that you got plenty of sex. Real star models and guardsmen from Wellington Barracks could command a fee, but most young guys were so eager to see themselves in magazines, they were happy to pose for just a free set of photos or a drawing as payment, being well aware that getting fucked in the process was always a strong possibility.

*Brigitte Bardot and Basil leaving the Royale Cinema*

# A New Lover and a London Home

Ray and Ian still called to see me occasionally, and one evening Ian told me he had fallen madly in love with a guy called Jim, who he had met in a Holborn pub. What really surprised me was that apparently the chap was married, and had two little boys, one of whom was disabled and had to live in a special home in Tonbridge Wells.

Shortly after Ian and Jim had met, Jim's wife deserted him and their three-year-old son, Mark. Luckily Jim's mother lived on the opposite side of the street to him, and had agreed to care for the boy. With no wife to worry about, the affair with Ian really began to flourish.

For several months all went well, then one night Ian came to see me in a state of utter depression and told me that Jim had finished with him. Near to tears he told me it had all been a dreadful misunderstanding. I gave him a drink, and told him to tell me what had happened.

He explained that the previous night they had been in a pub, and wanting to pee he had gone to the toilet, but there he had been interfered with by a total stranger, but before he could do his trousers up again, Jim had walked in and blamed Ian for what had happened, calling him a two-timing rat and telling him he wanted no more to do with him, then he stormed off out of the pub. Later he had returned in the company of some woman, and flirted with her right under Ian's nose.

Poor Ian was completely heartbroken and asked if I would see Jim on his behalf and try to bring about a reconciliation. At first I said no, I did not want to get involved, but after a little persuasion I finally agreed.

Ian suggested we go to Jim's favourite pub the following Saturday night, and he could introduce me, he said Jim had always wanted to meet me. Then Ian was to move on to another pub, the William the IV in Battersea, where if I was successful in patching things up, I could take Jim and we could all drink to their happy reunion.

The following Saturday when Jim walked into the pub and saw Ian sitting at the bar with me, he hesitated for a moment, then completely ignoring Ian, he walked up to me, and reaching for my hand said, 'You must be Ron, the artist Ian has talked about so much. I have wanted to meet you for a long time.' He smiled broadly and offered to buy me a drink, while Ian tactfully withdrew to the other end of the bar, then left the pub with a couple of other friends.

After Ian had gone I tried to steer the conversation onto Ian and how upset he was, but Jim would hear none of it, 'If your only purpose in coming here tonight was to try and patch things up between me and Ian, you have had a wasted journey. That's all over now,' he said, adding, 'I want to talk about you instead.'

Clearly there was nothing I could do to help Ian's cause, and so I set about enjoying what was left or the evening with Jim, and I had to admit that I was smitten with him too, a small but handsome young man about my own age. Later when he walked me to Holborn Underground station and asked if he could see me again the following Saturday night, I was happy to agree.

All the way back to Hertford that night I was wondering what Ian would say when he knew that far from mending things between him and Jim, it now looked as though I might have replaced him in Jim's affections. I hated myself for the way things had turned out, but it had just been one of those things one can't control.

When Ian called to see me the next morning, he was very understanding, and shrugging his shoulders he said, 'Oh well, that's life I suppose. But if I can't have him, then I would rather you did than anyone else. Thanks for trying, anyway.'

The next time I met Jim, he suggested we meet every Sunday night as well as Saturdays, and next he was suggesting we also spend one evening together at mid-week, too. It seems I really had made an impression on Jim, and I was equally attracted to him.

As my infatuation with Jim grew, I felt the ever-increasing desire to sleep with him, and was jealous of the fact that Ian had, many times. When I hinted that I would be happy to stay overnight with him, he said the apartment was in such a mess he would feel too ashamed for me to stay there.

Eventually however there came the night when I had missed both the last train AND the last Greenline coach to Hertford, and so he had no alternative but to invite me back to his place.

I had never seen the street where he lived before, Ordehall Street, let alone his apartment, which occupied the ground floor and basement of a drab old Victorian house. He had two rooms on each floor, and shared a toilet with the two other floors above him.

Having fumbled for his key and unlocked the door, he said, 'I forgot to mention I have not paid the electricity bill lately, so they have cut off my power. You had better hang on to my coat-tail until I can find a candle to light.'

We groped our way down a long hall to a bedroom at the back of the house, then I stood in the doorway until he found the candle and lit it. The sight that greeted my eyes was pathetic. A small single bed pushed under the window without sheets or coverlet. An old scratched chest or drawers on which stood a couple of cheap plaster ornaments, an easy chair piled high with crumpled shirts and underwear, and a chipped and badly scratched wardrobe.

The room had no pictures on the walls, but over the fireplace, pasted onto a large sheet or pegboard, were a dozen pictures of naked girls he must have torn from various girlie magazines. There were no rugs on the floor, only some rather dirty looking linoleum.

Telling me to sit on the bed, Jim asked if I would like to hear his favourite poem? We had both drunk quite heavily that night, and somehow the combination of drink and these very humble surroundings, together with Jim wishing to read some poetry, made everything seem a bit unreal.

The poem about a woman's fisherman husband being drowned at sea in a storm, and with Jim reading it with so much feeling, brought a lump to my throat. A sense of overwhelming pity came over me as I realised that Jim associated himself with the woman in the poem. Deserted by his wife, his children living away from home, and the home itself in such a pathetic state. I felt a burning desire to help Jim and bring a little happiness into his life.

Having read the poem Jim began to undress, I did the same and naked we both climbed into bed. For a while we lay talking, then Jim slid a hand down to my groin to fondle me. I kissed him, and I tingled with pleasure as he began to explore the rest of my body. His own desire rising, he slipped both arms around my waist and crushing me against his body, kissed me and forced his tongue into my mouth.

For the next hour I was to experience a kind of lovemaking that was quite new to me. Sex with Roy had never been like this. With him it had just been animal lust. This was heated with the passion of someone who wanted me not as a substitute, but for what I really was, a man. When it was all over and he had slumped exhausted onto the bed, he remarked, 'That was bloody marvellous. You really ARE a beautiful fuck.' Then clasped in each other's arms, we fell into a deep, contented sleep.

I say contented, but in fact half way through the night, Jim was ready yet again to take his pleasure, and the next time I was woken by Jim caressing my body it was daylight and quite late on Sunday morning, but his sexual appetite seemed insatiable, and soon he was mounting me yet again. His desire then temporarily satisfied, I said I would get up and make a pot of tea. Did he have any? He told me where to find the necessary items and slipping on my pants I went down to the basement.

Later in the morning Jim took me across the road to meet his family, Italian mother, Irish father, nineteen-year-old brother Tony, and Jim's little son, Mark, a very pretty child, his dark hair cut in an American crew-cut style.

After the introductions and a cup of tea, Jim and I took Mark out for the day in the London parks, buying lunch at a cafe, and taking him back to his grandma's in time for tea, which we were invited to enjoy too. In the evening we accompanied his father to a local pub for a couple of pints and a game or darts. It was to be the first of many such weekends we would spend in that fashion.

As time passed, I found the evenings spent away from Jim increasingly hard to bear, and since I was spending so much time travelling backwards and forwards I suggested I might as well move in with him, and he agreed.

When I announced to my family that I was moving in with Jim, they all voiced the opinion that I was making a terrible mistake, but despite their warnings I went.

Previously Jim had spent all his evenings in public houses, but it was my hope that if I made things more attractive and comfortable for him at home, he would want to spend more time there. Jim's family were delighted with all the improvements I made with a little paint, some new curtains etc., and agreed that Jim seemed to be much happier and contented since he had come to know me. I have to admit that in the beginning I knew very little about cooking, but with the help of a good cookbook I soon learned to prepare some tolerable meals. Jim did not cook, and previously had eaten all his meals in pubs or cafes.

Our first few weeks together were absolute bliss, but knowing that my mother was missing me, I set two periods aside to visit her each week, Wednesday evenings, and all day Sundays when both Jim and little Mark would accompany me. In the winter months we mostly watched television with my parents, but in the summer we took Mark fishing and paddling in nearby rivers. We always returned to London directly after tea, so that Mark would be home at a reasonable time for bed.

Our financial arrangements were that Jim should pay the rent of the apartment, and I paid all the household expenses and food bills. Later Jim was also to suggest that I contribute to his son's support. While he continued with his window cleaning business, I continued working at the menswear store in Hertford as well as doing gay artwork for Basil and the magazines most evenings.

Then one day Josh Joshua invited me to dine with him at a smart West End restaurant and during the meal he said, 'Isn't it time you branched out on your own?'

'But that would be disloyal to Basil. He gave me my first big break in the magazine world', I replied.

'He only helped you for his own benefit' said Josh. 'He has had more than his fair share of the cake. He certainly could not blame you for wanting your independence. Why take only a portion of the profits when you could have them all? I can give you the name and address of someone who will photograph your work and supply you with prints. I will also give you three thousand names and addresses of people in the UK and United States who are keen to buy physique material. That should be enough to get you started. In addition, if you will allow me to publish some of your work free of charge, then in return I will give you free advertising space in all my magazines. How does that sound?'

It sounded wonderful, and when I told Jim about it, he was as thrilled as I was.

However producing three thousand circulars, plus the cost of envelopes and postage, soon made a considerable hole in my savings, and the need to devote more time to the project tempted me to give up my shop job in Hertford. What I should have done of course, was wait and see how the project fared before handing in my notice and throwing away a steady income. My parents thought me quite mad, and so did I later.

Right from the start everything went wrong. It took many weeks for my first orders to arrive, and I discovered I had far less money to manage on. Never mind I thought, things will improve. But they didn't.

Two months later Josh's editorial offices were gutted by a terrible fire that claimed the lives of two of his staff. Huge stocks of magazines and materials were destroyed, and it was clear that all publishing would be at a standstill until new premises could be found. This immediately put an end to my advertising and restricted my sales.

Jim was even more depressed than I, for recently he had come to rely on me more and more for money. Overnight a great change took place in him, and he became extremely bad tempered and moody. Nothing I could do pleased him any more, and he found fault with everything. Soon he hardly bothered to speak to me. The only time he cheered up was when we went to the pub in the evenings. We could not afford to drink quite so much now, although I for my part could quite easily have given it up altogether. However this was one luxury Jim was NOT going to do without.

One night Jim said he wanted to go to the William IV pub in Battersea, a notoriously gay pub that had live music every Saturday night. When we got there the band was playing, and a very effeminate-looking young man was singing a suggestive song. I did not pay particular attention to him until Jim said, 'What a lovely face that boy has.'

When the young man left the stage, Jim handed me his glass and disappeared in the crowd. A few minutes later I caught sight of him handing the singer what looked like a glass of whisky or gin. They talked for a while as I stood alone, then the singer returned to the stage and Jim returned to me saying he had just requested a song, and the next moment the band struck up with 'I can't give you anything but love baby', the singer obliging with the words, smiling and winking at Jim as he did so.

When the song was over, the singer got off stage and disappeared in the crowd. Almost at once Jim asked me to hold his glass again and walked off. Seconds later I saw him going through the door marked 'Gentlemen', hot on the heels of the singer. I felt as if someone was twisting my gut, and a feeling of desperation swept through me.

When they emerged, together, Jim brought the young man over and introduced him to me, although for the rest of the evening I was totally ignored as Jim centred his whole attention on the boy.

I was thankful when the barman called 'Time please' and everyone made preparations to leave, but when we went to get a bus outside, the young man came with us openly flirting with Jim. When we boarded a bus for Holborn, the lad sat next to Jim so that I was forced to sit behind them.

It was clear the young man was hoping he would be invited to spend the night with us, or rather with Jim, and I was fearful that Jim would do just that, but when I spoke out and made it clear he was not welcome, the lad got off the bus at Trafalgar Square, saying to Jim as he went, that he hoped to see Jim the following Saturday at the William IV. I then made it clear to Jim that if he DID go, then I would leave him and return to Hertford, but when the following Saturday did arrive, Jim just suggested we go to our usual pub in Holborn.

*Jim, 1957*

# Drink and a Woman

A few weeks later, Jim's young brother, Tony was married. I did not attend the wedding in case my presence should embarrass Jim, but I did attend the reception afterwards, held in rooms above a local pub. It was not long of course, before all the guests were drifting downstairs to the bars below.

I looked in both bars for Jim but could not see him. Instinct told me that he had gone off to his favourite pub a short distance away, and sure enough that is where I found him.

When I arrived he was sitting at a table talking to an old friend called Sid. I asked why he had left the party so suddenly, leaving me with a lot of people I did not know. His answer was evasive, but it was clear from his speech and manner that he was drunk. Even so, he called for another drink, and when I suggested he had had too many already, he showered me with a stream of scalding abuse. Sid looked most uncomfortable, and I decided to move away and leave him talking to Sid.

At closing time when Jim got to his feet, he was swaying badly, and I moved forward to assist him, but he jerked his arm away violently and swore at me. Following Jim and Sid outside, I stood a little way off as they said goodnight to each other, then I followed Jim as he began to stagger home.

Keeping my distance so as not to provoke him, I kept an eye on his every movement in case he should trip or fall. Crossing busy streets became a nightmare, and occasionally when I moved too close, he would take a swing at me with his fists, shouting out drunken abuse as he did so. I had never seen him like this before.

Having unlocked the door of the house, and staggered to the bedroom he collapsed half on the bed, half on the floor. I heaved him up, and he offered no resistance as I started to unlace a shoe, and when he lifted up his foot I assumed he was unconsciously trying to assist me. But a moment later he shot it at me with such terrific force, catching me in the groin, I was sent crashing backwards into the wardrobe behind me.

In great pain I started to get to my feet. Jim had raised himself on one elbow pulling a grotesque face and reaching for something beside the bed, said he was going to kill me. Not waiting to see what he had got in his hand, I fled to the next room locking the door behind me, for it was pointless trying to reason with him in that drink-maddened state.

In the adjoining room I listened as he swore and shouted abuse, tears running down my face as I prayed to God asking why our friendship had come to this.

In a lot of pain, only later, much later, did I discover that Jim had split the muscles, which formed the wall of my stomach.

After a while all was quiet in the next room, and I guessed he had fallen asleep. I tried to make myself comfortable on the settee, but it was a cold night and I had nothing to cover myself with. For several hours I lay there awake, then I thought I could hear Jim moaning, and thinking he might be ill, I unlocked the door and went cautiously into the bedroom. I found him clutching his tummy, saying he felt sick. There was no time to run downstairs to fetch a bowl, so I threw up the window and helped him to the ledge so that he could vomit into the backyard.

He had sobered up a lot now, said he felt terrible, and his head was aching. I fetched him some aspirin, and he allowed me to undress him and put him to bed, then I got in beside him, though I got little sleep, partly from caution, but mainly in case he wanted to be sick again.

Next morning, Jim remembered little of what had passed. He said he was sorry he had kicked me, and thanked me for looking after him, adding that he still felt, 'bloody awful.' He promised he would never drink as heavily as that again, and he kept his word, for although he continued to drink, it was always in moderation.

A couple of weeks later we were sitting in Jim's favourite pub talking with his old friend Sid, sitting on stools at the bar, me in the middle. Sid and I were in conversation, when glancing into the mirror behind the bar I noticed that Jim was talking to a woman sitting on the other side of him.

In her fifties and not particularly attractive, she was wearing spectacles and a fur coat. She was holding her head close to Jim's and he was whispering something to her which was making her laugh. It was also apparent that she was really rather drunk. The barman, who knew me well, nodded towards Jim and the woman, and then winked an eye at me.

While Jim continued to whisper to the woman, I walked to the end of the bar, and calling the barman over, asked who she was? He was surprised I did not know her, since he said she was a regular customer, and in fact an alcoholic. Since Jim had been complaining recently about our financial difficulties, it made me angry to see him squandering money on a complete stranger, buying her drinks as fast as she could consume them.

Going back to my seat, I overheard Jim whisper to her '...and I will follow you outside.' Moments later the woman got up, bade everyone goodnight, and tottered out of the bar. Almost at once, Jim complained that he was not feeling too well and would step outside for 'a breath of air.'

'Then I will come with you,' I remarked.

He looked at me sharply, and in a firm voice said, 'You had best stay here! I shall be alright.'

I was about to protest, but Sid put a hand on my arm and stopped me. Jim left, and when he had closed the door, Sid said, 'We both know he is feeling fine and that he has gone after that woman. This is something you will have to get used to Ron. I have known Jim a lot longer than you, and he NEEDS a woman occasionally. Don't interfere.'

Ignoring Sid, I waited a few moments, then putting my drink on the bar, went out into the alley. There was no sign of Jim or the woman, but hurrying to the end of the alley where it connected with a main street, I saw the two of them about a hundred yards away, just about to enter another pub. I stood and waited for about five minutes, then I followed.

I found them at the bar with glasses in their hands. Jim looked surprised to see me, but smiled and asked me what I wanted to drink? I said I wanted nothing but to know why he had just lied to me and sneaked off in that fashion? Quite calmly, he said he could hardly have explained his real intentions in the other bar with everyone listening, could he? And although the woman HAD drunk rather a lot, he was not seducing her WITHOUT her knowledge. She was not a child. At this the woman laughed loudly and told me not to be so puritanical, inviting me to have a drink with her too.

Reassessing the situation, I thought perhaps I WAS being a bit straight-laced. Jim was after all bisexual, and if a woman encouraged him to seduce her, why shouldn't he? Having sorted this out in my mind, I accepted her offer of a drink and started joking with them. After a few more drinks I even began to get a sexual urge myself, and thought that if Jim intended to enjoy himself with the woman, why shouldn't I? Sensing what was in my mind, Jim seemed very pleased.

When the barman called 'Time please', Jim told the woman we would help her home - where did she live? She couldn't remember, but the barman knew her address, and chuckling to himself, told us.

She was extremely drunk by now, swaying so violently on her feet that we had to bodily carry her most of the way. Luckily she lived close by. Jim asked for her door key, and she handed him her handbag. As he released her to take the bag, she promptly collapsed in a heap on the pavement.

The door unlocked, we carried her up to her apartment on the third floor, I say apartment, but actually it was a large bed-sitter. We dumped her on the large double bed in the corner of the room, and she immediately raised her head and asked for another drink.

To the reply, 'There isn't any more,' she answered, 'Yes there is. There is plenty under the bed.'

Sure enough there was. Several dozen bottles!

After giving her a drink and lighting the gas fire, Jim told her he would make her 'nice and comfortable'. He helped her off with her coat and switched out the light. In the glow of the gas-fire I watched as he removed all her other clothing as well, and when she was naked, he stripped himself and climbed onto the bed beside her. I heard her say: 'I don't mind YOU screwing me, but I don't want your friend - he's too fucking respectable!'

I sat in an armchair by the fire, and in the semi darkness watched as Jim mounted and proceeded to fuck her. I listened to the grunts and groans of satisfaction for a while, then turning over in my mind what the woman had said, I crept out or the flat, down the stairs, and out into the street... Though not before I had taken my revenge on the woman by peeing in some of the empty bottles and replacing their caps!

It was eight o'clock next morning when Jim came home. I apologised for my behaviour in the pub, and asked him if he had enjoyed the woman?

'Not really. The old bitch was really too drunk to perform properly.' Then pausing for a moment he said, 'I am sorry I walked off like that leaving you with Sid. I promise I will never do that again.' Then he added, 'I am sorry I have treated you so badly of late, but I needed to know you really DID love me. Now I know you do, because no one else would put up with what I have been dishing out to you lately.' Then he took me in his arms and kissed me.

# Jim Finds Me a New Lover

A few weeks later Jim chanced to run into an old girlfriend he had not seen since his schooldays. She was married now, and was the mother of a small baby boy. Her name was Ruby, and Jim told me he had invited her round to our place the following night, 'for a little fun.' He said she was a highly sexed girl, and he knew he would have no trouble seducing her.

When I asked if he was not ashamed of playing around with married women, he said they were the best ones to fuck. They were always more eager than single girls, and if they should get pregnant, well, then they could always blame their husbands.

'Who will be looking after the baby while Ruby visits you?'

'Her husband,' replied Jim.

It was a Wednesday that Jim chose to invite Ruby round, the evening I always spent in Hertford with my mother. By the time I got back to the apartment, Jim had already seen the girl home, and was making a pot of tea for the two of us. He had thoroughly enjoyed himself, and was anxious to tell me all the details. In a way I was pleased too, for he was more cheerful than he had been for a long time. After that they met regularly every week for sex.

Then one day Jim came home and said, 'Ron, how would YOU like to have sex with somebody else for a change?'. For a moment I thought he was joking, although several times he had said he would fix me up with a girl one of these days. However it transpired that on this occasion he was offering me a MAN.

Jim explained that it was his habit each morning to go to a certain cafe about ten o'clock for a cup or coffee with other window cleaners who worked in his area, and who subsequently exchanged general news and gossip. One of these, a man named Johnny, was bisexual and although married with a ten-year-old daughter, still enjoyed sex with men. In fact he was sex mad, frequently touching-up all the boys in the cafe and eager to seduce Jim, who thought it all very amusing until Johnny become too persistent.

On this particular day, Johnny had told Jim that if he would be 'nice' to him, he could put some extra window-cleaning business his way. Jim wanted the extra work, but NOT John, and so had suggested that he had a friend at home, who would be happy to oblige. Johnny had been delighted, and promptly said he would call round at 4pm when he finished work for the day.

At first I was annoyed that Jim should take me so for granted. He replied that he had thought he was doing me favour. He was enjoying sex with Ruby each week, and thought I might welcome sex with someone different for a change. Jim said he had told Johnny we were cousins and there was nothing sexual between us.

Promptly at four o'clock Johnny's car pulled up outside the house, and Jim went to the front door to let him in, while I went over to the window to see what he looked like. Quite handsome, with sleek black hair, he was a big rugged man, wearing a black tee-shirt and blue jeans. He did not look at all the type of man you would suspect was eager to jump into bed with another man. Suddenly I felt nervous and very excited all at the same time.

A moment later Johnny was standing in front of me and Jim was making the introductions. A broad smile spread across the man's sunburnt face as he shook my hand and his eyes roved approvingly over my figure. Jim asked me to go and make some tea, and when I returned Johnny was seated on the settee under the window, with Jim sitting on one of the arms, they stopped talking as I entered.

'Doesn't Jim ever have any sex-fun with you?'

'He is only interested in women,' I replied.

'Women are alright when there isn't a good man around, but I would sooner have a good man anytime. Jim doesn't know what he is missing,' said Johnny, making a playful grab for Jim's nearest leg.

Jim jumped away from the settee laughing, 'Keep your hands to yourself, or else play with Ron!'

I poured the tea. Johnny suddenly jumped up and drew the curtains, remarking that the settee was much too public in front of the window. Jim switched on the light, and Johnny patted the seat next to him and told me to come and sit down.

Tea consumed, I got up to clear the crockery away, but to my surprise Jim offered to do the washing up, suggesting that I entertain Johnny. Almost  before Jim had left the room, Johnny had grabbed my wrist and dragged me down on the settee.

'All right. Come on, lets have a look at you.' I started to unbutton my shirt, his big bronzed hands were eagerly unbuckling my belt and un-zipping my jeans.

Seconds later as he gazed with pleasure at my naked body he purred, 'Jim didn't exaggerate. You really do have a lovely body, and boy, you certainly were not on the end of the queue when they gave THOSE out, were you?'

Without saying more he lunged at me greedily, his hands groping and squeezing, his eyes glistening with lust. There was nothing gentle about him, and I could see now the reason he had so many lovers. He was simply too much for one person to cope with. He seemed to be everywhere at once, not just with his hands, but with his lips, teeth and tongue. However it was my cock that seemed to fascinate him the most, and he kept muttering, 'Boy, what a beauty. What a fucking beauty.'

Suddenly springing to his feet he frantically started peeling off his tee-shirt, and throwing this on the floor he urgently unbuckled his belt at the same time kicking off his shoes. Then, unzipping his jeans, he eased them down over his hips, and standing first on one leg, and then the other, he yanked them off.

His glorious muscular body was covered with thick black hair. He was like some magnificent animal as he stood there proudly naked, hands on hips, feet astride, his big penis dangling heavily and half erect.

'You are not exactly small yourself!' I exclaimed.

'I wish I was as big as you,' came the reply. 'Come on. Let me see if I can take it.' He reached for his jeans, and taking a tube of KY lubricant from a pocket, handed it to me. 'Here, use this.' Then moving to one end of the settee, he stood with legs apart, body bent forward at the hips, hands resting on the arm of the settee for support, and waited.

Smothering myself with a thick coating of the jelly, I positioned myself behind him, and taking a firm grip on his shoulders, I thrust hard with my hips. The feeling was like nothing I had ever experienced before as my cock slid into his warm tightness, and I pressed my groin hard against his muscular bum.

'Go on. Shove it all in,' Johnny commanded, groaning with pleasure, and we settled into a steady rocking rhythm, he moving back to meet my every thrust. I tried to make it last as long as I could it felt so wonderful, but finally, unable to hold back any longer, I shot my load into him and fell shuddering onto his back, satisfied and exhausted.

'Thank you Johnny,' I said, 'Do you know that is the first time I ever fucked anyone. I've always been on the receiving end in the past.'

'Well now you are going to be on the receiving end again!' declared Johnny, 'I want to fuck YOU. Lets have it in the bedroom this time.'

I led the way to the adjoining room, and Johnny climbed onto the bed, and lying flat on his back, instructed me to squat over him, a leg on either side of his body, my hips directly over his own. Then propping himself up on his elbows so that he could see what he was doing, he plunged a rigid cock savagely into my eager arse, and I gasped as he thrust his hips upwards again and again. Loving every minute of it, I ground my hips down to meet every penetration, bouncing up and down in ecstasy.

At this point the bedroom door swung open and Jim peered in. Continuing his measured strokes, Johnny shouted out, 'Where the hell have YOU been? You should have some of this. You don't know what you're missing.' Closing the door Jim came over and sat on the edge of the bed to watch.

For some time Johnny kept the pace steady, then moaning and groaning he started to speed up the action, the bed creaking noisily under the quickening onslaught until his body began to tremble and shake violently as he shot his cum into me.

His energy now completely spent, Johnny collapsed back onto the bed with a satisfied sigh. 'Boy, that was fucking great,' he gasped. Then glancing at his watch he said, 'Gosh, is that the time? I'm supposed to be taking the wife out this evening,' and jumping up from the bed he hurried through to the adjoining room to get his clothes, while I hurried downstairs to get him a bowl of water, some soap and a towel.

Johnny became a regular visitor to our apartment after that, and we were constantly trying out new positions to add spice and variety to our sex. I was usually alone when Johnny called round, but on the occasions when Jim was at home too, he never failed to get a kick out of watching us perform, and Johnny never gave up in his attempts to get Jim to join in the fun.

Sometimes Jim would be so excited by what he had witnessed, that the moment Johnny had left, Jim would be desperate to fuck me himself, and this all helped to improve things between us.

# My First Threesome

Six months after I had been living with Jim, he received notice from the council that the property was to be demolished, and he was offered alternative accommodation, a house in one of the new satellite towns around London, or a renovated, older apartment even nearer to the West End. Jim chose the latter and soon we were installed in a very smart area of Bloomsbury, Torrington Place, on the first floor of what is today Waterstones famous bookstore.

Jim said we simply MUST get some cash from somewhere. All kinds of new things were needed for the apartment and he was fed up living on a shoestring budget. Suddenly he proclaimed the solution to all our financial problems was simple, why not start selling pornographic photos to the gay customers on my mailing lists? They had always asked for photos as well as drawings.

I told Jim I did not like it, it was too dangerous. The last thing I wanted was trouble with the police. Jim flew into a rage and said that if I truly loved him, I would do this for him. Not wanting to wreck our relationship, I finally gave in.

But having consented, there were problems to face. It would be a simple task to photograph each other, but my clients would want duos. Who was going to take these? I certainly did not want anyone in the physique business to know what we were up to.

Jim said we could use a cable release to take photos of the two of us having sex together, no third party was needed, and as far as the developing of the film and its printing was concerned, Johnny had a friend called Sonny who was an amateur photographer, and if we gave him a small share of the profits, Jim was sure he would handle the work for us.

The photos taken, we passed the negatives on to Johnny, who in turn passed them on to Sonny, and we were informed that the first batch of prints would be ready for collection in a week's time. Jim was to pick them up from Sonny's home in Stockwell, South London. Jim had spoken to Sonny on the telephone several times, but they had never actually met face to face before.

Having collected the first lot of prints and brought them home, Jim remarked what a very sexy wife Sonny had. 'She's about thirty, with long dark hair, a smashing figure, big tits, and guess what? I think she fancies YOU!'

Laughing, I asked why on earth she should, and he said, 'Well when she saw these photos and what you have got between your legs, she kept right on talking about how "well endowed" you are. In fact she has insisted that YOU must collect the next batch of photos!'

Only half believing Jim, I said, 'It's all very well you saying she "fancies" me, but I should think her husband would have something to say about that!' Jim answered, 'According to Johnny, Sonny would welcome a lover for his wife so that it would leave him free for affairs of his own. Anyway, you go down and see what happens. They are obviously a very broad-minded couple, because while I was there Sonny showed me a lot of nude slides of his wife. You might do all right there! I wouldn't mind fucking her myself, but I wasn't invited to. I suppose my cock's just not big enough for her!'

It was with a mixture of nervousness and excitement that I went down to Stockwell the following week. Arriving at 8pm, the door was opened by Sonny who shook my hand and led me into the front sitting-room where Peggy his wife and their two small children were all watching television. I was introduced to Peggy, who immediately put the children to bed so that Sonny and I could talk business.

Once I had inspected the prints, Sonny said: 'Would you like to see some of MY pictures?' Peggy who had by now returned to the sitting-room with forced coyness remarked, 'Oh you don't want to show him THOSE!' wriggling her hips seductively she gave a little giggle.

A few minutes later Sonny had put out the light and was projecting various nude colour slides of Peggy onto a screen. Each time he came to a particularly sexy one, Sonny would nudge me and say, 'What do you think of that then? A bit of all right, eh?'

When the light was switched on again, Peggy was looking a little flushed and excited, 'Whatever did you show Ron those for? I looked awful.' But Sonny with a trace of pride in his voice said, 'I bet Ron thought you looked smashing. Didn't you Ron?' Then after a slight pause, 'How would you like to pose WITH Peggy for a few pictures, just for my private collection of course.'

'Now you have embarrassed him. He's too shy,' said Peggy.

'OK' I said, 'I'm game.'

Peggy was delighted and so was Sonny. I stripped off my shirt and Peggy ran her fingers over my shoulders saying how broad they were. 'Well you might as well take off the rest of your clothes and we can get started,' said Sonny.

Unzipping my jeans I eased them off, and by the time I had peeled off my underpants, my excitement was very obvious. Starring at my stiff cock, Sonny said to his wife, 'Well, are you satisfied NOW!'

'I hope I soon WILL be,' she giggled.

While Sonny set up his camera and some lighting, Peggy left the room but returned a few minutes later wearing nothing but a South Sea Island grass skirt, and a garland of artificial flowers. I was mesmerised by her huge and beautiful breasts, which although large were very firm. She came over and stood by me, pressing one of her rose-coloured nipples against my arm. My head swam, and my cock throbbed even harder.

For the initial pose Sonny suggested I stand sideways to the camera, while Peggy knelt in front of me, grasped my cock in her hand and opened her mouth as if on the point of devouring me.

He took several variations of this pose, with her sucking me in several. Then he said it was time we had a drink, and leaving the room for a moment, returned with some bottles of beer.

We all sat down on a big sofa-bed, which Sonny had opened up, Peggy in the middle, and between drinks Sonny kissed and fondled Peggy intimately, while I looked on in amusement. Then leaning towards me Peggy kissed and fondled me. I thought I must exercise caution, not knowing how far Sonny really wanted me to go, and all too soon it was time for me to leave, but before I did, Sonny had extracted a promise from me to come down again the following week.

Jim was highly amused when I got home and described what had happened. 'Well, I said you would be OK there, didn't I?' he said.

On my next visit to Stockwell things went a stage further. Commencing as before with drinks and general conversation, Sonny said to Peggy, 'Where is that Baby Doll nightie I bought you the other day? Show it to Ron!'

Delighted with the suggestion, Peggy left the room and Sonny said, 'She looks really sexy in it.' Then, moving closer, he said, 'When you come to see us I want you to really enjoy yourself', and patting me on the back said, 'why don't you take your shirt off and make yourself more comfortable.'

I stood up to unbutton my shirt, and as I did so, Sonny opened up the sofa-bed again. When we had sat down, Sonny poured us more drinks and a moment later the door opened and Peggy walked in wearing the short see-through nightie. Quite naked underneath, she had brushed out her hair, and applied more make-up to her face. She had also dowsed herself liberally with a heady perfume.

'Well, what do you think, Ron? Isn't she gorgeous?', asked Sonny, and telling her to turn round, he lifted the hemline and gave her a resounding smack on her bottom, making her giggle. Then putting an arm round her waist, he pulled her down onto his lap, kissed her, and putting a hand under the nightie stroked her between her legs.

Suddenly he remembered, or so he said, a promise to develop a film that night for a friend, he must go and do it immediately. As he left the room her instructed Peggy to 'Keep Ron entertained!'

She immediately lay down on the bed and asked me to take the rest of my clothes off. I did, and at the sight of my rock-hard cock she grabbed my nearest arm and pulled me down on top of her, smothering my face and neck with kisses. I told her how beautiful she was, and she asked me to help her remove the nightie. After she had flung this on the floor we resumed kissing and fondling each other, exploring all the soft and firm parts of each other's bodies.

Finally, unable to resist the temptation any longer, I manoeuvred my hips between her wide-parted thighs, and allowing her to grip my throbbing cock and guide me into position, I plunged into her as hard as I could, tingling all over as her lush warm moistness enveloped me. She wrapped her legs around me, and lost in a world of sexual bliss I plunged in and out of her as she squealed with delight and I groaned with pleasure.

I had been pumping away for about five minutes, when suddenly the door flew open and Sonny walked into the room. For a moment I was panic-stricken. What would he say? What would he do? Had he really intended me to go this far?

I need not have worried however, for after picking up a packet of cigarettes from the coffee table, he simply said, 'Sorry, I forgot these,' and left the room leaving Peggy and I to carry on grinding away to an explosive climax.

Afterwards, happy and satisfied, Peggy got up and went to make some tea and sandwiches. I clambered off the bed and was in the process of pulling on my underpants when Sonny walked in. 'I'm glad you took my advice,' he said slapping me on the backside. 'The next time you come I will join in the fun, too.'

Jim was tickled pink when I related the latest episode.

'Well how does it feel to have fucked your first woman?'

I said of course it had been great, yet as nice as it had been, the slackness of Peggy's vagina did not compare with the tightness of Johnny's arse, and I could see why the ancient Greeks took boys for their lovers, and kept wives for breeding purposes.

Jim said I only felt like that because Peggy was the first woman I had experienced. 'You will feel different in time,' he remarked. However the fact that both Jim and Johnny, for all their experience with women still enjoyed sex with men, seemed to prove that this was not so.

My visit to Stockwell the following week began much as before. A chat, shorter this time, drinks, and Sonny suggesting the sofa-bed be opened up. After that we ALL stripped off and lay down naked, Sonny in the middle. Having kissed and fondled his wife for a while, he turned his attention to me, groping and fondling me. Then returning his attention to Peggy, he pulled her legs apart and began fucking her. It was exciting to watch Sonny plunging in and out of Peggy. He was more ruthless than I had been, and she twisted and writhed in ecstasy, groaning and moaning as he poured a stream of obscenities into her ear.

After a while they changed to a different position. Ten minutes later they changed to yet another, doing their best to get the utmost satisfaction. My excitement as I watched was almost unbearable, and my stiff cock was oozing pre-cum. I wanted to wank, but thought I had best save myself, and it was just as well I did, because a few minutes later after the two lovers had climaxed, Sonny turned to me and said, 'OK Ron, now its your turn.'

Crawling between Peggy's wide parted thighs I wasted no time on preliminaries I just plunged straight into her. Sonny hadn't used a condom (neither did I), and Peggy's cunt seemed moister than ever. I did try my best to put on a good show for Sonny, while he knelt behind me on the floor so as to get the best possible view of the action, but not content with this, he put a hand between Peggy and me so that he could actually feel each penetration and withdrawal, and I felt my cock sliding through his fingers as well as into her. This got Sonny so excited that a few minutes later I was aware that he was parting my buttocks and pushing couple of fingers up my arse, and after a few minutes of finger-fucking, he slid his prick into me. So Sonny was yet ANOTHER bisexual!

It was an amazing sensation being sandwiched between the two of them. The ultimate in sex, playing both active and passive roles at the same time!

After that, this kind of threesome became a regular feature of our weekly get-togethers, with Sonny continually thinking up new ideas for our maximum excitement and pleasure.

That Sonny too was bisexual, caused me to wonder how many men were really honest about their sexuality. To be acceptable to society most men might claim to be heterosexual and pretend to despise gays, but as time went on I was to discover that far more married men were happy to jump into bed with another men than might be imagined. Perhaps there was a little bisexuality in ALL men and those who protested the loudest simply had a guilt complex?


Someone who definitely seemed to have a complex was Dirk Bogarde. One day when Jim's young brother Tony came to visit us, he told us that as he had walked down Gower Street, Dirk Bogarde had tried to pick him up. Bogarde was at the time making one of the 'Doctor' series of films outside London University. Bogarde had been sitting in his car during a break in filming, and as Tony walked by had invited him to get into the car.

When Tony had said, 'Fuck off, you creep,' Bogarde in astonishment had said, 'You DO know who I am, don't you?'

Tony replied, 'Yes, and you can STILL fuck off!'

A few days later I happened to be sitting in the bar of the Red Lion pub in Red Lion Square, Holborn, and Bogarde walked in accompanied by two burly bodyguards. They sat at the bar, and because he WAS very good-looking, I could not help but stare at him in admiration, but this only appeared to make him angry and he said very loudly to his minders, 'Can't I even have a drink without being stared at by some bloody poof!' and he immediately got up and walked out leaving me feeling terribly humiliated.

What a bloody hypocrite I thought. It certainly took one to know one!

# Enough is Enough

By mid-summer Josh had resumed publishing his magazines again, indeed he had even asked me to create a new, fourth one for him which we called SIR GAY, and I became it's editor. Once again I was able to sell prints of my artwork, and orders came in from fans in no less than 37 different countries throughout the world.

Some of these people were keen to know if I could also supply pornographic photographs and so we had quite a prosperous business. I had given up the shop job in Hertford some time ago, and was now working full-time on the magazines.

Once we had bought new furniture and furnishings for our new apartment in Torrington Place, I told Jim I wanted to stop selling the pornography, it had been useful when I had no money coming in from Josh's magazines, but things were back to normal now and there was no need to risk getting into trouble with the police.

Jim was adamant that we continue with the pornography a little longer. The truth was that Jim was getting both lazy and greedy. He was giving up more and more of his window-cleaning business, and having bought lots of new clothes and shoes etc., wanted to spend more and more time drinking in local bars or sitting at home with his feet up.

I seemed to be working night and day. When I wasn't busy creating work for the magazines, I had housework or cooking to do. Jim would do absolutely nothing around the house, he just wanted to be waited on, hand and foot.

Jim was still seeing Ruby once a week for sex, until she got pregnant, then he finished with her. Then one day another of his old window cleaning fraternity, another married man, asked if he might bring a girl round to our place for sex - he couldn't very well take her to his place, and they could not go to her's either, she was a married woman and her husband was at home all day. Jim agreed on one condition, this guy, Bill, must bring a second girl with him for Jim to have sex with.

When Bill and the two girls came round, Jim fancied the girl that Bill wanted himself, and row ensued which culminated in Bill and the two girls leaving in a storm slamming the door behind them.

About an hour later, Bill's girl turned up at our flat again on her own. It seems she had taken a real fancy to Jim, but had not wanted Bill to know, now she had returned to give Jim the sex he had wanted.

I had hoped she would only stay for the afternoon- I had a lot of work to do for the new issue of SIR GAY, and Josh was due to be collecting it the following day. To my annoyance the girl wanted to spend the evening with Jim too, so I went off to a cinema in the West End.

When I got back to the apartment it was around 9pm and the girl was still there, and Jim suggested we all go to the pub together. At the pub they sat together at a side table, gazing deeply into each others eyes, both clearly completely smitten with each other, while I had a game of darts with Jim's old pal Sid.

After about half an hour had passed, Jim told he was taking the girl back to our apartment, and she was going to stay the night. They would have the bed, I could sleep on the settee in the lounge. I asked what the girl's husband was going to think when she did not return home until the morning? Jim said she would think of some excuse.

Jealous and deeply upset by the intrusion into our lives by this woman, there was little I could say in front of her, but I could sense trouble lie ahead. Next Morning Jim took her part of the way home- she lived in Tottenham, and before he arrived back Josh came to collect the latest work I was supposed to have ready for him.

When I said it was not ready, and wouldn't be for another couple of days (I had domestic problems), he guessed that Jim was at the root of it, and remarked that he had never liked Jim, and that I deserved someone better, someone who really appreciated me. He said Jim was just a leech. He added that he was not desperate for the work, take a little break to sort myself out, and deliver the work to him in a week's time. Adding that if I had any sense, I should finish with Jim and return home to Hertford.

Deciding that I could not put up with things the way they were, I intended to have it out with Jim as soon as he came home. However when he DID return a couple of hours later, it was WITH the girl. I couldn't believe it and I asked what had happened? Jim said the girl's husband had refused to believe her excuses for being away all night and had kicked her out in the street, and as she now had nowhere to go, and only the clothes she stood up in, she would have to move in with US.

I could not believe it was happening. I said although I had in the past been willing to financially support Jim and his son, I was NOT prepared to keep his mistress! After all, the apartment was also my place of work, and I could not possibly produce work with HER under my feet all day as well as him. Either she would have to go, or I would. To my utter amazement and surprise, he said: 'OK then. Goodbye.'

# My Body for a Meal

My parents were so pleased when I walked in carrying my suitcase and announced that I was home for good. I got no sleep at all that night, persistently reviewing my life with Jim over the past twelve months. It had been the most bittersweet relationship of my life to date, and I vowed that never again would I commit myself to any one person like this. Previously I had always viewed Ray's "love'em and leave'em" attitude to life as rather cynical, now I was not so sure.

I wondered how long it would be before Jim tired of Brenda. Money, or rather the lack of it, was going to be his biggest problem. I had little doubt that he would soon send her out to work, not simply to support herself, but him also.

As far as the porn sets of photos were concerned, that business was now at an end. Sonny still had the negatives, and he could keep these for his private collection. I did not want them. Neither did I intend to visit Peggy and Sonny again, for I knew they would soon get to hear about Jim and Brenda through Johnny, and I had no wish to discuss the matter with them. In any case, living in Hertford again, the journey to Stockwell was too tedious to make it worthwhile.

My first few days at home were spent in a haze of grief and self-pity. My family said little, understanding my need to be left quietly alone so that I could gather myself together again.

After a few days rest I set to work completing as quickly as I could, all the drawings and layouts Josh was waiting for. When they were ready I delivered them to him, bringing him up-to-date with my latest news and receiving prompt payment for my efforts, I had money in my pockets once more to go to the West End the following Saturday night and get stinking drunk.

Josh still gave me advertising space in all the magazines, but the bulk of my income was derived from private commissions I accepted. Whilst living with Jim, he had never allowed me to meet any of my clients personally, but once I had returned to Hertford, all that changed.

One of my most regular patrons was a man named Paul Gerrard, and the thing that intrigued me most was that his commissions always had to be sent to him care of the plush Waldorf Hotel in London. Then one Sunday morning I received a telephone call from this man saying he had just flown in from the United States, would I dine with him that evening? I agreed and we arranged to meet in the lobby of the Piccadilly Hotel at 6pm.

A tall and beautifully built man with shiny black hair and a swarthy complexion, he looked decidedly Spanish. In his early forties I guessed, his handsome features had a very aristocratic look about them, and his immaculate suit was beautifully cut, a large diamond sparkling on his silk tie.

It was too early for dinner and he suggested we walk for a while. As we strolled in the direction of Piccadilly Circus, he asked many questions about my work and the physique world in general. He also mentioned that he was in the diamond business and said his work constantly took him all over the world. The fact that he also had a girlfriend currently appearing in the New York production of WEST SIDE STORY indicated that he was yet one more bisexual!

We turned off Shaftesbury Avenue and were walking down Gerrard Street, when suddenly he noticed two blonde women a little way ahead of us talking together at the kerbside. 'Damn!' he cried. 'I know one of those women, and she is the last person I want to bump into at this moment. Let us hope she won't notice me as we pass.' She didn't, and after we had gone safely by he explained, 'She is Sally, a prostitute I have known for many years. She is a nice girl but she drinks, and when she drinks, she talks, and talks, and talks! Thank goodness she didn't spot me.'

Turning a corner at the end of the street, we passed a door with the words 'Coronation Club' above it, and Paul asked if I was acquainted with the place? I said no.

'Right, I'll take you in there then for a drink, it used to be a very elegant little bar, but its a bit tatty now I am afraid, but I still like to pop in occasionally when I am in London, because such interesting types use the place.'

The club had not yet opened for business, so Paul suggested we walk around the block once more. Returning about fifteen minutes later, we passed through the street door, and climbed a narrow staircase. At the top, Paul pushed open another door that gave access to a large wood-panelled room, which had chairs and tables around three of its walls. The floor was thickly carpeted, a juke box stood in one corner, and heavily draped windows overlooked the street below.

There were only half a dozen people in the place that early, all men except for one lone woman sitting on one of the high stools arranged along the front of the bar. Paul stopped dead in his tracks. The solitary woman was Sally! He hesitated for a moment, as if wondering whether to beat a hasty retreat, but she turned and saw him.

'Why look who's here,' she cried with delight. 'It's Paul. Haven't seen you for months. Suppose you have been round the world a couple or times since then. How's your love life?'

Paul kissed Sally on the lips and introduced me. Then calling to the elderly man behind the bar to serve all three of us with drinks, Paul said, 'Ron, I would like you to meet Max who owns this club. A nicer man you could never hope to meet.'

Max offered me a hand saying, 'Any friend of Paul's is a friend of mine. The trouble is we see so little or him! Hope we are going to see more of YOU. Tell you what, I will give you a year's free membership to the club, then I KNOW you will come to see me again.' I thanked him and a moment later he was busy serving someone else.

Paul proceeded to bring Sally up-to-date on news about himself, then added, 'What about you? Have you had any unusual or amusing experiences lately?'

Between drinks she gave us all the details. The girl was a born comedian, not only impersonating the voices of her clients, but their actions as well. She also had a rather loud voice, and clearly enjoyed an audience, which she soon had, for by now all conversation in the bar had ceased. Simply everyone was listening to Sally, who as she was talking, still continued to drink heavily.

Her performance was suddenly interrupted by the shrill ring of a telephone behind the bar. Max answered it, relaying information that the Madame of the brothel where Sally was employed, was asking if she was in the bar? The blonde made motions to Max to say she wasn't, and this he did. Her performance continued. More people came into the bar, all men, and Sally gradually got more and more intoxicated.

Fifteen minutes later there was a second call from the Madame and again Sally instructed Max to say she wasn't there. However Madame was clearly suspicious, for ten minutes later while Sally was in the middle of yet another drink, the door burst open and into the room stormed a short, fat and very formidable-looking woman, black haired, and dressed all in black wearing a lot of gold jewellery.

In a broken French accent the woman let fly a stream of abuse at Sally. Drawing attention to a very handsome and well-dressed young man who had walked in with her, the Madame let Sally know in no uncertain terms that this lad had been waiting patiently for more than an hour in her apartments for Sally to return. The poor young man was beginning to look very embarrassed by all the fuss.

Swaying violently on her feet and hanging onto the bar for support, Sally let fly an even more startling stream of obscene abuse at her employer, ending with, 'I'm a married woman, I don't HAVE to work for you, you old bag. If you're not satisfied with me, then fucking well get somebody else!'

Sally's unexpected retaliation made Madame hastily reconsider. The tone of her voice immediately changed, and in quite soothing tones she said, 'Now come along, dear. Be a good girl. I do know you like a little drink, but do show poor Micky here some consideration. If all the girls behaved like this I would soon be out of business.' Turning to the young man she said 'Come on Mickey give me a hand with her.' Both supporting Sally, they helped her towards the door. She was really too far gone to resist. In fact I would have thought she was too far gone for anything!

It was already 9pm and I was beginning to feel very hungry and wondering when I was going to have the meal I had been promised, although I had no wish to appear impolite and mention it. We continued chatting until 10pm and then I felt I really must say something about my making tracks for home.

'But you haven't eaten yet!', my host exclaimed. 'You cannot go until you have had the meal I promised' When I mentioned I would miss the last train home if I delayed any longer, Paul said, 'Oh don't worry about that. I'll find you somewhere to sleep. You don't HAVE to go home tonight, do you? The night is still young and it is a pity to cut it short.' I considered for a moment, then said I must telephone my parents to let them know what I was doing.

Having made the call, Paul told me to finish my drink and have another. On an empty stomach, I was beginning to feel quite intoxicated. As the evening wore on, Max invited Paul and I to stay behind for a private drink with him after he had closed the club. We did, and during the conversation I felt flattered when Max said, 'You are not THE Ron Wright, the artist, are you? I have often admired your handiwork. Well fancy meeting you in the flesh, so to speak!'

When we were finally ready to leave, Paul invited Max to join us for a meal too, and we all went to an expensive Italian restaurant in Greek Street. It was a delicious meal with even more drinks, and we didn't leave until about 1am, when Max said goodnight and went off in a taxi.

'Well,' said Paul, and now we had better see what we are going to do about YOU for the night.' Moments later we too were seated in a taxi heading for the Waldorf Hotel.

As we were going up in the lift Paul said that although he only stayed in London a few days each month, his room at the hotel was always reserved permanently so as to be available at all times.

It was a large and luxurious twin-bedded room, and having allowed me to say which bed I wanted, he said, 'Right, but first I want you in mine for a while.' Immediately he started to undress and when he was naked he sat down on the bed to watch me remove my last garment. Then taking hold of my nearest wrist he pulled me down roughly beside him, remarking that I had the finest legs he had seen on any man.

Putting an arm under my legs, he lifted them up and swung me round to lie full-length on the bed, caressing and stroking my body in a very rough manner, and making it quite clear that having wined and dined me, he was intending to get the utmost satisfaction for his money. SO rough was his lovemaking he hurt me considerably. But I was flattered that this man, sophisticated, intelligent and wealthy, should desire me like this. So instead of complaining, I felt a certain pride, and responded with my body in ways I knew would please him.

'Am I hurting you', he asked at one stage, and when I replied 'Yes,' he remarked, 'Good. Pain is all part of the pleasure!' and getting more and more excited he flung me roughly onto my tummy and plunged his eager cock into me with brutal force.

Fucking me savagely for what seemed like hours, he paused for a moment and I felt relieved that he was at last satisfied. But he wasn't. I had turned over on my back to rest, but now as I faced him between my parted thighs, he suddenly lifted my hips level with his waist, and putting one of my legs over each of his shoulders, he proceeded to make yet another ruthless attack on my now tender arsehole.

After pounding away for another ten minutes or so, he withdrew, and although he appeared as fresh as ever, I felt totally exhausted. 'You make a wonderful partner,' he commented. 'That was quite fabulous. You have a beautiful body, and you certainly know how to use it. I have fucked men of all races, and you are among the best I have ever had,' then he added, 'I had already made up my mind that I WAS going to fuck you tonight, but I did not realise it was going to be QUITE so satisfying. However we must get to sleep now as I have to go to Birmingham in the morning.' I clambered off his bed, crept into my own and fell asleep almost immediately.

When I awoke, sunlight was streaming through the windows, and I could hear the hum of a vacuum cleaner in the adjoining room. I looked at my wristwatch, it was 10am. Nudging Paul I told him the time, and we both bathed and dressed.

Before I departed Paul said how much he had enjoyed our few hours together, saying he would like to repeat them again next time he was in London- after Birmingham he had got to go to Paris, Rome and then Athens, but he would give me a ring.

I thanked him for the nice time he had given me, and he said, 'There is just one thing I would like to make clear. I make it a rule never to give presents, presents of money that is.'

'Well, that's OK then, because I make it a rule never to accept any!' I replied indignantly, and stalking out of the room I slammed the door behind me. Paul may have wined and dined me generously, but I hadn't given any LESS than he had!


Sometimes it could be a risky business meeting potential clients. On one occasion a man calling himself John Lewis asked me to meet him outside Goodge Street Underground Station with a selection of my original drawings, saying he would like to buy one or two.

A huge man aged about forty-five, he hailed a taxi to take us to his flat near Harley Street. I was wearing a black polo shirt, and tight-fitting hipster flare trousers in grey.

As the Taxi moved off, the man placed a hand on my nearest thigh and said, 'You have a beautiful body.' Pushing his hand away I said, 'Let's get one thing straight, I am here to sell drawings, not myself.'

Later, as we sat on a settee in his apartment, I started to open my portfolio, but before I could do so, the man suddenly lunged at me in a state of frenzied lust and attempted to get my trousers off.

As I struggled to fight him off, he said, 'Be nice to me and I WILL buy some of your drawings, you have a lovely body and everyone should be allowed to enjoy it!' I had my own opinions about that!

Picking up the portfolio from the floor, where it had fallen, I swung it as hard as I could across his face. The shock made him let go of me, and I jumped to my feet.

'Look what you have done to me,' I shouted, pointing to my ripped trouser-front. 'I'm sorry, I don't know what came over me,' the man said. Please stay, I will pay for the damage,' and pulling out his wallet he flung a number of bank notes at me.

Grabbing them I made for the door and beat a hasty retreat. Out in the street I found myself shaking like a leaf, but pulling myself together headed for Carnaby Street to buy a new pair of trousers to change into before going home.

The next day Mr. Lewis phoned to apologise for his behaviour, and asked if I would meet him in the West End so that he could buy me a meal to make amends, but I told him I never wanted to see him again. Once had been quite enough, thank you.


A few weeks later I was to have a much pleasanter experience with a handsome young man named Harry Woodman. Tall and blonde, Harry had recently been discharged from the army for admitting he was gay. He wrote to me from his home in Aldershot, saying how much he admired my work, adding that he liked to draw male nudes himself. Could he visit me in Hertford with samples of his work with a view to getting some published?

I invited him down the following week, and was at once impressed with both his looks and work. He told me he was new to the gay scene, and so far had never had sex with another male.

He seemed terribly shy and extremely nervous and agitated. I told him I would see that some of his work DID appear in print, and out of gratitude he invited me down to Aldershot for a meal at his apartment.

Harry lived alone, and when I did visit his place, I discovered that he was not only a good cook, but good in bed too. I soon realised that his agitation was really nothing more than pent-up sexual frustration, which needed releasing, and boy, by the time he had got me into bed, did he know how to make up for lost time! We spent the whole afternoon fucking like rabbits.

We had a fantastic time, but unfortunately it would be two years before I saw Harry again, and then it was in very different circumstances, which I will relate later.

# The Axe Falls

Four months after I had parted from Jim he telephoned to say he would like to meet me for a 'chat '. There really seemed little point, but I was curious about his motive and so arranged to meet him next day at a small cafe in North London.

The conversation was friendly to start with, each enquiring after the other's family members. Then I asked how he was getting along with Brenda. 'Fine. The only trouble is I cannot get her to go and work. She says it's my place to keep her! Frankly I am running into debt. I suppose you couldn't loan me twenty pounds, could you?'

Feeling triumphant but bitter, I said, 'No Jim. You turned me down for her. What kind of fool do you take me for?' I pointed out that he had not concerned himself about me for the last four months, only now when he was in need of money did he think to contact me!

'So you won't help me then?'

'Not this time. I am afraid this time you will have to look elsewhere.'

Furious, he shouted, 'You lousy bastard. A fine friend you turned out to be. Now I can see just how much you REALLY loved me.'

Shocked by this outburst in a public place, I got up and walked briskly out of the cafe leaving him sitting there. Shaking with anger myself, I made for the nearest Underground station wondering why I had been foolish enough to meet him. I might have known what he wanted. Never mind, finally all the sentimental debris about him had been driven from my mind once and for all.

How wrong I was however in my assumption that I had heard the last of him. A month later two plain-clothed policemen called at the house to see me. The more senior or the two took a small packet from a briefcase.

'Are these photos of you Mr Wright?'

Looking at the pictures in deep shock I saw they were the photographs that Jim and I had been selling.

'Who is the man in the photos with you?'

Thinking I must keep Jim's name out of it if only for the sake of his two children, I stammered, 'I don't know. Just someone I met casually one night in a pub who volunteered to pose for a few photos. How did you come by them?'

The detective replied, 'They were being sent through the mail, but the envelope got torn, and when a postal worker saw the contents, they were passed on to us. You DO know who the man is, don't you, Mr Wright? It is no use you trying to protect him, in fact we already have him in custody.'

Since the sale of the photos had ceased when I left Jim, I wondered why it had taken the police so long to trace their source. Then I learned that when discovered, the photos had been in transit between a client and his friend. Subsequent inquiries had led to Jim and myself.

By now I was trembling. Whatever were my family and everyone else going to think? The police wanted to know where the negatives were and although I did not want involve Sonny and Peggy, I felt I had no choice. Later when the police searched Sonny's home, they found some three thousand negatives, all of Peggy. Since these were classed as 'personal' and for his own amusement, the police took no action against Sonny. Where OUR negatives had gone I just could not imagine. Sonny must have destroyed them when I left Jim, or else sold them to someone else.

At the local police station, I was subject to further questioning and asked to make a statement. Out of my mind with worry I told the police everything they wanted to know. I just wanted to get the whole rotten business over as quickly as possible. I knew I would have to be punished, but my greatest concern was for my family. What had they done to deserve the disgrace I was about to bring down upon their heads?

The police, pleased with my cooperation, seemed quite sympathetic, remarking that it was a tragedy that someone with a good public image, a good home and background, should have blemished his character in this fashion. They added what a pity it was that I had ever got involved with Jim in the first place. They also asked if my family knew I was gay. When I said no, they suggested I should tell them as soon as possible, otherwise they would not understand what the case was all about.

I was left to quietly contemplate my fate in a cell while the police got in touch with Grays Inn Road Police Station, London, which was conducting the investigation. About 7pm the two policemen I had earlier spoken to, came to the cell and told me I was to be taken to London immediately.

We drove quickly to the city, and on the way I asked, 'Shouldn't I see a solicitor?'

The senior officer replied, 'Oh no, not at this stage.'

'My family will be wondering where I am all this time.'

'A policeman has already called to tell them you won't be home until tomorrow morning,' I was told.

I had my fingerprints taken, and from the conversation I overheard, gathered that Jim had been in custody for most or the day. Again I asked, 'Shouldn't a solicitor be present to represent my interests?'

Again I was told, 'At this stage it is not necessary,' and was put in a cell for the night.

Next morning Jim and I were brought together, cautioned, and formerly charged with 'buggery'. We were also told that we were released on bail of £100 each, which my father had put up. We were warned that we were not to contact or speak to each other before the day of the trial. Then told we were free to go, and left the building separately.

Naturally as soon as I reached home, my parents were eager to know all that had happened, and my poor mother was in a most dreadful state. I told them I had been charged with selling blue photos since I did not have the courage to say what the REAL charge was. I knew they would not understand the meaning anyway. How do you explain that kind of thing to your parents? Today the task would not be difficult, but in the beginning of the 1960s it was a different story.

My parents were deeply upset, but to my relief they were willing to stand by me. However the more I thought about it, the more I realised the need to explain the real charge.

That evening I sat alone in my room trying to work on the layouts for Josh's new magazine. When mother came in with a cup of tea and told me not to worry, I said I had something to tell her, would she please sit down.

For the next hour while my mother quietly listened, I explained to her that I was gay. I explained the meaning of the word, and the way I searched for love amongst members of my own sex. I also told her about all the little experiences in my life, which had led me to discover what I really was. I told her about the man who had wanted to lure me into the woods when I was a schoolboy. How I had been rebuffed the first time I ever took a girl to the cinema, and my love life with the various men I had known since.

I explained that when I was born, the desire to love or be aroused sexually by the opposite sex was missing in me. This did not mean however that I lacked the emotions and desires of a so-called normal man. Simply that I could only feel them for a man.

I explained that the need to love someone and have them love me, was as great as in anyone else, maybe greater. Homosexuals, REAL homosexuals were at a disadvantage from the day they were born and, as if their lives were not complicated enough, society, instead of trying to understand them and their problems only sought to make them outcasts. In more civilised countries like Sweden, Denmark, and Holland, homosexuals were allowed to lead happy, useful lives. Here in this country of contradictions and hypocrisy, it was perfectly all right for two women to make love, but not two men. All right, so some gays were promiscuous, but didn't normal men like to sow THEIR wild oats too? A few gays (unfortunately) committed sex crimes, but here again, did not heterosexuals do exactly the same thing, AND to a much greater degree?

By the time I had stopped talking, my mother was quite overwhelmed, and tears were streaming down her face. 'Why SHOULDN'T you be allowed to find love and happiness like anyone else?' she asked.

'Because the law forbids it,' I told her.

'Then the law needs changing,' she remarked, adding with her simple logic, 'If it is wrong for you to go to bed with someone you love, then it is wrong for me to go to bed with your father!'

Getting up from her chair she said, 'Oh Ron, I feel so sorry for you.

I never knew there were THREE sexes before. Perhaps it is my fault you were born this way?'

I told her not to blame herself, it was just one of those tricks nature plays on us sometimes. Then she said, 'You will have to explain all this to your father and Shirley.'

'I will tell Shirley, but I cannot tell dad. I couldn't even begin to,' I said. 'You know we have never been able to talk to each other at the best of times. We are simply not of the same wavelength. In any case I know he is quite incapable of understanding something like this. I only wish I COULD talk to him.'

Mother said she would try to explain to him herself, but when I went downstairs later for supper, father said nothing to me, just buried his head deeper in his newspaper.

Next morning when my sister called round and I attempted to tell her about myself, she said, 'Don't worry about it. There are thousands of people like you. The public doesn't worry too much about that sort of thing these days. Anyway you look after yourself, and damn what anybody else thinks. WE know what you are really like, and that is all that matters. No one had better say anything to ME about you, that's all.'

My sister had chuckled as she said the last few words, and her good-natured acceptance of the facts, her easy understanding and good humour all worked like a tonic on me, and for the first time since the trouble began, I felt more like a human being.

After breakfast I telephoned Josh. He was shocked when I gave him the news. When he learned that I had not yet engaged the services of a solicitor, he made an appointment for me to see his own. When I met this gentleman he asked why I had not engaged someone sooner, immediately after I had been arrested in fact. I told him I had TWICE inquired about a solicitor, but each time the police had told me, 'You do not require one at this stage.'

'That is just the sort of thing they WOULD say. They deliberately took advantage of your ignorance of the law and your rights, to get you to talk and commit yourself. You have told them far too much, and played right into their hands. Take my advice, another time you are in trouble, but let us hope you never are, do not tell the police ANYTHING at all, until you DO have a solicitor present.'

Surprised that the police had charged Jim and I with buggery, the solicitor remarked, 'That is an extremely difficult thing for them to prove, photographs can be faked. I would have expected them to make a more simple charge. So long as the charge remains one of buggery, you have not got much to worry about, and we shall enter a plea of "not guilty".'

'What happens if things go against us?'

'Well, since you have never been in trouble with the police before, you are likely to be fined or put on probation for six months. As this is your first offence you will certainly not go to prison.'

When my father heard my trial was to be at the Old Bailey, he remarked, 'Your case must be a very bad one if it is to be held there!' Later I mentioned this to my solicitor. 'There is no need for your family to get alarmed. Although many famous cases have taken place at the Old Bailey, it is really no different to any other court in the land. You were charged in Holborn, and the Old Bailey being the court for that area, it is only natural your trial be held there. If you had been charged in Hertford, then you would be on trial there. It is as simple as that.'

Possibly because I was so ignorant of the law and my rights, the police may have assumed they would win their case easily, but once they became aware that a well-known queen's councillor was to defend me, they quickly withdrew the original charge, and changed it to one of 'gross indecency', a charge my solicitor told me he had expected them to make in the first place.

Since I could not deny the new charge, my solicitor said I should plead guilty. There was really very little he could do for me other than expound my previous good character, and hope that being my first offence, the judge would be lenient. However, later when my solicitor discovered that the judge I was to appear before, was a man who was notoriously homophobic, he tried to get the case postponed so that I might at least be dealt with by a less biased individual, but he was unable to do so and warned me that I must now be prepared to go to prison for three to six months.

I was stunned by this news, but thought, 'Oh well, I suppose it is no more than I deserve, but for goodness sake let us get it over and done with as quickly as possible.' The suspense was killing me.

There was a gap of six months between my time of arrest and the day I was actually to be sentenced. They were six or the most nerve-shredding months I was ever to experience. At the time the waiting and anticipation became almost unbearable, and every time I saw a policeman in the street my tummy would do a somersault and I would feel dreadfully ill.

Most evenings I would travel up to London to drown my sorrows in drink and sex. Some nights visiting five pubs or clubs in fewer hours. I drank far more than was good for me, and while under the influence was frequently picked up by men looking for a casual night's sex. Sometimes they were kind and considerate, at other times brutal and demanding.

When the day of the trial arrived, my parents came to the court with me. Since Jim and I had both pleaded guilty, our case did not last long. The facts having been put forward, defending council could do little but expound my previous good character. The judge passed sentence on me first, and in his summing up said that despite my good behaviour in the past, and the fact that I came from a respectable home and background, there were far too many crimes of this nature being committed at the present time, and so as a warning to others, he intended to make an example of me by sending me to prison for EIGHTEEN MONTHS. I could not believe my ears, for it sounded like a life sentence at the time.

I just stood there stupefied. Unable to move until hands on my shoulders steered me towards stairs leading from the dock to the cells below. A few minutes after I had left the dock, I was joined in the cell by Jim looking equally stunned.

'What sentence did YOU get?'

'Nine months.'

'NINE? Why only nine for you?'

I felt it was all a ghastly nightmare, not reality at all. It was just a horrible dream and any moment now I would wake up. But I knew this was for real, and we just sat there, two people suffering from shock.

Sometime later, our solicitor came down to see us, and in a most unconcerned voice, said he was sorry for the way things had gone. I asked why I had received double of Jim's sentence?

'Because Jim is a married man and a father. You are a self-confessed homosexual. Although you have both been in this together, in the judge's opinion you have been a bad influence on Jim. He probably considered you had wrecked his family life.'

'My God,' I thought. 'They call this JUSTICE? Just because I am gay I am given twice the sentence!'

What seemed like several hours later, Jim and I were taken to a room, where through tiny wire-mesh windows, we were allowed to see our relatives and say our last farewells. We all tried to put on brave faces for the sake of each other, but inside our hearts were all being torn to shreds.

Later when the courts had finished dispensing justice for the day, Jim and I, together with all the other prisoners, were handcuffed and put onto buses for transportation to various prisons. It was dark by now, and the brightly lit London streets were thronged with people. Thankful that there were no lights inside the bus, I was grateful for being spared the humiliation of being 'on show' as we made our journey of shame. My head was filled with thoughts of my family, and I was doubly grateful for the darkness as hot tears filled my eyes and ran down my cheeks.

Later I was to learn that providing I behaved myself in prison, one third of my sentence would be deducted. As welcome as this news was, at the time it did little to compensate for the fact that my life now lay completely in ruins.

*Eddie*

# Twelve Months of Hell

Those twelve months that I was to spend in Wormwood Scrubbs were to be a nightmare I would never forget, and no film, play or book can adequately convey the feelings of fear, degradation and utter despair that inmates were subjected to at times. It was something you actually had to experience yourself to properly understand.

I had done wrong, and it was only right that I should be punished, although I was extremely bitter about the harshness of the sentence. What upset me more than anything, was the shame and disgrace I had brought upon my innocent family. At least my friends and neighbours would have their memories dulled somewhat by the time I was released, but my poor family would have to endure the looks, the whispers, right from the start.

The conditions prevailing in the Scrubbs at the time were extremely tough, particularly for 'short-termers' like myself, who were treated far harsher than those serving long sentences or even 'life'. The reason for this was simple. It was felt that if those having their first experience of prison were treated harshly enough, once they were released they hopefully would never return.

Those men who were serving five years and more were given more relaxed conditions and better food for fear that they might otherwise continually make trouble or even revolt. On the subject of food, during the whole twelve months I was 'inside', I was to see only one egg (at Easter), and receive only one rasher of bacon (at Christmas).

After serving a couple of months I was lucky enough to be selected for one or the outside working parties, and this meant that at least we were able to see something of the outside world for a few hours each day. Early each morning we were taken by bus to a young boys Remand Centre at Ashford in Middlesex. For a few weeks I worked in the laundry, then I was told to assist a civilian painter whose job it was to look after all the doors and windows in the home.

Being a Remand Home none of the youngsters, some only children, had actually been convicted of any crime, all were awaiting trial. Yet some had been there as long as six months already.

One of the wardens was a particularly sadistic brute, and when in charge or the exercise yard, I often saw him kick the heads of youngsters not doing 'press-ups' to his satisfaction. On one occasion when a fourteen year-old boy managed to escape from the Home, when recaptured, this brutal warden, along with another, beat the boy up so badly as a punishment, that the next time I saw him he was hardly recognisable. I would stress that this had taken place without the knowledge of the Governor. It was also a practise I was told for the older boys to rape the younger ones in this home.

Working on this particular outside working-party also brought me into contact with no less than FIVE murderers, one of whom was a child-killer, who having served his sentence and been released, then murdered another child. None or the other prisoners would even speak to him, for the killing or harming of children in any way was considered by the prisoners to be the ultimate crime anyone could commit, and frequently if given the opportunity, prisoners would themselves exact punishment on such men.

One way was to throw a quantity of petrol over the intended victim (collected in small amounts over a long period of time), set the victim on fire, then push him into his cell slamming door shut behind him, self-locking doors that can only be opened by prison officers, all busily engaged elsewhere at the time.

On other occasions the intended victim would be knifed whilst we were all exercising in the yard of the prison. Those chosen to carry out the attack would wait until in a position close to the victim yet maximum distance away from the screws (warders) on duty. Then they would surround the man and stab or beat him up, leaving him to grovel on the ground in agony as they quickly dispersed to mingle with the ever circulating crowd once more. The victims knew better than to reveal the names of their attackers.

As well as having to tread carefully with some of the prisoners, one also had to be careful of certain warders who were sometimes even more vicious thugs than the inmates, having sadistic tendencies, which in the seclusion of a prison they could indulge in. This kind of thing instead of encouraging the right sort of response from inmates merely instilled fear amongst the more sensitive, and rebellion among the more hardened cases.

One had only to be in prison a very short tine to sense that as a human being you counted for absolutely nothing. To the outside world you were completely non-existent, and therefore anything that happened to you in prison did not matter. You felt that even if you died through the fault of the prison system, SOME suitable excuse would be given by the authorities to satisfy relatives.

Inside each cell, high up on the wall, was a button. This, when pressed, rang a bell downstairs by the duty officer's desk. Since certain times were allocated for the emptying of the slops etc., these bells were only to be pressed in cases of dire need, a visit to the WC was not deemed necessary by the screws, who felt our tin pots answered all our needs, regardless of the fact that it might be a very hot night and perhaps you were sharing the cell with three other men.

One reason why bells were only to be rung in an emergency was that once prisoners had been locked up for the night, most of the prison staff went home, leaving only two screws, on duty in each huge hall. Occasionally the screws on duty would be considerate at other times they were not, particularly if several men rang bells during a relatively short period of time.

I remember one occasion hearing a bell ring continuously, and when it was not answered, there were frantic shouts and hammering on the steel door. I was terribly upset by all the din, my cell being situated close to the source of all the noise. But the screws on duty were quite unconcerned. After shouting several threats to the offending prisoners, they allowed them to carry on with their hammering.

Finally, after what seemed like ages, the noise which at later stages had been intermingled with heartrending cries, ceased. Next morning word spread by word of mouth that one of the prisoners had died in the night of a burst appendix, the frantic ringing and shouting had been made by the man's cellmates calling for help.

The matter was hushed up, and of course none of us had any idea what the man's relatives were told, but no doubt a suitable statement tendering sympathy was issued. Who was there to challenge the prison authority's statement?

I know that some hardened criminals need severe discipline, but did one need to make a man forget he was part of the human race? To prisoners who were really hard cases, having grown up in poverty, and spent several years in borstal as youngsters, this kind of treatment and brainwashing makes little impression, but to people like myself, coming from a good home and having a love for the more civilised and sophisticated things in life, then the mental reaction was quite shattering. One being reduced to the status of a vegetable.

Sex, or rather the lack of it, is something else that caused prisoners great frustration and created a certain amount of violence. Sex and GBH (grievous bodily harm) cases were housed in single cells, while others were usually three or four to a cell, but since a man might be gay and yet been convicted for a driving, tax or theft-offence, he was quite likely to be sharing a cell with three or four heterosexuals and quite happy to relieve the sexual frustrations of his fellow inmates. However there were cases where a man was not gay at all, and if he was handsome or had a nice body, he would be regularly raped by his cellmates.

On occasions it was the screws who did the seducing, and when I was in the Scrubbs there was a screw who regularly bribed young prisoners in 'A' Hall- the building housing all the teenage offenders - with cigarettes. For a few fags they were quite happy to give him oral sex, or even more.

Being one-sex establishments, prisons encourage intense relationships between men, and during my spell in the Scrubbs I became involved in three very close relationships myself. The first was with Karoly, a young Hungarian. In his teenage days he had been a freedom fighter in Budapest, and when the Russians had entered the city and killed his father and brother, Karoly had fled to Britain. But unable to speak English, he quickly turned to crime for a living with the result that by the time he was twenty, he had landed in prison. A mutual love of art and drawing had first attracted us to each other, but the friendship was short-lived, for after only a few weeks he was transferred to another prison in Kent. My next relationship was with a young Maltese man named Elinor. Rugged and with dark good-looks, I earned his respect and friendship when, outnumbered by a group of prisoners verbally attacking his homeland and people, I rose in defence of the Maltese. After that he was to treat me like a brother, and said that when we were both released from prison, he wanted me to go and live with him. He added that I would make a wonderful 'front' for his business with my gentlemanly manners and general air of respectability. When I enquired just what kind of business he was in, I was informed that he and his three brothers ran a group of gambling clubs and brothels in the East End.

As an added enticement to join him, Elinor told me I could have the pick of any of his girls for sex, but on no account would he allow me to have men-friends, if he ever caught me with another man he would beat me up!

We did meet up again after we had both been released, but when he introduced me to his long-term girlfriend, and she quietly told me (out of his hearing) a few facts about Elinor and his brothers, I was convinced I should end our friendship and not get involved, so when I left his apartment next morning, it was with the intention of not returning.

My third and final friendship in prison after Elinor had been released and I still had another two months to serve, was Eddie. Young, blonde, and extremely handsome, he had been intrigued by the friendship between Elinor and myself. Being such contrasting types, he was anxious to know what had attracted us to each other.

A construction worker from Plymouth, I never did discover just what crime Eddie had committed. He told me he was married and had a young son which surprised me, for he looked so extremely young. An artful charmer, once I had been released from prison he persuaded me to send money to his wife and child in Plymouth. I stopped when I realised he was only out to use me.

The most feared people in prisons were always the 'tobacco barons', today probably replaced by drugs barons. They would manage to get tobacco smuggled into prison, then barter it for other commodities or favours, gaining both power and status. Although I did not smoke myself there was one occasion when, through a case of mistaken identity, I thought I was going to end up in hospital over a few ounces of the stuff. Ironically too this happened on my very last night in prison.

After twelve long months in the Scrubbs I was so thankful to have eaten my last meal in the place, and now sat waiting for the final ritual or the day, 'slopping out', before we were finally all 'banged up' for the night.

As I waited I could hear the voices of prisoners already opened up, on their way to the washbasins and toilets. After a while I was aware that someone had slid aside the cover of the eyehole in my door. All the cells were fitted with such a device so that screws could see what was happening inside at any time.

At first I had assumed it was a warden about to unlock my door, but then an unfamiliar voice called out, 'Have you got my snout ready?'

Puzzled, I just replied, 'Snout? What snout?'

'You know what I am talking about. You were given some tobacco to pass on to me, and I want it. No messing about.'

'I really don't know what you are talking about. No one has given me anything for you.'

The voice on the other side or the door was getting very angry now. 'Don't fool around with ME, mate,' it declared. 'You have got some snout that belongs to me, and I mean to have it.'

Then in more subdued tones I heard the same man talking to others, 'I wish the screws would hurry up and open this fucking door. What the hell does this fucking bloke think he is playing at? If he thinks he is going to cheat me, he has got another thing coming.'

I really was quite alarmed now. What on earth was going on? At first I had thought it some kind of joke, but now I knew it wasn't.

Once more the voice called out, 'The screw will be here in a minute to unlock this door, and when he does, we are coming in after that snout, so you had better have it ready for us if you know what's good for you.'

'But I HAVEN'T got it!' I shouted. 'You have made a mistake. It is someone else you want.'

The angry voice lashed out, 'You work on the Ashford party don't you?'

'Yes.'

'Then it IS you,' the man shouted. 'You fit the description.'

'Who claims to have given it to me?'

'One of the blokes in "D" Hall.'

All the time we had been talking, the noise or the warder unlocking the doors got nearer, I had never been so scared in my life for I knew just what these boys were capable of if they thought someone had crossed them in a tobacco deal. WHO could have set me up like this? And on my last night in prison, too. What on earth was I going to do? If they beat me up, I would not be going home tomorrow after all, I would be detained for inquiries to be made, and maybe get blamed of something which I knew nothing about.

'Look, be reasonable,' I begged, 'I really DON'T know what you are talking about. No one has given me anything for you. I am being released tomorrow, why would I bother to cheat you on my last night in this place?'

'You won't BE going out. You won't be going ANYWHERE if you don't hand over the stuff.'

I was panic-stricken now. Oh God, had I endured a whole year in this dreadful place only to have something like this to happen in the last few hours?

Then I heard a different voice, 'Perhaps he really DOESN'T know anything about it. He sounds genuine to me. Perhaps we HAVE got the wrong guy.'

'Well, I am waiting here until the screw does unlock him.'

A moment later I heard the cell door next to mine being unlocked. A vision flashed through my mind of my parents waiting outside the prison gates in the morning, ready to take me home in the car, whilst I lay in a hospital bed with cuts and bruises, and possibly broken bones.

As I heard the warder turning the key in my lock, I braced myself against the wall, waiting for the attack on me that I expected to take place once the warder had moved further along the landing to unlock more doors.

Nothing happened. I waited for a few minutes, standing near to my doorway across which prisoners kept passing in their usual manner with water jugs and tin pots in their hands.

'Where are they?', I asked myself. Surely they were not waiting to attack me out on the landing!

Very cautiously I crept to the door and peered out, and to my utter relief there was no one waiting to pounce on me. Getting my jug, I hurried along the landing to fetch some water for the night.

In the washroom I mentioned briefly to another prisoner what had happened, and he said, 'I did hear a couple of blokes talking about it just now as I came in. Must have been them. Seems they DID make a mistake, but found the right guy after all.'

Back in my cell once more, I slammed the door shut and lay down on my bed, and allowed my eyes to wander round the bare walls, and over the few furnishings the cell possessed.

'My last night in this bed,' I thought. 'Tomorrow I shall be home.' It seemed too good to be true. Undressing and climbing into bed, I closed my eyes to enjoy the happiest and most contented sleep of my life.

*My parents around the time I was in prison*

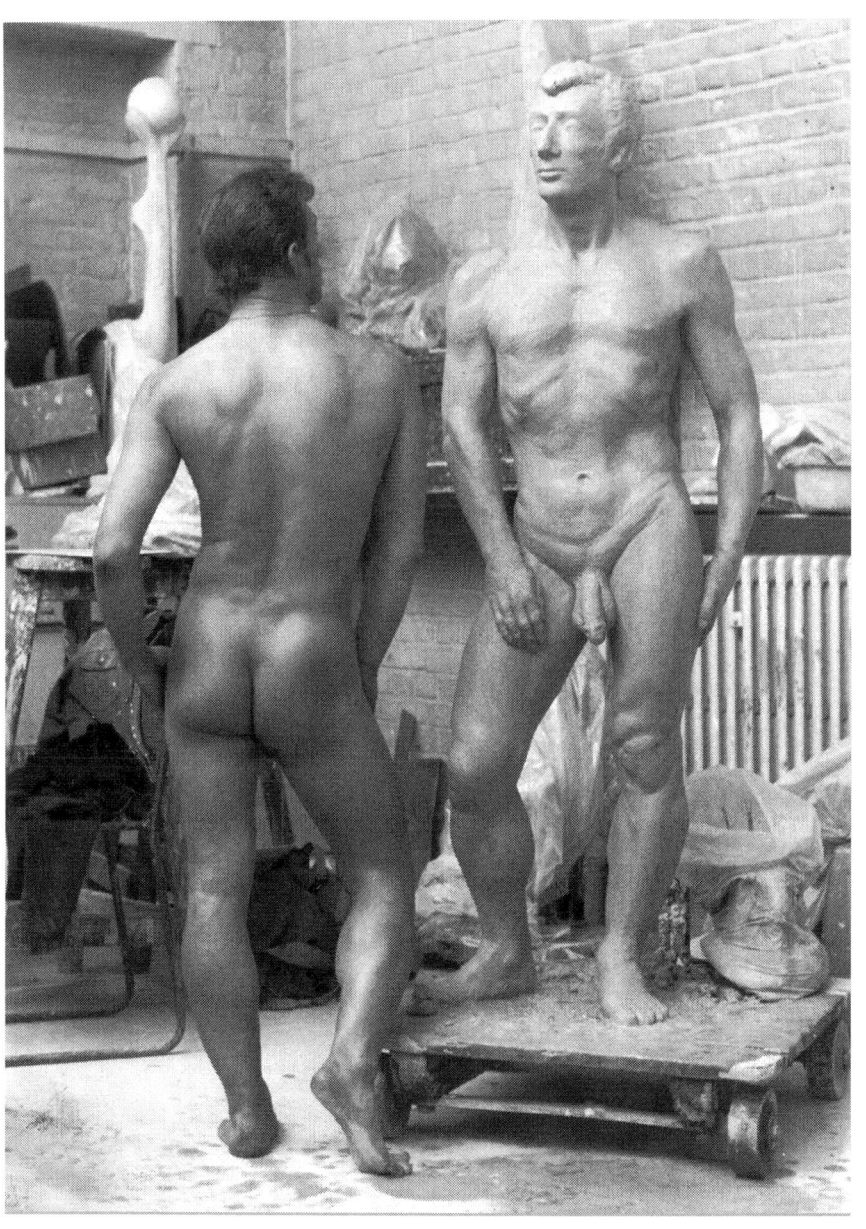

*Posing beside "my torso" sculpture*

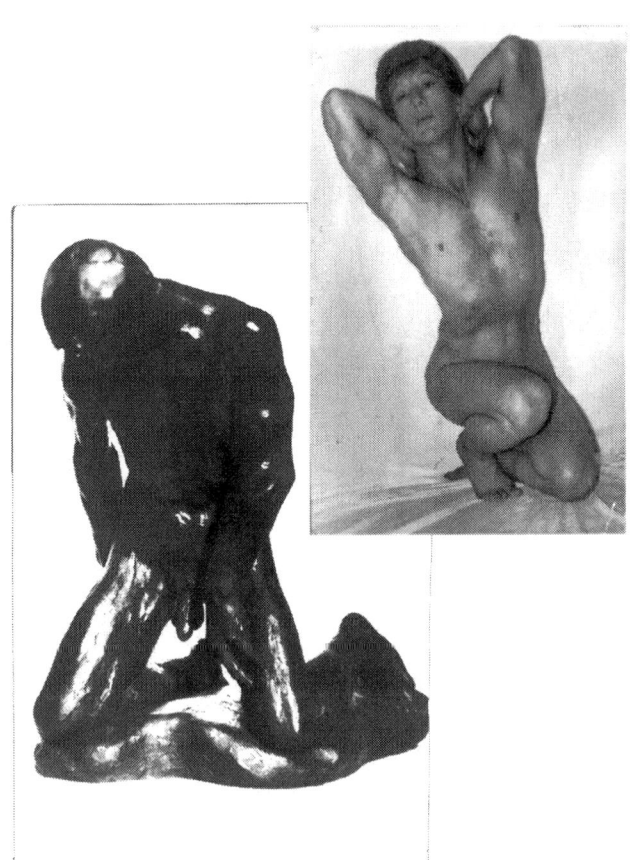

*Ronald by James
Mathieson, Archer
Galleries, Mayfair
1973*

# Toast of the Art World

Released from prison in the autumn of 1962 my most pressing problem was to find employment, Josh making it perfectly clear when I called to see him, that now I had acquired a criminal record I was no longer welcome in his organisation. He said that in any case since I had gone to prison for longer than had been expected, it had been necessary to look elsewhere for someone to replace me, and I felt particularly angry when I discovered exactly WHO had replaced me: Harry Woodman, the young man from Aldershot I had given a helping hand to, in more ways than one. I felt I had been stabbed in the back.

Not having the courage to take a job locally in my home town, I dreaded the prospect of a new employer asking, 'And where were you last employed?', and as week succeeded week without my finding work, relations between my father and I steadily worsened, reaching a point where had it not been for my dear mother, I would have been quite ready to commit suicide.

Then, down to my last few shillings one day, I happened to pick up an art magazine, not the pseudo kind of publication I had worked for, but a highly respectable publication called THE ARTIST and the idea came to me, 'Why not be a model?'. Artists and sculptors were a broadminded bunch and not the kind or people to worry about my past indiscretions.

So it was that from 1963 until 1973 I was to work in every major art school in London, including the Royal Academy schools, Royal College, the City & Guilds of London, the Slade, Camberwell, St. Martin's, Goldsmiths and several others. They were to be ten of the happiest years of my life. I really enjoyed the work, and quickly established myself as the most sought after male nude in the London art world.

The reason for my popularity was really quite simple. Most art school models were extremely lazy, only willing to sit or lie down, often falling asleep in the process. I on the other hand loved to do poses that were athletic, classical, even erotic, and this delighted both the students and their tutors. At one point in my career I was actually booked up FOUR YEARS in advance. Most other models would complain that they did not know where they would get work the next season!

During the art schools long summer holidays, I accepted work from both professional and amateur artists and sculptors. It was a great honour to pose for the famous ones, and gave me a lot of satisfaction to walk into galleries and see items I had posed for, there on display.

Amongst the favourite things I posed for was a huge fibreglass by Lorne Mackean, which showed me seated naked on the back of Pegasus, the mythical flying horse. The work entitled, 'The Taming of Pegasus' was originally exhibited at the Royal Academy, and later at the Alwin Gallery in Brook Street, Mayfair, before it was moved to its permanent home in the United States.

Lorne shared her studio in Mayfair with her boyfriend Edwin Russell, another sculptor, and on one occasion when Edwin had asked me to pose for a figure of Hercules, I arrived at the studio to find Lorne working on a bust of Sir Michael Redgrave. The star of stage and screen was sitting there cigarette in one hand and a glass of whiskey in the other, and I was able to chat to him for about half an hour.

Another work I was proud to pose for was a huge bronze figure of Jesus ascending up to heaven on a ball of fire by the Austrian sculptor Uli Nimptsch RA. This can be seen in the church of St. Wilfred in Bognor Regis, Sussex. Quite an amusing little story is attached to it: Nimptsch always created his originals in wax, and the figure of Jesus being so large, some seven feet in height, the wax was placed over a core or plaster-covered wire and wood. Securely bolted to several large wooden planks, it was placed upright in what appeared to be a concrete base.

My visits to the famous man were spread over several months, and on the final day at mid-morning when Mrs Nimptsch brought two cups of coffee into the studio, her husband said we should take a break. While I stood in front of an old fashioned iron stove warming my bottom and sipping my coffee, the sculptor decided to fill a small spirit lamp which he used to soften the wax before pressing small pieces on to the big figure with a metal tool.

Accidentally Nimptsch poured too much liquid from the bottle, and it ran down all over the sides of the lamp and onto the stand on which the lamp stood. Next he struck a match and lit the wick of the lamp before turning away to enjoy a pipeful of his favourite tobacco, then stood gazing out of the window into the garden which lay between the studio and the house. Suddenly my attention was drawn to the spirit lamp for the flame had spread from the wick to envelope the whole lamp. Alarmed, I called Nimptsch's attention to it. He glanced round in a very leisurely manner and said not to worry, it would burn itself out in a minute. Then he went back to gazing out of the window.

A few moments more, and the whole top of the stand was burning, coated with the accumulated drips of wax constantly dropped on it over the years. Almost immediately the melting wax began dripping onto the wooden floor, and where it fell, so it continued to burn, forming a complete circle of flame around the base of the stand.

I hesitated to worry the sculptor a second time, for the great man was not the type or person one could easily speak to, but it was obvious that the flames were taking a hold, and they were NOT going to 'burn themselves out' Risking his annoyance, I called his attention to the situation again. He did not appear unduly worried, although he walked over to the stand to deal with it. Then he did a stupid thing, he attempted to BLOW out the flaming lamp and merely blew more particles of flaming liquid and wax all over the floor. Wherever they landed, so they continued to burn.

I stood wondering what I could do, but since I was wearing nothing to protect me, and did not know where there was any water in the studio, I felt completely helpless. I had visions of the whole studio going up in flames, the room was filled with numerous wax figures, and I would have to dash naked into the house to summon help.

As the sculptor continued blowing loudly, one flame leaped into the air and fluttered down again right on top of his head! Almost immediately his fuzzy white hair began to burn.

'Mr. Nimptsch, your hair is on fire!' I shouted in panic, wondering if I DARE throw the remains of my coffee over him. He began beating his head with his hands and moments later it was out.

In a state or frenzy by now, Nimptsch rushed wildly over to the window-sill, knocking over a couple of objects in his haste to get at a water jug that was apparently kept there. He threw the contents of this over the lamp and stand putting most of the fire out. Then he proceeded to stamp out the remaining flames with his feet. Soon it was all over, the worst damage being to the sculptor's head, and he spent the rest of the day rubbing this very scorched area.

Later I posed for a wax figure which was put on display in the famous London waxworks exhibition 'Madam Tussauds'. The well-known sculptor James Butler RA had been commissioned to make four new figures for the exhibition, General de Gaulle, Don Cordobes the bullfighter, fashion model Twiggy, and Rudolf Nureyev, the Russian ballet dancer. All the subjects had agreed to pose for Mr. Butler with the exception of Nureyev who it seems felt that were he to do so, then his spirit would leave his body and take up residence in the wax figure instead.

Since Butler wished to depict the dancer wearing tights and performing an exercise, Nureyev's figure was of prime importance and since I was already working for Butler at the time, and was of similar build, I was asked to step into his shoes. Or rather his tights!

When I told my mother I was going to be placed in the waxworks exhibition, she laughed and said, 'Oh yes? In the Chamber of Horrors I imagine!'

Although I frequently worked very long hours, I still found time to lead an exciting social life meeting lots of interesting people, not all connected with the art world, an exiled Russian Princess, Betty Marsden, Katie Boyle, Gerry and Sylvia Anderson (producers or the popular puppet TV films THUNDERBIRDS and TERRAHAWKS) and Belinda Cadbury, a member of the chocolate-making family. Belinda was student at the City & Guilds of London art school at the time, and had a lovely house in Chelsea to which I was invited several times.

This being the 'Swinging Sixties' era the attitude to frontal nudity had become very relaxed and every stage show, film, and magazines included nudes, and it was inevitable that I should be approached by photographers, and now that it was safe to pose for such pictures I was happy to oblige. I was even invited by the producer of a 'blue movies' company to appear in a number of his films, but they were not half so exciting to make as one might imagine, a single camera having to be continually repositioned.

The sixties was also a time for lots of really wild parties, often held in large and elegant houses, and being an artists model the hosts would invariably expect me to entertain their guests with a display of classical and erotic nude poses.

Fancy dress parties were all the rage and I went to one of these dressed, or rather undressed, as Bacchus the God of Wine. My costume was a tiny G-string, its elastic hidden by plastic vine leaves, the crotch area covered by a bunch of grapes. I wore a circlet of leaves on my head at a drunken angle, and trailed more leaves over one shoulder. As I entered the main room there was lots of laughter and one wit shouted out 'Look, he's been G-raped.' Before the evening was over I had been!

The more elaborate parties had cabarets and at one of these I was asked to perform a sensual Afro-style dance to the accompaniment of music played on bongo drums and flutes. I wore heavy black fringes around my neck, upper arms, and below the knees, a small black G-string and an exotic golden mask.

For my act the room was plunged into darkness and two spotlights illuminated my well-oiled body as it writhed and contorted to the throbbing of the savage music. As the tempo increased, so my dance became more and more abandoned, and in response to calls from my audience seated in a large circle around me, one by one I tore off the fringes, and then finally the G-string.

Sexually aroused by now I taunted them with my wildly gyrating hips and bouncing erect cock, and unable to restrain their pent up excitement, those seated around me immediately began to tear off their own clothes and person's next to them. Moments later the floor had become a sea of naked bodies all indulging in a frantic sex orgy, two women and a lusty young man quickly claiming me for their own gratification.

So successful was this particular evening, I was asked to repeat the dance several more times for other party-givers, and always they would end in the same frenzy of furious abandonment.

I had lots of requests to pose for amateur artists and photographers, some were genuinely interested in art, although in the main I must admit they mostly just wanted to fuck me. They included the smart frustrated wives of husbands constantly away on business, liberated single women, and of course a horde of gay men.

When posing I always coated my body with oil, partly to accentuate the flesh tones, partly to keep me warm in cold studios. My oily skin always looked sensual of course, and on occasions my clients would be tempted to ask if they might apply an extra coating to me themselves. The effect this had on me as they gently massaged and squeezed can be well imagined, and of course this was just the result they were after.

There were 'kinky' suggestions, too, like the lady who asked if I would stand on the arms of her armchair while she sat directly below me - 'to get an unusual angle!'

I commenced facing her, and had been given strict instructions not to look down as her pencil scraped away at the drawing on her lap. After a while she asked me to face the other way round. I did, and there was more frantic scratching for a few minutes. Then all went quiet until she could pluck up the courage to say, 'It's no good, I can't concentrate any more. Can I touch you?'

I never refused sex if that is what the client wanted. Sex was more pleasurable than posing, and I WAS getting paid for it.

When booked to do some serious posing however, I always behaved in a very proper manner. So much so that on one occasion the late Eric Winters, head of the Sir John Cass College Sculpture Studios, said to me, 'Ron, you are quite the best model I have ever known, and I think the greatest compliment I can pay you is to say that you are a REAL professional.' A remark that made me very proud.

But the line between sex and art is very thin as was illustrated by a remark I overheard one day when some friends had called at the studio of a well-known sculptor I happened to be posing for. Looking at the sculpture one of the men remarked, 'You have overdone the genitals a bit, haven't you?'

The sculptor replied, 'If the model has a well developed cock, and Ron has, why NOT devote suitable attention to it?' Then, with a wicked gleam in his eye, he added, 'Let's be honest, some collectors will want to buy it for that VERY reason!'

On one occasion when I was posing for students at Camberwell School of Art, Lord Anthony Armstrong-Jones (husband of Princess Margaret) walked into the studio with a tutor-friend, and proceeded to take photographs of me. Since I was of course nude, and had not given him permission to do so, I thought it a bit of a liberty, the school may be paying me a fee, but HE wasn't, and so I asked him to leave. He did, but I could see he was not very pleased.

*Myself and Dinah Sheridan, 1970*

*Mother with Dinah Sheridan, 1976*

# Dinah Returns

Some eighteen months after I had commenced my modelling career, my friendship with Dinah Sheridan began to flourish again. We had not actually seen each other since her departure from Welwyn Garden City in 1953, although we had exchanged letters and cards at Christmas.

In early December 1964, I received a Christmas card on which she had written, 'Many years of anxiety are nearly over. Legal proceedings take ages, but one day we three will be settled again somewhere.'

What on earth was she referring to? What HAD happened? Dinah was apparently assuming that I already knew what it was all about, but I was at a complete loss.

I wrote to her immediately asking for some kind of explanation, but before she could reply, a friend sent me a copy of the DAILY MIRROR which carried a picture of Dinah and her husband on the front page and the headline, 'Dinah Seeks Divorce'.

The newspaper went on to say, 'Mr John Davis, 57 year-old "Boss-man" behind many British films, is being sued for divorce by his wife, film star Dinah Sheridan. News that the couple had parted came as a complete shock to their many film star friends. For when Dinah gave up her sparkling career to marry the chief of Rank films, it seemed that she was more than happy with her two roles, as a housewife and as First Lady of the British Film Industry. Friends now predict that 41 year-old Dinah will make a return to films.'

A letter from Dinah arrived shortly afterwards, the contents of which were much too private to be revealed here. I will only say that what she related, made my heart ache for her, although frankly it was no more than both Dinah's mother and I had anticipated some twelve years earlier.

In July 1965, Dinah got her divorce, but it was to take a further twelve months before the financial side of things was resolved, and the national press had quite a field-day reporting all the various details of the case. Once it had all been sorted out, Dinah lost no time in buying a beautiful apartment for herself and her two children in the smarter part of Kensington.

Jeremy, now twenty, was studying accountancy, and in the years ahead would not only have his own business, but enter politics, becoming first Conservative MP for Richmond and Barnes, then Minister for the Armed Forces, and Chairmen of the Conservative Party, finally receiving a Knighthood from the Queen.

Jenny too became very successful. Now grown to a tall and willowy blonde, she had inherited her mother's beauty, and after leaving her finishing school in Switzerland, became a photographic model, appearing on the covers of countless magazines and in television adverts. Later she became an actress and appeared in a number of films for cinema and TV. But it was as a television presenter that she was to score her biggest success in the very popular children's programme MAGPIE.

The mid 1960s was quite a traumatic period for Dinah. First the divorce, then the deaths of her sister and her mother Lisa. Only six months earlier Lisa had taken her last set of Royal photographs at Windsor Castle. These included several charming shots of the young Princes Andrew and Edward, which had been widely published in newspapers and magazines everywhere. Both the Queen and the Queen Mother sent personal letters of sympathy to Dinah.

In one of my own letters to Dinah around that time, I posed the question, 'WAS she intending to resume her acting career?'

In her reply she said, 'I cannot just sit and knit, and just do housework. I long to get back to work, and have already had a few feelers out in my direction. It is good to know that I have not been forgotten, and probably this is due to the fact that I have been seen regularly at Premiers etc. Just let me get settled and I shall be back - perhaps as Shirley Temple's grandmother! But I do feel I must start once more. Must stop now. Have masses of letters to write. Tapestry to do, sewing, and then the supper to cook. Never stops. Much Love, Dinah (Sheridan again!)'

Reading the final part of her letter it crossed my mind how very different Dinah's circumstances had now become. Married to John Davis and living in the greatest style and luxury with homes in Kent and London and a large staff to cope with all the household duties, the only time she needed to go into the kitchen was to hand a menu to her cook.

In 1968 when Dinah was finally ready to resume her career, she went along to her old agent, Al Parker, and soon discovered the bitter price of her retirement fifteen years earlier. At the time Dinah had told him to turn down all offers no matter how good. Now she learned that the offers had included several from Hollywood to appear opposite the likes of Gregory Peck and Danny Kaye.

Her new career was to concentrate mainly on the West End stage and television, and she was to become particularly popular with London theatre audiences, starring in one successful play after another. Her leading men including Sir Douglas Fairbanks Junior, Sir John Gielgud, Peter O'Toole, Donald Sinden, and Tony Britton. She was also to star in one more classic film, THE RAILWAY CHILDREN, and made a brief appearance in another, THE MIRROR CRACKED.

Whenever Dinah was starring in a new play, my family and I would always go to see the show, then go backstage afterwards to have drinks with Dinah. On one occasion when I happened to mention that I was redecorating the lounge at home, she asked me to send her a sample of my wallpaper. At the time I thought she was merely curious to see what it looked like, but a few days later through the mail I received a beautiful pair of fingerplates for my lounge door. Made from pressed flowers from her garden and placed under clear sheets of perspex they were truly attractive, and such a lovely gift.

On another occasion when I had spoken of my fondness for jam, she went to her storage-cupboard and produced a jar of apricot and almond jam she had recently made herself, and told me to take it home for my tea. So typical of Dinah. Not just a very beautiful star, but a very human being too.

For this reason, I was very pleased when, after two broken marriages, Dinah found the ideal companion to share her life with. After a long and happy relationship they would finally marry in 1986. The lucky man was John (Jack) Merivale, actor stepson of actress Gladys Cooper.

Previously, Jack had been married to Hollywood star Jan Sterling. He had also been the companion of beautiful Vivien Leigh right up to the moment she died so tragically in 1967.

Dinah first met Jack in 1968 when she was starring with Gladys Cooper, Evelyn Laye, and Hugh Williams in a play called LETS ALL GO DOWN THE STRAND. Jack used to escort his stepmother to and from the theatre each day.

Jack himself had been very successful, touring all over the world with Sir Laurence Olivier, Vivien Leigh and their Old Vic Theatre Company. Jack had also starred opposite Vivien on Broadway, New York. His films had included A NIGHT TO REMEMBER, KING RAT, 80,000 SUSPECTS, THE FILE OF ADRIAN MESSENGER, and ARABESQUE opposite Gregory Peck and Sophia Loren.

Sadly as Dinah's career began to flourish again, so Jack's began to decline due to ill health, and eventually he was forced to give up acting altogether and spend several days a week attached to a kidney machine. Typical of Dinah, she learned how to operate the machine (it was in their home), so that for most of the time she could nurse Jack herself.

Sadly Jack died in 1992, and six months later Dinah was married for a fourth time to American businessman Aubrey Ison. They married in Las Vegas, and settled in California.

# Variety, the Spice of Life?

During the 1960s my life swung from one end of the social scale to the other and although the limited space prevents me from describing all the colourful and weird characters I encountered, I must just mention a few.

One was 'Tiger', or at least that is what he liked to be called. In his early thirties, Tiger ran a small motorbike shop in the Whitechapel area of London. Indeed he was a mechanical wizard who personally built all the motorcycles he sold. He was also a 'leather and chains' fanatic who was looked upon by the leather fraternity for miles around as their acknowledged leader.

I first met Tiger at a drinks party given by a mutual friend, and when the rather scruffy leather-clad figure was introduced, he seemed to take an immediate liking to me for some reason. During my conversation with him I learned that he was a frequent guest at a certain stately home, the owner of which, an earl, was also secretly kinky about leather and chains. It was this earl who had bought Tiger the premises he now owned and set him up in business.

Despite his butch and very rugged appearance, I soon discovered that under the show of leather and chains there lay hidden a quite gentle and tender heart. When he invited me to visit him one day for a meal, I found him working in a small yard at the rear of the shop surrounded by a group of doting young leatherboys.

We had a meal in his small apartment above the shop, then he took me into his 'den', a large room which overlooked the yard. Bench-type seating ran around three walls, and a small bar was built against the fourth. Here Tiger told me the group met each night to socialise and perform their initiation ceremonies. He said that every time a new lad wanted to enrol into the group, he had to prove his toughness by allowing all the other members to gang-bang him. Tiger said sex was a very important part of the group's activities, and the thing which personally gave HIM the greatest thrill, was to be fucked on the back of a motorbike doing a ton (one hundred miles an hour)

Some time later I heard that Tiger had been killed in a motorbike accident, and could not help but wonder if his kinky taste for sex had contributed to his death.

At the other end of the social scale was Mr. Hopkins, or Hoppy as he preferred to be called. A one-time wealthy Malayan rubber planter, he had now retired and built himself a large and luxurious house in a very secluded stretch of woodland just outside Guildford. Having seen a nude photo of me, Hoppy invited me to spend a weekend with him. The grounds of his house which covered four acres, contained both a swimming pool and a hard tennis court.

I had half expected that Hoppy would want to 'bed' me as soon as I arrived, but to my surprise he behaved in a most gentlemanly manner. After drinks and a super lunch, he took me for a long drive through the lovely Surrey countryside. Later he took me to dinner at a terribly expensive hotel en route to his home where there were more drinks. When it was time to retire he showed me to my bedroom complete with its own bath, shower, and fridge full of drinks, but somewhat to my disappointment made no demands on my body.

Next morning after bringing me tea in bed, he had given his staff the weekend off, he said that as the grounds were so secluded, I might wish to walk about naked? Clearly this is what he wanted me to do and since it was such lovely weather, I obliged for the rest of the weekend. Still he made no sexual advances or even attempt to touch me. I therefore assumed he must be a voyeur who got his kicks just looking at naked guys.

He invited me to return as often as I liked, and seemed to greatly enjoy taking me out to dine at all the most expensive restaurants in the area. Before setting out, he would always push a bundle of bank notes into my hand saying, 'That's just in case you want to buy me a drink while we are out.'

It was not until my sixth or seventh visit that he was to reveal what his real motive was. Having plied me with plenty of drink, he led me to a room I had not been into before. It was furnished like a schoolmaster's study, and on a side table were canes, whips, and a whole array of weapons used for corporal punishment.

Hoppy asked me if I would dress up as a schoolboy so that the headmaster could punish me! I told him that as a nude model I certainly could not appear in public, nor indeed in private, covered in lash marks or weals, and in any case I was not prepared to have him beat me.

Disappointed, he asked if I would agree to the roles being reversed? At first I said no, then feeling selfish after his kindness to me in recent weeks, I relented and said I would 'Give it a go', although I was not into that kind of thing.

The performance went on for hours, and by three o'clock in the morning I was feeling completely exhausted. He was not only wide awake, but getting more and more excited, but finally I begged to be allowed to go to bed.

I had only been asleep a short while when he burst into my room, flung me roughly onto my stomach, and savagely raped me. I was far too drunk and exhausted to resist, but next morning when he said he wanted to repeat the whole thing again, I felt enough was enough and made it quite clear that I would not be returning to Guildford again.


Another character I met in the 1960s was Rupert, the owner of two prosperous hotels in the Finsbury Park area of London. He had a lovely home in Southgate where he and his schoolteacher wife lived, and to which I was invited for meals when his wife was absent.

So very obviously gay, Rupert was in his mid-fifties, and with his speech and manners he could easily have doubled for the late Sir Noel Coward, their style and elegance being identical.

Rupert stands out in my memory for two particular reasons. One was the occasion when he turned up unexpectedly on my doorstep trying his hardest to look like a butch leatherboy. The sight was so hilarious I almost collapsed laughing, and quickly dragged him inside before any of my neighbours could catch sight of him. Even funnier than the sight of him trying to imitate someone like Tiger was the fact that he had not ridden down from London on a motorbike, but a little Lambretta scooter!

The second memory of Rupert concerns a little story he told me. It seems that he was in the habit most summer evenings of going to a certain area of Hampstead Heath to indulge in a little sex-fun. He explained that in a large area of woodland there was a certain pathway along which gays hid behind bushes and trees until such time as a dishy male came along, then they would either step naked in front of the walker, or drag them into the bushes for a little fun. Rupert said no one actually walked down this path at night unless they WERE looking for gay sex. He said you always knew just where the gays were stationed by the glow of the cigarettes they kept burning.

It seems that on one particular night in readiness for some anticipated fun, Rupert had stripped down to his underpants on the edge of the woods, and hidden his clothes under a bush until he should return, then walked boldly down the 'pathway of pleasure'.

Having enjoyed an hour or so of sex with a couple of men, Rupert returned to the spot where he had hidden his clothes, only to discover that someone had stolen them!

Poor Rupert! That night he had the embarrassment of having to ride his scooter through the busy streets of North London in his underpants, hoping that people would think he was wearing sports shorts! He pointed out that he could hardly return HOME in that state, especially as his wife was there, and so he had to ride to a nearby friend who was roughly the same size and shape as himself, to borrow some clothes. Just what his wife must have thought when he arrived home wearing different clothes to those he had left in, I cannot imagine.

Still on the subject or Hampstead Heath, there was a famous willow tree on the Heath known to gays as the 'yum-yum tree', the reason being that its heavy foliage touched the ground on all sides forming a kind of tent. Inside away from prying eyes, in the dusk of evening large numbers of gays would gather for sex orgies. I well remember on one occasion seeing a young man with an insatiable appetite for sex, fucked fifteen times by a variety of men.

Another place that attracted a lot of gays to Hampstead Heath during the summer months, was the famous all-male nude enclosure known as 'the ponds'. The place was actually supervised by the LCC which employed a full time attendant to look after the place and keep and eye on things.

It was a large expanse of concrete surrounded by a seven foot high wooden fence, which had bench-seating all round for those waiting their turn to do some sunbathing on the concrete floor. Unless you got there early on a hot summer's day, the floor area was absolutely packed tight with naked bodies all eager to get a tan, or a crafty little fondle when the attendant's back was turned! For most of the time he was as naked as everybody else, and so it was not always easy to spot him.

Everything was strictly above board, no hanky-panky allowed, and although men frequently took turns to oil each other's backs, it was not wise to linger on certain areas too long. Neither was it wise to take a camera into the enclosure. More than once I saw one snatched from the owner and flung into the lake, which had a doorway opening onto it.

There was a shower in one corner of the enclosure, and a certain amount of weight-lifting equipment when sufficient space was available. One was also permitted to swim in the lake, but had to wear a swim slip after 8am. There was always a dedicated core of genuine sun-worshippers amongst the men, but of course most went to see and be seen. I remember on one occasion being full of admiration for a truly beautiful young man, obviously a bodybuilder, and in the Mr. Universe class, who paraded up and down, large cock swinging and bronze muscles rippling to everyone's delight.


Before leaving the subject of strange and interesting people I was continually coming into contact with, I must mention just one more: Larry or Rita as he preferred to be called, a transvestite, and an art school model like myself. He was in his late twenties, not particularly good-looking, but with a trim figure and a small waist. He seemed most anxious to talk to me the first time we sat opposite each other in the canteen, telling me that he had a one-room flat in the East End, and had no friends whatsoever.

Feeling sorry for him I suggested we have a drink together one evening when we had both finished posing for the day, and it was then that he told me he was a transvestite. He said he had been married at one time for two years. Unknown to his wife, he often used to dress up in her clothes and jewellery. Then one day she come home unexpectedly and found him wearing her things. She was so shocked and angry she promptly packed her bags and left him.

Larry explained it wasn't simply a case of wanting to LOOK like a woman, he felt he was a woman trapped in a man's body. He said that every evening when he got home, he 'became' a woman, putting on women's clothing, make-up, and generally behaving like one.

He added that sexually he was terribly frustrated, and on the rare occasions he had managed to persuade a man to go back to his flat with him, there had not been a single one who would accept him as a woman. He said their attitude was always the same: 'If I wanted to fuck a woman, I would choose a REAL one.' This had hurt him bitterly, and he had considered having a sex operation.

Discussing his problem openly with me seemed to make Larry feel a lot better. We spent another couple of evenings in pubs together, and eventually he asked me if I would like to spend the night with him at his flat. Part of me objected to the idea, but another part felt sorry for him. I thought: 'Oh well, it WOULD be an experience, I suppose!' So it was that I arranged to go along to his place the following Friday evening.

When I had finished posing for my class at 9pm, I got dressed and went to the nearest pub for a stiff drink, to prepare myself for what was to come. I had told Larry I would arrive about 10pm, his flat being about a thirty-minute journey from the college.

Larry's door was opened by what in the dim lighting of the hall I took to be a woman. It turned out to be Larry, a curly wig on his head, masses of make-up on his face, complete with false eyelashes, a well-filled blouse, mini-skirt, and high-heeled shoes. Holding out a delicate hand with nails all neatly varnished, 'she' told me her name was Rita, asked me in, and then led the way to a room on the first floor.

The room was very neat and tidy, colourful and comfortable. I was offered a glass of wine, and we talked about art against a background of soft music coming from a record player. It was just as though I was being entertained by a REAL girl for the very first time.

Finishing my drink, 'she' offered me another, and I began to get quite a sensuous feeling creeping into my loins, and pushing Rita back onto the settee, I kissed and began to fondle her. At first I was disturbed by the hardness or her breasts, they were TOO solid, so I transferred my attention to the lower parts of her body.

Sliding my hand under her skirt and up the inside of her thigh, I reached to where Larry's cock should be, but it wasn't! I presumed he must have strapped himself down somehow. While I was doing this, Rita had unbuttoned my shirt, unfastened my jeans, taken out my hardening cock, and started to suck on it. We kissed, and feeling the urgent need for sex, I stood up to remove all my clothing. Rita stood up too, quickly removing her blouse, skirt, and stockings. In just a bra and panties, she hurried across the room, dragged an enormous full-length mirror out of a cupboard, and positioned it carefully opposite the divan. Next she put a table lamp on the floor beside it. Meanwhile I sat patiently waiting for her to sit down again. But accuracy in getting the mirror positioned just so, seemed all-important to her.

Satisfied at last, she came over to join me. But for me the frustrations were just beginning. Although I was desperately craving sex, she seemed to have her whole attention focused on her reflection in that damned mirror!

I stroked and fondled her body as she continued to stand there with her back to me, and lowering her black panties, I glanced over her shoulder at the mirror's reflection. With the wig, make-up, bra, and matt of air between the legs (cock and balls were tucked out of sight), it really DID look like a woman.

I caressed the shapely hips, which began to gyrate wildly, while at the same time she kept touching her wig and admiring her reflection all the time, completely ignoring ME. Indeed I felt I might just as well not been there at all, I was just another 'prop' in this fantasy.

Each time I tried to pull her down onto the divan she would pull away from me, go over to that damn mirror and lamp, and reposition them to get a different angle!

I became so fed up and frustrated I simply gave up, and pulled back the covers of the divan and made it perfectly clear that if I wasn't going to get anything, then I might as well go to sleep. She, seeing that I had lost interest, walked over to the divan and got in beside me, still wearing the bra, one shoulder strap of which kept slipping (revealing all the padding inside). Each time it slipped, she clutched it wildly, pulling it back into position. It was clear that she had no intention of removing her bra, the final illusion.

After a few minutes of petting, she turned her back on me so that she could again stare at her reflection in the mirror. Quickly I rolled over on my side, placed the tip of my rock-hard cock between her buttocks, and with one quick thrust forced my cock up her arse as hard as I could. She screamed, and looking over her shoulder into the mirror, I could not help smiling at the agony on her face! After all that teasing and messing about I had been subjected to, I WASN'T going to stop now.

Regardless of her squeals and groans, I belted away for all I was worth, my arms around her waist to make sure she didn't get away from me THIS time. Having kept me waiting for so long however, it did not take me too long to ejaculate, which must have been a great relief for 'Rita'- and finally satisfied I turned over on my back and went peacefully to sleep.

I left early next morning, and was not surprised when Rita did not suggest I visit her again, as lonely as she was. Perhaps she found she had bitten off more than she could chew? Anyway it was just as well, for I do not think I could have gone through all that charade again. I had to agree with my predecessors, there really was no substitute for a woman, just as there was no substitute for a real man. I decided I really must learn to curb my sympathy in future.


There were some interesting women in my life around that time, too, and one of them was Gylda, a sculpture tutor at the Sir John Cass College of Art in Whitechapel. With huge blue eyes and raven-black hair, she was very beautiful and had a child-like innocence that drew everyone to her like a magnet. In truth, beneath that gentle exterior there lurked a very sexual woman full of unleashed desire for the unusual.

Gylda was married to a young artist two years her junior and they lived in a sumptuous apartment in Chelsea to which I was invited on a number of' occasions for meals and weekends.

Gylda admitted to indulging in sex freely before she married Peter. 'Why not?', she said, 'I like it!'

As versed as she was in the delights of 'normal' sex however, she knew little or nothing about homosexuality, and so when she discovered that I was gay, she demanded to know in detail all that went on between male lovers. Not content with this, and in order to gain first-hand knowledge, she suggested I have an affair with her husband. He was not so keen on the idea however. I could see he felt uncomfortable about the whole thing, and I told Gylda I had no wish to become part of any triangle. As it happened, the couple were divorced shortly afterwards.

Another lovely girl who wanted my body for herself, was Nikki. A professional nude model like myself, she was an extremely sexy-looking girl, with long dark hair and heavily made-up eyes. She had a fantastic body, and whether clothed in figure-hugging dresses or stark naked, she knew exactly how to turn men on.

It seems Nikki first caught sight of ME when I had my clothes on, in the art college canteen. Apparently liking what she saw, and having heard that I was well endowed, she sneaked into my classroom one day so that she could see what I looked like naked. Seeing that I DID have a big cock, she made up her mind that she wanted sex with me.

As it happened, Gylda was in charge of the class at that time, and taking Nikki on one side whispered to her that she was wasting her time, I was gay! Undeterred, Nikki was determined she was going to get me into bed, and left a note with Gylda inviting me to meet her for a drink at a nearby bar after classes.

I was very flattered, because every red-blooded male at the college I was told, dreamed of fucking Nikki, with her voluptuous figure and enormous, shapely breasts.

We did have a drink together that night, and she did get me into bed where I don't think my performance disappointed her, because we carried on seeing each other for a further six months, right up to the time she decided to return home to Nottingham, where it seems she had a little daughter being looked after by her mother while she was in London.

During the six months I regularly saw and fucked Nikki, I got envious glances from men wherever we went, and I must admit it was a terrific boost to my ego. However, although sex with her was always fun, I knew that deep down inside me, women were no substitute for the kind of loving I really craved for.

Yet another female I had a long association with around that time was Mary, and although our relationship was purely platonic, I grew extremely fond of her. A very plain-looking woman in her fifties, Mary was married to a wealthy Greek restauranteur, and had two grown-up children. A cultured and charming woman, we had met when she was a part-time student at the Sir John Cass Art School, yes, in Gylda's class yet again!

Mary told me that although she had borne two children, her marriage had been a mistake from the beginning, and she had not known what it was to experience REAL love until she had recently fallen in love with another woman.

Suddenly she had become 'alive' and found depths of joy and emotion she had never experienced before, but sadly, just recently, her female lover had cast her aside. Mary had been so devastated she had attempted to kill herself. When I met her she had only just come out of hospital, and was badly in need of someone to talk to, particularly someone who could speak the same language, and I felt I was able to help her a great deal, and in return she introduced me to many of her cultured and interesting friends who frequently invited us to dine with them.

Whenever I think about Mary, I also recall an occasion when she and I had a rather bitter argument with a young Australian male student in the school canteen one day.

Until that moment Mary and I had always regarded the young man as a thoroughly charming and delightful person, but having got onto the subject of homosexuality, both Mary and I were deeply shocked by his very bitter attitude towards gays and lesbians. He was quite unaware that Mary and I were both gay.

For someone who had previously seemed so intelligent, his utter hatred seemed to push aside all common-sense reasoning, and after attacking what he called the lapse of standards in British people in general, he went on the say, 'We don't HAVE homosexuals in Australia!'

Looking at him in astonishment I asked, 'How on earth can you AVOID having them since something like one in every ten males throughout the world IS gay?'

'We drive them under the surface,' he replied.

'Don't you think that is a very dangerous thing to do?' Mary asked

'No,' he snapped in a very angry tone, 'I think all people like that should be shut away from decent folk!'

Furious, I retorted, 'If since the beginning of time your attitude had been universally adopted, then mankind and civilisation would have been the poorer for it. Think of the influence men like Michelangelo, Da Vinci, Plato, and Tchaikovsky have had on the world to name only a few. And they were all gay. By shutting away all homosexuals, do you honestly think you would eliminate all vice, murder and rape? Are these things only committed by homosexuals? People cannot help the way they are born. What would you do if you had a son yourself and discovered he was gay? Would you shut HIM away too?'

Determined to back up his argument, the young man said, 'Yes,

I would make no exceptions!'

As I walked away in disgust I put in my final shot. 'Then I think you are bloody inhuman, and if your attitude is typical of all heterosexuals, then thank God I am NOT one!'

# Nice Work, If You Can Get It

Towards the end of the 1960s more and more people were asking me to pose for photographs, one gay firm even sold sets of colour slides of me which proved to be very popular. Then a film producer, Elkan Allan of Tiger Films, asked me if I would like to feature in one of his movies for general release throughout the UK and Europe. Two of his films were already doing good business in arty type cinemas up and down the country at the time. Both dealt with sexual problems and featured lots of nudity which was the main attraction.

I went along to Mr Allan's house in North London to discuss my possible appearance in his latest film, which was to deal with homosexuality. Indeed he wanted me to play myself in some situations I had actually experienced in recent years. However when I discovered just how little he was intending to pay me, I decided not to go through with it. Not only would I be providing a large part of the film's story, he was intending to publish a 'book of the film' for which I would not receive a penny. Fun it might have been to 'star' in a film about myself, but not if it meant putting all the profits in someone else's pockets.

By now sexual morality was becoming very much broader and in consequence more and more people, both in the art schools and in private were asking me to pose for duos, not only with other men but with women too on occasions. In the schools I had to be careful not to get an erection, but with private clients the artist or photographer would usually be delighted!

I recall one artist who asked me to find another male to partner me for some wrestling poses, and seemed delighted when I turned up at his studio with a beautiful black boy. We started with quite legitimate wrestling poses, but it did not take the artist long to suggest we take it a stage further which made me realise that what the artist really wanted was to see us having sex together.

Telling me to get on all fours, he asked the black boy to kneel behind me, bend over and lie across my back. The artist then began making a sketch of us, but while he was doing this, the boy began first to nibble one of my ears, then kiss the back of my neck, this started to get me aroused, especially when I could feel the boy was getting an erection and his cock started throbbing between my buttocks.

When I glanced at the artist, he was getting excited too. He had put down his sketchpad and was unzipping his jeans. Moments later both the boy and I had given in to our desires, and carried away by the heat of the moment, the boy slid his cock into me and began fucking me in earnest, the artist, cock in hand, was wanking furiously as he watched.

Another time a famous sculptor asked me if I would be prepared to pose with a girl for a series of sculptures he was keen to produce. These were to show me having sex with the girl in a variety of positions. The idea had apparently been suggested to the sculptor by a wealthy patron for his own amusement, so that when he got fed up with looking at me having sex in one position, he could 'insert' me into another sculpture of the girl. Quite a novel idea if you are able to afford it!

By the beginning of the 1970s I was forty-two years old, and my family was suggesting it was time I gave up my modelling career. I was not getting any younger, and my figure would not last forever. They were right of course, but what should I do next? Then suddenly one day my brother-in-law who had become a director with a well-known Christmas Hamper company, came and asked if I would be interested in taking charge of their London office since their present manager was having to retire due to ill health.

Since the replacement was required quickly, I was given just twenty-four hours to make up my mind. I accepted. It would mean much shorter hours for equal or more money.

News quickly spread through all the art schools when I needed to cancel four years of advance bookings. Many tutors sent kind messages and good wishes for my future, and the students at my favourite school, City & Guilds of London, in Kennington, all clubbed together and bought me beautiful art book which contained all their signatures.

# A White-Collar Worker Again

It had been so many years since I had worked in an office, but it did not take me long to get into the routine of things. Originally the company had occupied offices in London's Upper Regent Street, by now it had moved to Smithfield Market. Not the actual market itself, but an office block on the corner of Farringdon Road, and Charterhouse Street known as Harts Corner.

For most of the time I worked alone in the small office on the first floor. Our business was selling Christmas food and wine hampers, and my particular function was to collate agents orders and payments as they were received, and keep records of these. At first I was kept extremely busy, but with the introduction of a computer, my workload was cut drastically.

I saw little of the company's four directors for most of the time, only during the busy Christmas season did they seem to put in appearances. The rest of the time they seemed happy to leave the running of everything to me, and that suited me fine.

However during my first six months at the office, I did get a lot of attention from one of our reps. A young man named Ray, who instead of canvassing the country as he was supposed to do, spent most of his time hanging around the office making sexual advances to me. A very masculine young man, married and with two young sons, he was eventually sacked for neglecting his duties, although he continued to phone me from time to time.

Then one day Ray invited to meet his wife and have a meal with them at their home in Redbourn, near St. Albans. He picked me up one evening from St. Albans railway station in his car, calling in at several pubs on the way home to buy me drinks. Indeed by the time we got to Redbourn I was feeling quite intoxicated. He introduced me to his wife and we settled down to eat.

After the meal and while I was having yet one more drink, Ray suddenly dared me to strip naked and show his wife my cock. Accepting the challenge I immediately started to take off my clothes, but before I had flung my last garment onto the floor, Ray's wife had also started to tear off her own clothes as fast as she could, Ray looking on in amusement and obvious satisfaction.

Completely naked, the wife then lay on the carpet, her thighs wide apart in invitation. I got down onto the floor to oblige, while Ray sat behind us to watch, but after a few minutes, the excitement of watching me fuck his wife proved too much for him and he took off all his own clothes to join in the fun. Moments later he had positioned himself behind me, and was thrusting his hard cock into me so that I was sandwiched between the two of them. It was great, and we all had a fabulous time.

Not long after this particular evening, Ray and his family moved to

London where he became the landlord of a popular pub in Chelsea's King's Road called 'The Hollywood.' Once established, he put a proposition to me. He was anxious to organise some live sex shows for his special customers, all male. Would I be willing to take part? He said he had already got two girls lined up, all he needed now was a guy with a big cock. He added that the profits would be shared four ways.

Well, it sounded fun, so I agreed. The 'performances' took place after the pub had closed for the night, in Ray's private sitting-room. Our audience would sit round in a circle, while I and the two girls had sex on a couple of mattresses that had been placed in the middle of the floor.

The men would continually grope and fondle us as we performed, shouting remarks like, 'Go on boy, give it to her hard!', 'Get stuck in there!', 'Lovely, they can't get enough of it!'.

The excitement proving a little too much for some, one or two of our audience would get their cocks out and have a good wank, and there was usually at least one guy who would strip off and join in.

These evenings were a great success, and everyone had a lot of fun until Ray gave up the pub a year later to move up North, these shows became a regular monthly attraction.

# Sex, Sex and Yet More Sex

Now that I had more free time in the evenings, I began to socialise even more than previously, and one of my most constant companions and lovers at that time was Harry. A little older than I was, he was a married man with two grown-up sons, one married and living in Bristol, the other single and working in a goldmine in South Africa.

When I first got to know Harry, he was manager of a block of luxury apartments just north of Marble Arch. It was popular with wealthy Arabs, film and pop stars, 'The Who' had just moved out, and because such people are continually on the move, it was not uncommon for at least one apartment in the block to be vacant, as a result often when I went out with Harry I would end up spending the night in one of these luxuriously furnished apartments.

Harry's wife, Edith, was a very nice but very plain-looking woman who often invited me to have a meal with them. I do not know if she realised her husband was bisexual. Harry said he had lost all sexual interest in his wife. He only wanted men now.

Whenever Edith went down to Bristol to visit their son, which he encouraged her to do as frequently as possible, I would stay in their apartment and sleep in their bed.

Like me, Harry had a great love of the theatre and cinema and we spent a lot of time enjoying both. He was also a great drinker and several times a week we would go on a pub-crawl among the many bars that exist in that area, our favourite being 'The City of Quebec' in a side-street off Oxford Street.

I had always considered myself very randy, but Harry was worse. Not content with getting me into bed at every opportunity, he would often call at my office during the day if he knew I was alone, and want sex either over the top of my desk or on the floor.

When we went out for a drink in the evenings, he was always trying to pick up good-looking men (age did not matter), to take back to his place or one of the vacant apartments, so that we might enjoy a 'threesome', and he got a particular kick out of fucking me just after I had been screwed by somebody else.

Another man I met around that time with an insatiable appetite for sex was Peter, a doctor at the famous children's hospital in Great Ormond Street. He too was yet another married man, his wife being a qualified psychiatrist with a practise in North London where they lived. They were a very broad-minded couple, both believing in sex outside of marriage, and both taking their lovers home to meet each other. On one occasion the wife actually suggested it would be nice if all four of us were to make love in the sitting- room at the same time! One better than a threesome, I suppose.

My longest affair however was with Henry, an important official working for the corporation of Norwich, and I became a frequent visitor to that lovely city during the 1960s and 70s, and well into the 80s. One of Henry's duties was to make arrangements for any royalty visiting Norwich, and during his long service he was to meet just about every member of the Royal Family. He was proud of the fact that whenever the Queen Mother attended a banquet he had organised, she would always send for him afterwards, to personally thank him for his efforts.

A charming and very educated man, he was unfortunately terribly pompous and stuffy, and on the few occasions he came to Hertford to visit me, he always managed to make my little mother feel so uncomfortable, she considering him to be 'such a REAL gentleman'. Certainly in manners and appearance he was always impeccable and everyone in Norwich held him in the highest esteem, but what I wonder would all those grand dignitaries have thought had they known as much about him as I did!

He was absolutely obsessed with my body, and from the moment I arrived at his attractive apartment close to the city centre for a weekend visit, I would become virtually a prisoner, the only time we ventured out being in the evening when he would take me to a nearby restaurant for a meal. The rest of the time he would spend worshipping my body, in bed, in the bath, in the living-room. I would even wake in the middle of the night to find him sucking or licking me from head to foot. I do admit I enjoyed it. Who wouldn't?

Extremely jealous he could not bear another man to look at me and was scathing whenever I chanced to mention any of my other friends. He was however very generous and bought me many lovely and expensive presents. Even so, I hated the 'imprisonment' I had to endure whenever I went to see him, and eventually we had a blazing row which ended our relationship. He died six months later.

Someone else I had quite a long sexual relationship with was Alf. A carpenter by trade, he lived at Tollington Park, Hornsey, North London, and his hobby was male nude photography, preferably pornographic. He was also a member of the 'Golden Circle' a pen-pal club where like-minded people exchanged sexy photos as well as letters with each other, and consequently he made friends with a very wide variety of men all over the country.

Having booked me once to pose for him, I soon became a regular weekly visitor to his home. An attractive, sensual man, he was about forty years old, with a muscular body, beautiful legs, and a good-sized cock, he made an excellent model himself, and it did not take him long to suggest taking duos of the two of us using a cable release on his camera. Sex with him was fantastic, and he was insatiable, and soon he was inviting various friends to join us for threesomes. He always provided plenty of wine, and made sure I was well 'oiled' in more ways than one.

Alf also owned a motorbike, and during the summer months we used to travel all over England to spend sexy weekends with his many pen-pals. One of the great things about Alf was, that like me, he liked to be both passive AND active, which is always more fun.

Yet another man I came to know (a friend of Alf's), was David. A professional optician, he had a shop in West Green Road, between Turnpike Lane and Tottenham. He lived above the shop on the first floor, and had two tenants, both gay, living in an apartment on the floor above.

David was in his early sixties, a Scotsman with a sharp wit and lots of charm. His hobby too was taking photos of the male nude, he also liked to make colour-slides and shoot movies. Whenever I visited him, he would invite me to stay the night, however he always provided me with my own room - he never expected me to sleep with him or even have sex with him. What he DID like was to suck me off in private, or invite his friends along to have sex with me while he simply sat in an armchair and watched.

He was a great party-giver, and every Saturday night would invite a dozen to fifteen young men round for drinks and to watch film and slide shows which always got them sexually aroused and would end up with an orgy taking place. Occasionally David would ask me to do a striptease or my 'Bongo-dance' routine to amuse guests who hadn't been to his parties before.

Eventually when David decided to retire from his optician business, he sold the shop to some Turks who turned it into a restaurant, but a few months later some Greeks fire-bombed the place and both the shop and the apartments above were completely gutted. Luckily no one was in them at the time, or it could have proved fatal. Nevertheless David lost everything. He was in his seventies now, and the shock and worry of it all, put him in hospital where sadly he died a couple of months later.

# From Hollywood to Kathmandu

I had always wanted to travel, there were so many glamorous and far away places I had never seen, and now that I had more time and cash I did just that. First I travelled extensively throughout Western and Southern Europe, visiting most of the major cities, then for more relaxed holidays I went to islands like Elba, Majorca, Mykonos, Rhodes or Paros.

Later I went to Morocco and visited Casablanca, Tangiers, Fez, and Rabat. In Marrakech I was astonished by the young Arab boys, some no more than children, who begged to act as guides around the city, and if commissioned would promptly offer sex. A young lad I hired aged about sixteen, first offered me his sister, then his brother and finally himself before he eventually realised I really WAS interested in seeing the city sights.

Even in small shops, I found that having bought a fairly expensive item, the young male assistants would offer to leave the shop and come back to your hotel for sex, all with the approval of their employers who I imagine got a large portion of whatever money they returned to the shop with.

One country I had always wanted to visit was the United States, and in 1980 I went for twenty-two days. Since I wanted to see as much as I could during that time, I booked nine internal flights. By the time I returned home, I had covered nineteen thousand miles. But what a trip! In New York I went to the tops of the Empire State building and the Statue of Liberty. In Washington I gazed in wonder at the enormous statue of President Lincoln and visited the Senate and White House. Then it was on to Philadelphia to see the Liberty Bell, before going out to Vermont to visit George Washington's old home on the Potomac river.

Next I flew down to Florida to visit first Disney World at Orlando, then Cape Canaveral to see the space station and rocket launch pads. A short rest, then I was flying over the vast swamps (the Everglades) to New Orleans where I visited the Jazz clubs on Bourbon Street, listened to Ella Fitzgerald singing in the Blue Room and the Fairmont Hotel, and travelled down the Mississippi river on a steam boat.

Taking another flight to San Diego I visited the great navel base and Sea world, before another flight to Los Angeles.

My hotel was the Roosevelt out in Hollywood where in 1928, the year I was born, the very first 'Oscar' had been awarded. Right opposite the hotel was the tabled Chinese Theater in whose forecourt one can view the hand and footprints of so many of Hollywood's greatest stars imbedded in concrete. While in Hollywood I also visited Universal Film Studios.

Then after a quick trip across the Mexican border to visit Tijuana, I took a coach going to San Francisco, visiting Santa Monica and Monterey on the way. San Francisco was, I thought, the most beautiful of America's cities with the sea on one side and the great bay on the other. While there I crossed over the Golden Gate Bridge to visit the enormous Redwood trees at Muir Woods, where the trunks of trees are so large a car can actually drive THROUGH them.

Next I was on a flight headed for Las Vegas. What an astonishing place, bursting with life twenty-four hours of the day! The spectacular hotels really are amazing and the entertainment offered equally so. A crazy, fabulous place with its gambling, showgirls and billions of electric light bulbs.

While staying in Las Vegas I took the opportunity to visit the huge Hoover dam and take a return flight down the Grand Canyon. In those days, you were actually allowed to fly BELOW the rim of the Canyon. It was stopped the following year after one of the small planes crashed into one of the huge rocks and everybody on board was killed. After Las Vegas, it was to New York for the return flight home, after what I think you will agree was a truly memorable first visit to the States.

The following year, 1981, I went to India and Nepal for three weeks. What a contrast. Wonderful palaces and temples amid SO much poverty. I visited the beautiful Taj Mahal at Agra, the Palace of the Winds in the Pink City of Jaipur, New Delhi, and the great fort at Amber reached on the back of an Elephant. At the ancient holy city of Banares I boarded a small boat for a trip down the River Ganges, where in the early morning the bodies of the dead were being cremated on large stone platforms beside the river. As we watched I and others were horrified to see one of the funeral pyres collapse, and as a body-part (someone's leg), rolled down the steps towards the river, two hungry wild dogs fought over possession of it.

The sight of so many maimed beggars in India also upset me, and I was told by a guide that many poor families deliberately maimed their children to attract greater sympathy, and money, from visiting tourists.

Leaving the dust and the heat of India behind, I headed north in a very old aircraft over what appeared to be endless ranges of high rugged hills covered in dense green forest. Later when the aircraft began to descend, I looked out of the window at the wonderful scenery below. Was this Shangri-La? It certainly resembled it.

A beautiful lush green valley lay beneath us, its floor dotted with hundreds of white and gold temples and shrines, many built on small hill-tops, and in the distance I could see a large exotic city. This was Kathmandu Valley, and as a magnificent backcloth to all this enchantment, all along the northern side of the valley the gigantic range of the Himalayas thrust their snow-capped peaks into the blue and sunny sky above.

A land of exquisite beauty and tiny charming, smiling people, this small kingdom was without doubt the loveliest country I have ever seen. Until thirty years before (the 1950s) it had been a land of great mystery, no foreigners being allowed to enter. One could only hope that in time these gentle charming people would not regret having relaxed their restrictions.

Kathmandu, where I stayed, was a great deal larger than I expected it to be, but apart from just one wide fairly modern thoroughfare, New Street, the rest of the city was a dream of medieval wooden splendour, intricately carved and gilded.

Later I travelled to other and even older cities in the valley, Paten and Bhuktapur, and saw exquisite temples and palaces which surpassed all that I had seen in Kathmandu, and I fell deeply in love with this magical little kingdom, wedged between its giant neighbours of India, Tibet and China.

Funnily enough one of the most interesting people I was to was meet in Nepal was in fact English. To everyone he was simply known as 'Freddie' and he managed the bar of the Malla Hotel where I was staying. A kind of ageing Noel Coward, he told me he had once managed the bars of the Ritz Hotel and the Stork Club in London, until a visiting Nepalese Prince had invited him to take charge of the newly built Malla's Hotel in Kathmandu, and after many years of faithful service, the king had granted him Nepalese citizenship, the only foreigner ever to be so honoured.

So respected by the Nepalese royal family was Freddie, that on two occasions that our own Queen and Prince Phillip had visited Kathmandu, King Mahendra had requested Freddie to suggest suitable drinks and food for his royal guests. Freddie had created a special cocktail for the Queen which he called a 'Pink Pearl' and he asked me if I would like to sample one? He said it was a mixture of various spirits, and a selection of herbs, which had to be gathered on the slopes of the Himalayas very early in the morning.

The sights and sounds of Nepal were all very memorable, not least the glimpse I managed to catch of Kathmandu's 'Living Goddess' when the young girl appeared at one of the windows of her palace, as she does from time to time, to gaze at the people below, all anxious to catch just a glimpse of her. Yes, Nepal was pure magic.

# A Miracle of Healing

Readers will recall that when I had been living in London with with Jim, there had been a night when he got drunk and kicked me violently in the stomach. At the time neither of us were aware of what damage he had done, but in later years the strain I exerted in that area with my posing (and probably sex!) caused a lump to appear, which at times was causing me pain.

An examination by my local doctor and confirmed by the local hospital, was that the muscle-wall of my lower tummy had split, and a small amount of intestine was beginning to seep through.

'There is only one thing to be done. The torn edges must be brought together and sewn up,' my doctor said.

I was still doing a lot of posing at that time, and so my reply was, 'But I am a life model. If I have a scar, no one will want to employ me!'

Bluntly the doctor said, 'Well I assure you there is no alternative. Your condition cannot possibly improve, and the longer you leave it, the larger the tear will get allowing more and more intestine to seep through until it will be impossible to repair and you will die in agony. If you choose to ignore my warning, as soon as you experience any sharp pains, you should head for the nearest hospital immediately.'

Ignoring the warnings of both doctor and surgeon I continued to get on with my life, and although I only chose to do more relaxed poses the pain began to increase to a point where I was actually walking with a limp to be more comfortable.

Then one day a spiritualist friend asked had I thought of seeking help from a healer, quite a few offered their services in PSYCHIC NEWS each week.

I expressed my opinion that something as physical as a tear, must surely be beyond the capabilities of any faith heeler. The suggestion seemed absurd, but my friend persisted.

'Well its worth a try. At least you won't be any WORSE off, will you?'

For no particular reason I chose to go to a healer at Hove, in Sussex. The moment she opened the door to me instinct told me she was a charlatan. Having invited me in she asked me to lie fully clothed on an examination table, and asked some questions about my condition. Next she told me that having gone into a trance she would be 'taken over' by the spirit of a Chinese doctor named Chang, who would operate on me.

A terrible actress, 'Chang' said he was about to give me a spiritual anaesthetic and to keep my eyes closed until told to open them again! Anxious to see what she was up to, I opened my eyes a fraction in time to see her pouring some liquid out of a bottle into her hands, then standing above me she gently placed her hands on my tummy, at the same time asking me if I could feel the effects of the anaesthetic working. Since I suspect that the liquid on her hands was in fact methylated spirits, it was hardly surprising that I DID begin to experience a certain coldness in the area, but I was amazed that she expected me to be fooled by such hokum.

Going through the motions of actually performing an operation with invisible instruments, she informed me some fifteen minutes later that the operation had been a success, I could open my eyes. I paid her the required fee and was then told I would need to return to her for a 'follow-up' treatment each week for the next month. Feeling no better whatsoever, I had no intention of returning.

Naturally I was very disappointed, but being openminded I realised that even if 99 out of 100 healers might be fraudulent, there was always the chance that one would be genuine, and when I told my spiritualist friend what had happened, she said, 'Well I did not want to influence you in any way, but having been unlucky with one, would you be prepared to go and see a man my family and I have used for many years with great success?'

Well I did go to see the man she recommended- a Mr. George Chapman of Aylesbury, but because people from all over the world were making demands on his time, I had to wait some six weeks for my appointment. In the meantime there were two occasions when the pain got so bad I felt I would have to head for a hospital for an emergency op. So scared was I, and so urgent had it become that Mr Chapman did move my appointment forward a couple of weeks.

Incidentally, Mr Chapman's spirit doctor was William Lang, who had been a surgeon and specialist at Moorfields Hospital in London, before his death in the 1930s.

Chapman's waiting room was full when I arrived at his home, and when it came to my turn, his receptionist showed me into a small dimly lit room where Chapman sat waiting. He got up to shake my hand and asked a few questions, then instructed me to lie down on a leather examination table, saying I need only remove my jacket.

I automatically closed my eyes, but he said I could keep them open. Standing over me - he was already in trance - he began the 'operation'. Not a word was said, but he was continually snapping his fingers and holding out a hand as if expecting to be given instruments by unseen assistants.

While all this was going on, the most weird sensations were taking place in my tummy, I could actually FEEL my intestines being moved about, although no earthly hands were touching me. Mr Chapman's hands hovering about four inches ABOVE me all the time. It was extremely eerie.

The whole thing lasted about twenty minutes, and when I got up from the table, my tummy felt strangely numb, although Dr Lang assured me that this feeling would soon wear off. Then he told me to make an appointment with his receptionist for a check-up in three months time. I thanked him most profusely, made the appointment with his receptionist, paid the fee, and left.

Glancing at my wristwatch, I saw that if I made a quick dash to the nearest bus stop, I might just catch the 3.30pm coach back to Hertford. Seconds later I realised I was actually RUNNING, something I had not dared do for more then a year, fearing the consequences.

Pulling up sharply, I passed a hand under my coat and over the area of my tummy were I expected a bulge to be. But it wasn't there any more! My joy knew no bounds. I had hoped and prayed for a miracle to happen, and now one really HAD!

It seemed too incredible to be true. Modern science declared that this sort of thing simply could not happen. Miracles may have occurred in the Bible, but not now in the twentieth century. Our modern thinking and our superior knowledge was far too advanced to believe in that kind of nonsense. Or was it?

The fact remained. I HAD been healed, and instantly, just as in the Bible stories of old. I could not get home fast enough to tell my family what had happened.

From that day forward I was able to revert to a normal active life. When I returned to see Dr. Lang three months later, he pronounced me perfectly sound and said he too was happy with the results. I certainly was, and I realised how wise I had been not to be disheartened nor disillusioned by my earlier encounter with the fake healer.

The discovery that spiritual power was as potent today as it had been two thousand years ago really set me thinking. What marvellous secrets were being withheld from men because of their blind arrogance and refusal to see beyond their own paltry abilities? Clearly the world of spirit WAS very real and vastly superior to our own. What really WAS the purpose of our life here on earth?

My curiosity and my thirst for knowledge now fully awakened, I started to attend regular demonstrations of clairvoyance and mediumship at the headquarters of the British Spiritualist Association in Belgrave Square, London. I also read as many books on the subject as I could lay my hands on.

Eventually I booked a private sitting with one of the mediums who are daily available at Belgrave Square. Unfortunately unlike the transfiguration medium I had been lucky enough to sit with in Manchester many years earlier, this one, like most, merely acted as a 'go between' speaking to quite invisible spirits who were present at the time.

My sitting lasted half an hour, and among the things I was told, was something that alarmed me very much. 'I know you are very close to your mother,' the medium remarked. 'Soon she will have great need of all your love and strength, and you will be called upon to show her more kindness, consideration, and understanding, then ever before, for I repeat, she will have great need or you.'

As I travelled home that night, I felt desperately worried. Was the medium predicting the approach of a serious illness, even death of my mother? 'Oh God, I hope not,' I thought.

The thought that I might shortly lose my dear mother, naturally did make me extra attentive to her in the days and weeks that followed, and I made arrangements to be in her company as much as possible.

I kept my dreadful fears to myself, but about a month later my parents were due to go to Spain for a holiday. I hoped and prayed that nothing would happen while they were away, and luckily nothing did. However a few hours after their arrival home, on August the 12th (1972), my FATHER had a heart attack. He made a rapid recovery, but then in the early hours of the 13th he dropped dead as he was preparing for bed.

The effect of his death on my mother was a complete revelation to me, and I realise just why the medium had been so insistent that I show her so much sympathy and understanding. During their life together my parents had never seemed particularly happy with each other, but now they were parted, my mother's grief was of such intensity that I was forced to recognise, for the very first time in my life, just how deep her love for him had been, and for many months afterwards she could speak of nothing else but how completely 'lost' she felt without him.

I also have to admit to being more affected myself by his death than I had expected to be. As is always the case when it is too late, there were many things concerning the past that I now regretted. In recent years things had certainly run a little smoother between us, and his temper had mellowed with increasing age.

Much later I was able to tell my mother what the medium had predicted. So intrigued was she, and my sister too, that they attended lectures and sitting with me at Belgrave Square, and suddenly the mediums were predicting that I would become a healer.

# Spirit Protection?

As time passed I was to become more and more conscious that spirit had work for me to do, although in the early stages they moved with such subtlety that I was not always aware of what was happening nor why.

In the summer of 1973 I was to fulfil a lifelong dream of spending a three-week holiday at a nudist resort on the Mediterranean island of Corsica. The resort which had a population of some three thousand nudists, was situated on the north-east coast about an hour's drive from Batista.

The village consisted of several streets of neatly kept whitewashed houses, and a collection of bamboo huts close to woodlands. I had chosen one of the bamboo huts. The village also had two restaurants, a food supermarket, and a couple of shops selling various holiday sundries. The beach was fantastic with mile upon mile of golden sands, fringed with woods and scrubland along its entire length. It really did seem like paradise.

One of the nicest things about the place, apart from all the beautiful naked bodies of course, was its complete naturalness, with lots of happy families to be seen everywhere - mums, dads, kids, and even a few grandparents. The only problem, at least for me, was one of language. The village was run by Germans, and 90% of the visitors were German, the rest being mainly Scandinavian, French or Dutch.

Although I cannot swim, the weather was so hot and the sea so inviting that I spent a great deal of time in the water, although on one occasion I ventured too far out and it almost cost me my life.

At the time I was walking parallel with the shoreline up to my neck in the sea. Suddenly to my horror I was aware that my feet were no longer treading on sand. I had stepped into 'space' with only water under my feet, and moments later I was being swept out to sea by the strong current.

In panic I shouted for help, fighting desperately to keep my head above water. There were lots of people on the beach, but my cries for help went unheeded, presumably because either they could not hear me or failed to understand just WHY I was yelling.

It was the most terrifying experience, unable to attract attention, finding it difficult to keep my head above the waves that kept washing over me, and swallowing so much water that I was finding it increasingly difficult to breathe, let alone shout. I felt sure I was about to drown, and my thoughts flew to my mother. A widow for only seven months was she now to lose her only son as well? The shock I knew would kill her.

Suddenly to my great relief I saw that a young man on the beach was aware of my predicament and had plunged into the see and was heading for me. However by now I was feeling so exhausted, and his progress towards me seemed so slow, I felt certain he would never reach me in time.

After what seemed like eternity he eventually reached me. He was German, but in English told me to relax and leave everything to him. Then putting an arm around me he headed for the shore where a crowd had now gathered, some of them wading into the water to give a helping-hand as we drew nearer.

Choking and spluttering I was laid on the hot dry sand, and my goodness how good it was to feel solid ground under me again. I owed my life to this young German, but modestly he had slipped away before I could thank him. Many times during the rest of my holiday I was to wonder how many times I passed him on the beach or in the village without acknowledging him, for in the panic of the moment, his face had failed to register in my mind. If by chance he should ever read this book, I hope he will accept my everlasting gratitude.

Three days later I was to have my second brush with death when an Englishman I got chatting to on the beach suggested we hire a car and explore the mountains we could see in the distance.

The roads in the mountains were extremely narrow with a sheer wall of rock rising on one side, and dropping away hundreds of feet on the other. The road also twisted and turned in a most tortuous manner with numerous hair-pin bends. Having driven for about an hour climbing steadily all the time, we eventually reached a point where the road suddenly began to descend steeply, and as we took another sharp corner we came face to face with two young men in an Italian sports car.

My companion, instead of braking, immediately panicked and swung our car to the right, heading straight for a big pile of rocks and debris which had obviously fallen down the mountainside earlier. Just how he expected to negotiate this obstacle I could not imagine, some of the rocks being larger than a football and it was madness even to attempt it.

'What on earth are you doing?' I yelled.

Almost before the words were out of my mouth, we had begun to bump and grind over the rocks and rubble. There was a ghastly metallic crunching noise, and seconds later we were, miraculously, on the other side of the heap, past the oncoming car, but headed for yet another sharp bend in the road, our steering gone and the car completely out of control, swerving crazily from side to side, as my companion frantically swung the steering wheel this way and that way to no effect. In seconds we would be plunging off the road and down the mountainside.

'Jump!' he shouted as he leaped from the car himself.

I needed no prompting and was already on the point of doing just that, but suddenly, at the very moment I was about to leap clear, the car came to a grinding halt, wedged on a piece of rock, the bonnet and two front wheels dramatically projecting out into space over the sheer drop beneath.

By the time I had joined my companion, the two young men we had passed, were out of their own vehicle and racing down the road towards us, probably surprised to see that we were still alive.

Between the four of us we managed to haul the damaged car clear of the edge and a quick inspection revealed that the front axle was broken. The two strangers offered to run my companion to the nearest village so that he could telephone for a breakdown truck and a taxi to take us back to our resort. I stayed behind to keep an eye on things until they returned.

For several days after that we were both worried about the size of the bill for damages we would be presented with, but eventually the manager of the resort informed us that the car hire people were fully insured and we would only be charged for a day's hire of the the car. We were both very thankful, but it had certainly curbed our enthusiasm for making any further excursions.

Thinking about it later, I thought it strange that twice in a matter of days I had faced death, and twice it had been averted. It was almost as though someone was watching over me and I was being intentionally protected. But for what purpose?

*Ahmed, 1974*

*Self-portrait with Ahmed, 1974*

146

# My Work Begins In Turkey

A few months after my holiday, a friend introduced me to Roger Baker, writer and theatre critic who was then working for a magazine called QUORUM. Roger asked if I would have any objection to him writing an article about my past career as an artist and model, adding that if I could supply him with a nude photograph by way of an illustration, he would be grateful.

As a result of this article, yet another magazine called Q INTERNATIONAL got in touch with me asking if I would allow them to republish some of my gay drawings? I agreed, and my work appeared in three consecutive issues.

The new publicity was to bring a lot of correspondence from interested people, among them a twenty-two-year-old Turkish student at Ankara University who told me he was keen on sketching male nudes himself, and thought my work 'fantastic' - would I mail him my latest catalogue of prints for sale?

I wrote explaining that I no longer did this kind of work, but at the same time sent him some spare prints I still had in my possession at that time as a gift. He wrote back expressing his thanks and asked if I would be willing to enter into a regular correspondence with him as he wanted to improve his English. With this letter he enclosed a couple of photographs which showed he was a tall, dark and very handsome young man.

His name was Ahmed, and subsequent letters revealed he was sensitive, gentle, and highly intelligent, and soon he was suggesting I visit his lovely country. To his great delight I promised to go for a fifteen day holiday tour the following summer, and since I wanted to see as much of Turkey as I could in the limited time at my disposal, I suggested that he accompany me, all expenses paid, as my guide.

A month or so before my proposed trip in June, 1974, Ahmed wrote and told me he had just seen Dinah Sheridan's film THE RAILWAY CHILDREN in Ankara, and it occurred to me that it might be a nice surprise for him if I was to take him an autographed photo of her as a present.

I called to see Dinah a few days later and told her what I had in mind. Not only was she kind enough to provide me with the photo, she gave me an illustrated book of the film, and recorded a personal message to him on my recorder.

I had asked Ahmed to meet me in Istanbul. It was late evening when I arrived, and the air was warm and filled with unfamiliar sounds as my taxi sped through the sprawling suburbs of the city. We passed through huge and ancient walls, and before long a breathtaking vista opened up before me: the Golden Horn, its waters looking pale gold under an enormous full moon, exotic domes and minarets of numerous mosques silhouetted black against the summer night's sky, and hundreds of trembling lights both in the city and on the bridges spanning the Golden Horn, reflected in the waters. Truly an 'Arabian Nights' setting for the start of my trip.

When I reached the hotel where Ahmed was waiting, and gave him the various presents, he was absolutely thrilled, and tearing a ring from his finger insisted I accept it as a token of his friendship.

I had a quick shower, then after a meal at the hotel we went out to sample the nightlife of the city and it did not take me long to realise just how deeply in love with Istanbul Ahmed was himself, confessing that one day he would like to set up home there.

Next morning we boarded a bus and headed for Ankara, the capital of Turkey, a bustling modern city made pleasant with lots of gardens and parks. We stayed for three days, then boarded another rather ancient bus for a journey across the hot dusty plains of Anatolia which were more like a desert.

Away from the cities most of the women and children still wore their national costume, but most of the men, especially the young ones, favoured European dress, indeed they were very up-to-date in their styles.

We stayed a few days at Avanos so that I could explore the fantastic rock formations at Goreme, the village itself a collection of pink and white houses built on the side of a hill. At the small workshop of a potter we looked at the wares and I bought a couple of items. We also watched the potter at his work. As we were about to leave, I noticed a dear old lady dressed in traditional clothes and veil sitting against one of the walls. So touched was I by her frail appearance, I walked over to her and taking one of her hands, I lifted it to my lips, kissed it, then raised it to touch my forehead.

Immediately this action sparked off great excitement in the old lady, and she jabbered away to Ahmed and the potter in Turkish.

'Ron, what made you do that?' Ahmed asked.

Surprised at all the fuss I said, 'Do what? I only kissed the back of her hand!'

'Is it an English custom to do such a thing?' Ahmed asked.

'Not really, more French, I suppose.'

Then Ahmed said, 'But you did MORE than simply kiss her hand, you did something else, think, think!'

Trying to cast my mind back to the gesture I had made, I said, 'Oh yes, didn't I touch my forehead with the back of her hand?'

'Exactly!' cried Ahmed. 'What made you do THAT?'

I had to admit I had not the slightest idea. Then Ahmed said: 'In this country such a thing is considered to be a very great compliment paid by one Turk to another. That you, a foreigner to both our country and our customs should do such a thing is really quite extraordinary. That is what so excited the old lady and the potter.' Then he laughed and added, 'You must have been a Turk in a previous life!'

From Avanos we went southwest to the holy city of Konya, home of the whirling Dervishes, then further south, over lovely mountains to the coast. A couple of days rest, then we flew back to Istanbul for the final four days of my tour. It was Ahmed's first flight in an aircraft, and he was very excited about it.

In Istanbul we visited the Topkapi palace where I gazed in wonder at emeralds the size of duck eggs, at clothes embroidered in gold and silver, and furniture and ornaments studded with precious stones. We also visited the famous St. Sophia and Blue mosques, and the city's amazing covered bazar with its reputed four thousand shops and two hundred entrances.

One evening when Ahmed and I were preparing to go out to dinner, Ahmed developed a terrible headache, he said he got them at regular intervals of about six months, and then they lasted for days.

'Perhaps if I lie down and try to sleep for half an hour I will feel a little better,' he said. 'Please wake me in thirty minutes.'

When I did, it was only to discover that he felt worse and he suggested I go out alone. However I did not like the idea of wandering around Istanbul at night on my own, and in any case did not want to leave him feeling like this.

It was then that a thought flashed into my mind. For nearly a year now various mediums had been telling me that I was going to 'heal'. Why not try it now?

Sitting down on the edge of Ahmed's bed I said, 'Do you remember me telling you about my interest in Spiritualism and the fact that mediums are constantly telling me that I shall one day do healing? Well, I am going to try it now. I do not suppose for a moment that anything WILL happen, but there is no harm in trying, is there?'

Telling him to close his eyes and pray to Allah, I placed my hands on his forehead praying hard myself that his head-pains would cease. I had closed my eyes too, and when I opened them again some ten minutes later, Ahmed looked so serenely peaceful and happy I felt certain he had dropped off to sleep. However the moment I withdrew my hands he opened his eyes, and looking at me in astonishment said, 'You HAVE cured me! It's fantastic. It really DID work! You must have holy hands.'

For a moment I thought Ahmed was simply trying to humour me, but when I realised he was doing nothing of the kind, then I was as thrilled and delighted as he was himself, and we went straight out to celebrate.

Next day when we chanced to meet a beautiful young woman Ahmed had known for several years, a cancer victim, we invited her to join us for coffee at a nearby cafe. While we were having this, Ahmed talked excitedly to the girl in Turkish and I was curious to know what their conversation was about since the girl kept giving me rather odd looks.

'I have been telling her how you cured my bad head, and I

suggested that maybe you could do something for her too.'

'What did she reply?'

'She said she has had so many operations, she feels no one can help her now. Indeed she feels nearer to death than life.'

I thought it heart-breaking she felt like that, but told Ahmed not to press the girl further, we must respect her wishes. In any case there was no guarantee that I COULD get results a second time. Perhaps it was only coincidence that his pains had ceased when they did?

Before parting from the girl she kindly invited us to join her and a couple of friends for a picnic on the banks of the Bosphorus the following day, and we accepted. During the picnic Ahmed was again to relate how I had 'healed' him, and the other young man in the party remarked that he had for some time been suffering constant pain in his left bicep, could I cure this?

Ahmed translated the request and looked at me eagerly. At first I said no, making the rather lame excuse that the area we were sitting in was too public, but the truth was that I feared I might not achieve success and I did not want to look foolish. However the young man looked so crest-fallen at my refusal, I relented and said: 'Well, I don't suppose for a moment it will work again, but OK, lets give it a try.' Ahmed repeated this to the young man who smiled appreciatively.

Placing one hand on his shoulder and the other on his elbow, I closed my eyes and prayed to God to send down healing power. Some minutes later when I asked how his arm felt now, he said the pain had moved down to his forearm. He had never felt it there before!

Still keeping one hand on his shoulder, I transferred the other to his wrist and concentrated hard again. Five minutes later the young man declared the pain had now disappeared completely and was shaking my hand violently in gratitude. I was staggered, and following this latest success his female companion announced that she needed help for tummy troubles, could I help her, too?

I asked her to join me in praying to Allah, and ten minutes later she claimed she felt much better too, kissing me in gratitude.

Did I really have healing powers? From the moment I had first helped Ahmed he was always to refer to me as his 'Holy man'. ME holy! Yet God does sometimes work through the strangest instruments as is clearly illustrated in the Bible where the chosen had included not priests, but taxmen, thieves and even prostitutes, so why NOT me?

There was also one other strange and very significant thing about the healing I had been allowed to do so far- all the people I had healed had been Muslim, not Christian! Here was absolutely wonderful proof, if it were needed, that ALL mankind are God's children no matter WHAT religion they might practise.

All too soon my wonderful tour of Turkey was at an end. I was distraught, for despite the difference in our ages we had fallen deeply in love with each other and had enjoyed wonderful sex over the past fifteen days and nights, and parting for goodness knows how long, was almost more than I could bear.

On the way to the airport Ahmed told me he had one more year of studies at Ankara University before graduating, after that he would come to England for a further two years of study, hopefully to obtain a degree.

I told him I would do everything possible to help him, and he could look upon my home as his for as long as he wished. Gripping my hands he said he would never be able to repay me for my kindness, but would try to be worthy of me. Then telling me that he could not bear to think of any other man having sex with me or even touching my body, he begged me to refrain from all sex until such time as we could be together again, and I gave him my promise.

Not for fourteen years had I felt such deep-rooted love for someone. The disaster of my relationship with Jim, and my spell in prison had killed off all desire for a truly deep relationship with anyone. Since that time I had been content to enjoy a constant stream of sexual affairs, while at the same time keeping rigid control of my emotions.

Now Ahmed had completely demolished my defences, and as he had requested, on my return home I informed all three of my current lovers that I would not be seeing them again. All were extremely upset, thought I was quite mad and tried to make me change my mind. But I was determined to keep my promise to Ahmed.

# Bill Has a Vision

On January 1st, 1975, I telephoned Ahmed in Ankara with my best wishes for the New Year. It was wonderful to hear his voice again, and I was so pleased when he told me that he hoped to be arriving in England on August 15th.

In the spring I redecorated the house in readiness for his arrival. I had always had a flair for the unusual, and decided to furnish and decorate the bedroom we would share in an exotic old Turkish style, since I felt this would make him feel less homesick.

When finished, the room fascinated all my relations and friends who came to see it, and when I sent Ahmed some colour photographs of the room, he was completely overwhelmed.

When all work on the inside of the house had been completed, I set to work on the garden, filling the borders with masses of new plants and buying new garden furniture, for Ahmed was as fond of gardens as I was.

As the time for his arrival drew near I also made plans to take him on a tour of Britain before he should commence his studies in the autumn. Much to our mutual disappointment Ahmed had not been able to secure a place at London University, and was having to go to Aston in Birmingham instead.

To get the best possible lodgings for him in Birmingham, I had obtained a list of prospective landladies from the university's accommodation officer and personally visited several addresses before selecting one where I felt Ahmed would be truly happy. Then I paid a deposit for the room so that it would be held for him.

With everything for his arrival now complete, Ahmed's letters suddenly grew less and less frequent, until finally they stopped altogether. Puzzled and worried I wrote to him asking what was the matter? A letter came back saying that only a few weeks prior to his final exam the university had gone on strike, and unless classes resumed quickly, there would be no possibility of him coming to England that year after all.

Another long break in his correspondence followed, then just a few weeks before he was due to arrive I received a letter which stated that since there appeared to be no hope of Ankara University reopening in the near or distant future, Ahmed had taken a job as receptionist in one of the city's better hotels.

He went on to say that he had written to Aston since all his plans to come to England must at least for the time being be abandoned. He added, 'You have kindly tried to solve some of my problems for me, but now I only want to get involved with my work. I like working in the hotel and might later take a hotel management or catering course. I will never be able to think of friendship and so many other things without thinking how much I have learned from you, and how good you have been, and are. I know that after reading this letter you will probably want to come to Ankara to discuss the matter, but since I have only just started work at the hotel, I would not be able to get time off to see you.'

I was shattered. However having read his letter several times I felt it left so much unexplained. All right, so the university was not intending to reopen in the near future, and we did live thousands of miles apart, but why bring our relationship to a sudden end like this?

I turned for advice to a gentleman who during the past two years had become a very dear friend, the Rev. William R. Butler of Hornsey, London. 'Bill', as he preferred me to call him, was a well-known minister of the Baptist church who was deeply interested in Spiritualism and had a gift for reading palms, indeed so accurate was his palmistry that many famous people came to see him including Enoch Powell, Rudolf Nureyev and Cliff Richards. Bill was also a cousin of Lord 'Rab' Butler, one-time Chancellor of the Exchequer in the Conservative Government.

I had first met Bill when he officiated at the funeral of David Angus, and it was later as we sat chatting over a cup of tea that we discovered our mutual interest in Spiritualism. After that I became a regular visitor to his home in Hornsey, and he visited me in Hertford a couple of times.

Rev. Butler had worn spectacles for many years, but soon after I came to know him, his sight began to deteriorate very rapidly, so much so that finally he was forced to use a magnifying glass when wishing to read someone's palm. Then came the day when even this was inadequate and he remarked, 'Oh dear, Ron, what AM I going to do. So many people come seeking advice, especially about money or business ventures. Now I will not be able to help them anymore.'

The next time I called to see him he was very excited and said, 'Ron, the most amazing thing has happened. A few days ago a friend came seeking advice on a business enterprise, and not being able to see her palm I said a silent prayer. "Please, Lord, help me give this woman good advice", and the next moment, there on the wall of my study was a LARGE MOVING PICTURE which I could see clearly! It was just like looking at a big television screen, and what I saw in this 'vision' enabled me to help the woman. More remarkable still is the fact that it was not an isolated incident - it happens EVERY TIME I have a problem to solve for someone. Isn't that amazing?' I had to admit that it certainly was.

Now that I had a problem myself, it was to Bill that I went. I had mentioned Ahmed to Bill on many occasions and also shown him photos of the young man before his sight had started to fail so rapidly. Having explained the current situation to Bill he said, 'Let me go, into my study to meditate on your problem, then maybe we will have the answer.'

'Did you have another of your visions?' I asked him when he re-joined me some fifteen minutes later.

'Yes. When you go to Ankara, although you WILL experience a few ups and downs, I am happy to say things will turn out better than you expected. However you HAVE got to be prepared for your life to possibly take a different course to the one you had planned.'

Then Bill asked, 'Has Ahmed had his hair cut recently? In all the photographs you showed me I recall he had long shoulder-length hair, but the young man I saw you with in the vision had his hair cut short. There was also something about one of his wrists, the left one; I could not be sure exactly what it was because the wrist was 'blurred', appearing on the bottom border of the vision. It could have been a deformity, or it could have been a piece of jewellery, I don't know, but you will know when you come face to face with him.'

Then Bill said, 'I also had another vision, and again it appeared to take place in what must have been Ankara. You seemed to be in a large store or shopping arcade, and a man, not the one I have just described, but a slightly older one, was forcing his attentions on you, and you were very annoyed, pushing the man away several times. I do not know how this episode ends, for the vision faded away at that point.'

Two days later I received a letter from Ahmed in which he said he was sorry if he had given the impression he wanted to end our friendship, this was not so, although he stressed most emphatically that I should NOT go to Turkey to see him. I immediately sent a telex to say that I WAS going, and would arrive in Ankara on October 3rd, staying for a period of one week at the Mola Hotel. Surely he could spare me just thirty minutes during that time? That was all I asked.

On Friday morning the 1st of October as I was working in my London office, I received a telephone call from Rev. Butler, 'Ron, have you had a telephone call from Ahmed this morning?'

When I said no I had not, he continued, 'Well you WILL get one, and he will try to persuade you to change your mind about going to Ankara.'

Incredibly, within half an hour I DID receive a call from Ahmed insisting I should not go. However I told him my mind was made up, my flight booked, and if he was in some sort of trouble I wanted to know what it was.

# No Turkish Delight

From the moment I commenced my journey to Ankara on October 3rd, everything went wrong. My plane was delayed an hour at Heathrow Airport and I missed my flight connection in Istanbul, the last one of the day to Ankara. On the way into the city from the airport next morning the taxi broke down and I eventually reached the hotel about midday.

When I checked in at the reception desk the clerk said, 'You have a friend waiting for you in your room. He has been there all night. I will ring to let him know you are on your way up.'

Delighted by this unexpected news, I hurried to my room.

Ahmed stood waiting for me in the open doorway and I gave a gasp of surprise as I looked at him- HIS HAIR HAD BEEN CUT SHORT and around his left wrist was a CHUNKY SILVER CHAIN I had never seen him wearing before. So it HAD been Ahmed that Bill had seen in his vision after all.

Giving me a wonderful smile Ahmed said, 'Hello Ron, Welcome to Ankara. What happened to you? I have been waiting for you all night.' We embraced, then I explained all that had befallen me since leaving home. I also told Ahmed about Rev. Butler's visions and how accurate they had been. He was astonished. Incidentally a few days later Bill's second vision also came true when I WAS pestered by a man in a shopping arcade who wanted me to go home and have sex with him.

But back to Ahmed. I requested the hotel send a meal and a bottle of wine up to my room, and over these Ahmed told me his problems. Apparently the closure of the university had been only one of several problems and the least important, for it seemed that since my last visit he had met and had an affair with a young male dancer who had developed a deep infatuation for him, and as Ahmed's departure for England had drawn nearer the boy had become very possessive, and finally in a fit of depression taken poison.

Rushed to hospital his life had been saved, but ensuing enquiries had naturally shed light on the dancer's relationship with Ahmed, whose very strict Muslim parents had been shocked and horrified by the affair, and since then they had put him under what amounted to a virtually twenty-four hour surveillance and threatened to force him into an arranged marriage with a girl he had never set eyes on, a relative living in Eastern Turkey.

Ahmed said that at the moment he was playing for time, explaining to his parents that he had quite enough to cope with over his education, without them adding the responsibilities of marriage to his problems.

For the moment his parents were prepared to accept this argument, although they had made it quite clear that at the first sign of any trouble, they would insist on the arranged marriage. Under the strict laws of his particular sect, he would have no choice but to obey or be cast out of the family forever.

He said he would like to spend as much time in my company as he could while I was in Ankara, but his hotel duties would make it difficult, and on no account must we be seen together in public. He fucked me before he left that morning and on the three other occasions he managed to pay me visits.

I telephoned Ahmed on the morning of my departure, and it was agreed we view things in the worst possible light so as not to raise any more false hopes. He said it could be another two years before he could come to England if the university did not reopen in the next few months. At least now I felt I knew where I stood, or did I?

With the arrival of the new year, 1976, Ahmed wrote to tell me the university had at last reopened and he had resumed his studies. Now there was every possibility that he would arrive in England by late summer. This was good news, but experience was teaching me not to get too excited prematurely.

He continued to write regularly, almost daily, until May, then there was an alarming gap of six weeks. When I mentioned this latest breakdown in Ahmed's correspondence to Bill, he said, 'I am surprised you have not received a letter from him this week. I know he HAS written to you, although I feel he may be holding it back for some reason. I think he has something to say to you, and he does not know how best to express himself.'

Feeling most upset, I said, 'Are you telling me that Ahmed has changed his mind yet again about coming to England?'

'Yes, I am afraid so.'

Angrily I retorted, 'Well, if you are right, I shall offer him no further help. My efforts simply are not appreciated. I feel even God has let me down!'

A few days later I DID receive the letter from Ahmed, and this is what he had to say:

'Dear Ron,

I am sorry to say this will probably be the last letter I ever write to you. So many things have changed here and maybe you realised this when I did not write for such a long time.

I am sorry to disappoint you yet again, for you have been so good to me, been so patient. Always you have tried to comfort me when I needed it. You planned your life to suit my future. Decorated your home the way you knew I would like it. Made a beautiful garden because I like flowers, in short, you showed me pure love.

I know this is a holy and valuable thing, and I realise its importance, but    Ron, I have thought about it for months and months, and now I know I do not want these things. I know this letter will come as a shock to you, but as I also know you care about my feelings, you'll understand me. Yes, Ron, I really do not want to come to England any more. The truth is I have fallen in love with a Dutch girl who works in her

Embassy here. We have had a year-long relationship, and we love each other very much. We plan to marry shortly, leave Turkey and go to live in Holland.

She is a very humble and loving girl, and I feel comfortable in this new situation. My family accepts this girl and agree to my marrying her. This then is the situation, Ron, and I know you will understand and forgive me. Please keep the Turkish room you created for me as reminder of what we once meant to each other. I am sad that I shall not see it after all. Really, Ron, we had a very good relationship, and I would like to remain your friend for the rest of my life if you are agreeable. If you have any questions please write to me. One other piece of news- I have now graduated from the university and most probably will continue my studies in Holland. Please give my best regards to your mother, tell her of my love for her, and tell her that I am so sorry that I disturbed and destroyed your life.

Also tell her that all my life I will pray for her and you to my God.

I send you a kiss Ron, and I am so sorry,

Ahmed

How do you reply to a letter like that? I made several attempts but was so dissatisfied with the results that I tore them up each time. Finally I decided not to reply at all.

For weeks the pain and utter despair I felt were almost more than I could bear. I felt my faith in a merciful God was sorely tested. Then suddenly one morning I woke to the realisation that God IS loving, that life WAS good and that as painful as my pathway may have been, it was perhaps leading me towards my ultimate destiny after all. Just how true this was would be revealed a few months later, and none was more pleased by my peaceful acceptance of the situation and my new-found calmness, than Rev, Butler who was more than ever convinced that I was being prepared for some special spiritual service.

# Spirit of Light Speaks

My relationship with Ahmed now at an end, I booked a coach tour of Wales for my mother and I feeling she needed a change as much as I did, and it was during this holiday that I struck up an acquaintance with an Australian lady, which was to trigger off a most astonishing sequence of psychic experiences.

The lady's name was Carol, and discussing her one day with our courier-driver, I discovered that six months earlier she had lost both her husband and only son in two identical car-crashes, only days apart. To get over the shock her doctor had suggested she take a long holiday abroad, and following his advice Carol was touring Europe for four months, Britain was the final phase of this long holiday before she returned home.

Armed with this knowledge, one evening after dinner when our group of fellow travellers had gathered in the hotel bar for a drink, I steered the conversation onto the subject of Spiritualism, hoping it might afford Carol some comfort. Naturally I made no mention of the recent bereavements.

As the evening wore on, so people around the table began to excuse themselves and retire for the night, including my mother, until only Carol and I remained. Then Carol decided to unburden herself, confessing that every night she was now afflicted with violent headaches, indeed she had one at that very moment.

Suggesting that one last drink might help her to sleep better, I went over to the bar to place my order, and as I waited for the drinks, I turned to face the smart but sad and lonely woman. I thought of all the suffering and anguish she must have endured in recent months, and overcome with pity I remembered how with the aid of the holy spirit I had been able to help Ahmed and his friends in Istanbul. Wouldn't it be wonderful if I could help Carol, too?

Immediately I began to concentrate, hard on a spot midway between and above her eyes, the position of the so-called 'third eye'. Silently I prayed, 'Dear Lord, hasn't this poor woman suffered enough with the loss of both her husband and son. Must she now endure this physical pain as well?'

A moment later my concentration was interrupted by the barman handing me the drinks, and walking over to Carol with these, I noticed how much brighter she had suddenly become.

As I reached the table she smiled and said, 'Ron, when you were standing at the bar just now, did you try to help me?'

A little surprised and amused I replied, 'What makes you ask that?' 'Well, I noticed you seemed to be concentrating hard on me, and as you stared, so my headache seemed to simply melt away. Now I feel absolutely fine!'

Delighted, I admitted trying to help her, and so impressed was she by my little 'performance' that she was keener than ever to know more about Spiritualism and psychic powers. She told me that after the tour of Wales she would be staying with a sister in Watford and asked if I could arrange for her to visit a medium. The poor woman was desperate to get messages from her husband or son.

After the holiday, I booked an hour-long sitting for her with a medium named Mrs. Olive Orde at the headquarters of the British Spiritualist Association in London's Belgrave Square. I accompanied Carol to comfort her should she get distressed.

On the appointed day Carol received what I personally considered excellent evidence that her husband and son were certainly not 'dead' but simply living in another dimension. At one point Mrs. Orde told Carol that her husband was describing her bedroom in Australia, and mentioned that in a certain drawer in one of her bedside cabinets there was a small box containing a sapphire and diamond ring that he had once given to her. Carol was absolutely astonished, and agreed that this was so.

Unexpectedly half way through the sitting, Mrs. Orde turned her attention to me and made several unsuccessful attempts to pass on a message to me. I say 'attempts', because she seemed to have difficulty in finding the right words to express herself adequately. Finally she stopped speaking altogether, and gripping the arms of her chair slumped forward as if going to fall, but then just as quickly she regained her balance and straightening up, went into a much deeper trance. What on earth is happening I wondered.

When Mrs. Orde spoke again, it was abundantly clear that she had been 'taken over' by a very superior entity, and in relaxed and most beautiful tones it spoke as follows:

'Greetings, my brother. It had been our intention to relay a message to you through the mediumship of Mrs. Orde, however it seems the good lady found difficulty in expressing that which we wished to convey to you. We have therefore decided it would be best to take over our sister completely and speak to you ourselves, direct.

My brother, you have known much suffering and disappointment in your life, and I must tell you there is more to come in the future. However the hardships and disappointments of the past have all served their purpose in building up your character to give you the wonderful strength, courage and resilience which you possess today, all qualities you will have need of in the future.

The loss of the one you loved so much in the Middle East was a great sorrow to you, but that relationship had served its purpose and the time came for you to part and go your different ways, but not before you had taught each other much about the lessons of love and life.

I must tell you that you have a bright and very wonderful future ahead of you if you will but take advantage of all the opportunities that will be offered to you. You are to heal, to write and to teach, and many opportunities will be given to you to promote yourself and travel in many countries.

You have been chosen to help in the WRITING OF A BOOK which is of great importance to the world. Mankind is facing the crisis of its existence, and you and a few others throughout the world have been selected to pour oil onto troubled waters. The task is enormous and will continue long after you yourself have passed to spirit, but you are to sow the seeds which others will harvest, and God will give you a long life to accomplish all that you are to do.

You have been chosen because you combine practical earthly qualities with those of great spiritual understanding, which will grow ever deeper with the passing of time. Throughout all your life the material world will march hand in hand with the spiritual, and to further what you must do, you will from time to time wish to carry out certain projects, and there will always be money available to carry out these projects, God will see to that. Although your rewards will be great, you will encounter much disappointment and heartbreak. People will attack your ideas from all directions, but you have courage and great understanding, and these qualities will enable you to survive. Do you have any questions?'

I had sat listening, deeply humbled by all that had been said, but reflecting how human relations had played a major part in my life to date, I asked, 'Must I accomplish all these things alone? Is no one to share my life, my love?'

The spirit caused the medium to lift one of her hands and drawing attention to the wedding ring she was wearing said, 'THIS must have no meaning for you. You must have no need of others. You must give your love to ALL mankind, not just one chosen person. In return you will receive all the love you will need. It will flow in from all directions. Already there is a great deal of love surrounding you from both the material and the spiritual worlds. Now the time has come for us to leave you. I have not visited to earth for many, many years, but I wished to come on this occasion, so that I might give you the message that was intended for you. It has given me much pleasure to do so. I am the Spirit of Light. God's blessings be upon you, and know that He is always with you.'

So saying, the spirit departed, and a few minutes later Mrs. Orde came out of her trance completely unaware of all that had taken place, although she did remark that she felt 'something wonderful' had taken place.

When I reached home and told my mother what had been said, she remarked, 'Ron, you have already had so many disappointments and heartbreak in recent years, and mostly in your efforts to help others. It seems a little unfair that God should now call on you to make even more personal sacrifices.'

When I told Rev. Butler what the Spirit of Light had said, he remarked, 'This does not surprise me at all. You have been steadily moving towards this situation for the past two years. However, to be certain that this message HAS come from God, I want you to arrange two more sittings with different mediums at Belgrave Square. Things should always be done in threes to symbolise the Holy Trinity, and I will come with you as a witness to hear what is said.'

Accordingly, I booked private sittings with a Mrs. Hilda Holiman for November 10th and Mrs. Minnie Bridges for November 22nd. But before either of these could take place, a couple of strange things happened .

One morning as I sat in my London office, I received a telephone call from a complete stranger, a man who had obtained my number from a magazine that had recently published some nude photos of me. After first complimenting me on the pictures, he said: 'May I ask you a personal question? Does the Star of David mean anything to you?'

A little surprised, I replied, 'If that is a round-about way of asking me if I am Jewish, I'm not.'

'Well, I DID think you looked Jewish in a couple of the photos - I hope you did not mind my asking?'

The following evening, accompanied by my friend Harry and his wife Edith, I attended a demonstration of clairvoyance at Belgrave Square. There were about forty people seated in the hall at the time, and the medium, a man named Richard Dancer who I had never encountered before, suddenly asked, 'Is there an artist the hall?'

Harry nudged me, but since the medium had not been looking in our direction at the time, I felt he must be referring to someone on the other side of the room. When there was no response, Mr. Dancer asked again, 'Is there NO one here who paints or does drawing?'

Nudged by Harry again, I called out, 'I used to be an artist at one time, but I gave it up years ago.'

Turning his attention to me now, Mr. Dancer asked, 'Do you have a friend called Harry? I feel you and he are very close.' There were gasps of surprise, and chuckles of amusement when I replied, 'Yes I do have a friend called Harry and yes he IS close, he's sitting next to me now.'

Smiling, Mr Dancer continued, 'I feel you have recently been drawn into a spiritual situation that will require great personal sacrifice, and I have an elderly gentleman standing beside me who could be your father, and he warns you to give careful thought before committing yourself, saying you have done far too much for other people already. Do you understand his advice?'

I said I did. Then, after telling me that I would do healing work, he asked, 'Tell me, does the Star or David mean anything to you?'

Startled, I replied, 'It's strange you should ask me that. I am not Jewish, but yesterday I had a phone call from a complete stranger who asked the same thing.'

Mr Dancer replied, 'All I can tell you is that I SEE a Star of David shining brightly above your head.'

Later when I went to visit Rev. Butler and recounted the various things to him. I had the distinct feeling he was one step ahead of me.

'Why did you smile when I mentioned the Star of David?' I asked him.

'Because for some time past I too have seen this star hovering above your head,' he explained, 'The first time I saw it, it was quite high up in the air above you, but each time you came to see me the star appeared lower and lower. Tonight it is actually resting ON your head. Just what it all means I do not know, but God will make all things clear in His own good time.'

# Confirmation Is Given

On November 10th, 1976, in company with Rev. Butler, I went to Belgrave Square for the sitting with Mrs. Holiman, and what she had to say confirmed to Rev. Butler's satisfaction that I had indeed been selected for some special task.

Before the sitting ended Mrs. Holiman remarked, 'You know, you are a very old soul. You have lived on earth many times before and over the centuries you have built up enormous wisdom and one of the things you must learn to do is bring this forth for the benefit of others. You will also do much healing of bodies as well as minds.'

Then Mrs. Holiman said: 'This may sound odd, but tell me, does a DONKEY mean anything to you? I frequently see people's pet cats and dogs, but a DONKEY sounds a bit odd, doesn't it?'

I told her my mother was particularly fond of donkeys, and on her last birthday, I had bought her a framed print of one. Only half listening to what I was saying, Mrs. Holiman said very softly, as if speaking to herself, 'No. That's not it. Ah, now I see. It's symbolic. When Jesus wished to enter Jerusalem, they fetched him a donkey to ride on, saying to the little creature, "The Lord hath need of thee". Yes, that's IT!' Mrs. Holiman declared with confidence now. 'The Lord hath need of THEE my friend.'

Just before the session ended, Mrs. Holiman also said something else which, although it seemed of little importance at the time, was to have real significance at my later sitting with Mrs. Bridges.

Smiling at me, Mrs. Holiman said, 'There is a beautiful little baby floating over your head. A really lovely child, and it is sending down so much love to you. Who, is it?' I had to admit that I did not have the faintest idea. I had never produced any children and neither had my sister, but when I told the medium this, she merely remarked, 'Well, I can only tell you it is someone very close to you.'

On November 22nd I telephoned Rev Butler in the morning to remind him that we had an appointment that afternoon with Minnie Bridges, but to my disappointment he told me he had a cold and suggested it would be better if I went alone to Belgrave Square.

'But the whole purpose was for you to be there as a witness,' I said. 'Don't worry,' Rev Butler replied, 'I know you will give me a truthful report, and at least you will have the full attention of the medium. I could not help feeling on the last occasion my presence may have disturbed the medium to some extent. Alone you may get even better results.'

That afternoon Mrs. Bridges said to me, 'In the last two years you have had a lot of heartbreak and disappointment brought about by someone in the Middle East. Never mind, it was all for the best, and your suffering has made a better, stronger man of you as a result. And ask yourself this, if he had REALLY cared about you, would he have treated you the way that he did? You must sweep away the cobwebs of the past and go forward all the time. The past is the past.' I was astonished at this reference to Ahmed, for I had made no mention of him, nor had any thoughts of him entered my head that day.

Mrs Bridges continued, 'You have always had a deep understanding of spiritual matters, and this stems from the fact that you, like myself, once lived amongst the mystics of the East, studying their ancient wisdom and learning. In recent months your character has undergone immense changes, and I must tell you that these changes will continue, indeed, they will accelerate to such a degree, that were you to come to me again in eighteen months time, I would not recognise you as the same person who sits before me today. Do you like to travel? You are going to do a great deal of travelling in the future, and I feel that if you make wise decisions on the opportunities offered, you will have a bright and wonderful future ahead of you.'

Then to my amazement Mrs. Bridges declared, 'You have a brother.'

'No, a sister,' I interrupted.

Ignoring what I said, she insisted, 'You HAVE a brother.'

'I'm sorry,' I protested. 'You are quite wrong, I am an only son.'

Sounding a little annoyed now, Mrs. Bridges said, 'It is YOU who is mistaken. You DO have a brother. I am not ASKING you, I am TELLING you, and you are spiritually aware enough to know what I am talking about. NOW do you understand?'

Completely stunned but recalling the lovely little baby that Mrs. Holiman had referred to earlier, there was only one explanation. At some time during my mother's life she must have had an abortion I knew nothing about.

Confirming my thoughts, Mrs. Bridges continued, 'You know, once a life has begun, it makes no difference at what stage it is terminated, a life is a life, and you DO have a brother whose name is John. Younger than you, he has grown to manhood in spirit. I would say he is in his early thirties now.'

Intrigued, and full of love for this brother I had never known, I felt very emotional. Mrs Bridges continued, 'In fact, you are a very lucky person, for such people as your brother who are not born into the world and contaminated by sin, remain completely 'pure' spirit' and exist on the same plain as Jesus himself, which also means that they are among those nearest to God.'

Then, oblivious to my surprise at learning of my brother's existence, Mrs. Bridges asked, 'Have you ever seen your brother?'

She may have thought he had appeared to me at a sitting and I was unaware of who he was.

'No,' I replied.

'Well, you ARE going to,' she said. 'However, when he does first appear you may have difficulty in seeing his features clearly, for his face is so bright, so full of purity, it is not easy to look upon him. He loves you so much, and is pleased with the great change that has taken place in you recently. However you must spend more and more time in quiet meditation, and you must also learn to humble yourself, perhaps the hardest thing for any of us to do. Remember, in ourselves we are absolutely NOTHING, merely the instruments of God. But you are more fortunate than most, having this direct link to the Almighty through your brother.'

Then, after telling me a little more about the healing and writing I would do in the future, Mrs. Bridges gave me her blessing and brought the sitting to an end.'

Arriving home I related to mother all that had been said. At the mention of my brother, she looked very sad and said, 'It's true, I DID have an abortion many years ago. I carried it out myself, not knowing the risk I was taking at the time. Your father had been out of work for such a long time and we simply could not afford to have another baby. There was no such thing as family allowance in those days. At the time I had no way of knowing if it was a little boy or a girl.' By now mother was in tears and I put an arm around her shoulders to comfort her. 'Now I feel like a murderer,' she sobbed.

I asked how old my brother would have been had he been born on earth, and after a moments calculation she answered, 'Thirty-three.'

'What name would you have given him?'

'John, after your grandfather.'

Rev. Butler was absolutely fascinated when I related my latest news, but like me he was curious about the role I was to play in the future. 'We shall have to be patient,' he said. 'God will make his wishes known to us in due course. You can best help by setting a little time aside each day for meditation and prayer.'

I did. Not just at night and morning as I travelled by train to and from my office in London, but each lunch hour I would also spend forty to fifty minutes quietly praying in the nearby church of St. Bartholomew the Great.

More and more I tried to let thoughts of spiritual love filter through into my everyday life, at work, at play and travelling, too. I wanted to be conscious of God ALL the time, not just at selected periods or on certain days. I was trying, not always successfully, to allow God to enter my whole day. Sometimes I failed dismally, but at least I was making the effort, and that was the important thing.

Something I did develop with passing time was patience. In years gone by I had displayed a distinct lack of it, but now I seemed to possess even more than Rev. Butler, for as time drifted by without any further striking changes taking place, it was he who suggested I arrange another private sitting with Mrs. Olive Orde, the medium through whom the Spirit of Light had first spoken to me. I was delighted I did, because yet again this exalted spirit did speak to me.

Speaking for a shorter period this time, he thanked me for

accepting the duties I had been asked to perform, adding that the world of spirit was very grateful to me. Then he said, 'The ways of ploughing the soil change from time to time. In the old days they walked behind a plough, today they sit on a tractor. HOW the soil is ploughed is not important. It is the SEED that is the vital factor. For without the seed there will be no food.

There are so many paths to God, and which one we choose is really unimportant (a reference to the various religions and numerous sects), for the goal is the same in the end. Men search for that thing which you on earth call God, and some of you take comfort in imagining God to be in the form of a human being, because this is more easily grasped by the human mind, but God is an ENERGY FORCE from which everything in the universe is made up. And to understand this we MUST have harmony with everything around us, for God is in every tree, in every blade of grass. If you find God, God will find you. And in finding God you will have found yourself and that deep spiritual happiness and harmony that comes with the knowledge and the understanding. ONLY this harmony will solve the problems of your world.'

What incredible wisdom those few short sentences uttered by spirit contained, for there in a nutshell were all the solutions needed to resolve the problems we face in the world today if ONLY men were not so greedy and selfish to apply them. One has only to look at the world today to realise that if the planet IS to survive, then as the Spirit of Light had warned in his first message to me, mankind has no alternative. We MUST listen or destroy ourselves.

Before leaving, the Spirit of Light asked if I had any question and I said: 'Some time ago I was informed that I have a brother in spirit, and was told that one day I would be allowed to see him. When will this happen?'

In kindly tones, the voice replied, 'We are fully aware of how much you desire to see your brother, but the time is not yet right. There will come a time in the future when you will be faced with a great problem and will have need of spiritual guidance on the matter. Then it is that your brother will appear to you. He will come to you as a small ball of light, which as you watch it, will grow larger and larger. Finally from this ball of light shall step your brother. So bright will his face be that at first you will have difficulty in seeing his features clearly. At the same time that your brother shall appear to you, so shall your problem be solved. Have patience my brother, have patience.'

# Automatic Writing: I Speak Out

A few months later in the spring of 1978, I was seated at my office desk when suddenly for no apparent reason I stopped what I was doing, and picking up a blank sheet of paper and a pen, commenced to write furiously, not stopping until I had completely filled one side of the sheet, and then I stared at what my hand, quite independent of my head, had just written.

I rose from my desk and walked across the room to where our managing director sat. Handing him the sheet of paper, I said, 'Read this Mr. Burr and tell me what you make of it.'

A few minutes later he looked up end said, 'Well I know this IS your handwriting, and I do not mean to be rude, but I also know your own phraseology and never in a thousand years could you ever write something like this! Is this what you were scribbling away at just now?'

'Yes,' I replied. 'Isn't it fantastic? Clearly my hand was aided by some outside force.'

My boss, fully aware for some time past of my keen interest in Spiritualism (although viewing it with a certain amount of scepticism himself) asked, 'What do you intend to do with it?'

'I don't know,' I answered, 'I will take it along to Rev. Butler and see what he suggests.'

When Rev Butler had a chance to read it, he was dumbfounded.

'There is no denying its beauty and wisdom,' he said, 'But what are you to do with it?'

'I was hoping you would be able to give me some guidance there,' I replied.

Looking thoughtful for some minutes he said, 'Let me sleep on it.' Next morning when he spoke to me over the telephone he said, 'Ron, there is SO MUCH concentrated truth and wisdom in this message that each line is equal to a whole sentence, and THAT is what you have to do, dwell on each line carefully, then expand its meaning.'

Taking his advise I worked on it for several weeks, and blending it with some of the beautiful truths which the Spirit of Light had also expressed, I eventually produced a thirty-two page manuscript a portion of which read as follows:

'The material miracle of nature is all around you. The spiritual miracle is no less wonderful for those who take the trouble to search. Knowledge, real knowledge, will only come when all man-made ideas and concepts have melted completely away. If you seek only the fragments as the churches do, then you will be caught up in those fragments. Instead search for the "inner meaning", the inner stream or truth that is the basis of ALL the religions.

Man must abandon his fear of the spirit (invisible) world. Science in the 20th century has helped man to understand that things are not always what they appear to be. A hundred or so years ago, you would have looked at a glass of water and sworn that the glass contained COMPLETELY TRANSPARENT liquid. But look at a single drop of water under a microscope and you will see that far from being "clear" it contains thousands of minute forms of life too small for the human eye to detect. The same can be said of the air you breathe, the "empty" space between you and other planets. THERE IS NO SUCH THING AS NOTHING AND NOWHERE. Simply because your incredibly poor eyesight cannot see something, it is no proof that a thing does not exist.

To know "God" you must understand Him. Just as to know Jesus you must understand what he really attempted to teach. So few are capable of understanding because they have allowed themselves to be blinded by the doctrines and creeds of religious men.'

Rev. Butler was absolutely delighted with the manuscript when he saw it. 'But now comes the hardest part,' he declared. 'Trying to get it published!'

Just how difficult this would be, I did not realise at the time. In my innocence I assumed that all Christian churches no matter what their denomination, would be eager to have this wonderful message from spirit (Heaven), but I had reckoned without the prejudices that taint the minds of so-called 'religious' folk.

Throughout the summer I went from one religious publishing body to another, and although each expressed interest, always the manuscript was rejected as 'not suitable for us'. I was amazed by their blindness. Truly they were unable to see the wood for the trees!

Soon it became abundantly clear that men were much more interested in retaining their own man-made dogmas and creeds than they were in real spiritual truths or knowledge, and after two thousand years, the Pharisees were still rejecting the message of the Almighty. I felt in utter despair, although Rev. Butler told me it was no more than he had expected.

Eventually, feeling it was my personal duty to see that this message DID reach the public, or at least some of them, I arranged at my own expense to have ten thousand copies printed in the form of a small booklet entitled A MESSAGE TO MANKIND. It meant that I had to go without a holiday that year plus a few other things, but I felt this was far more important. Sadly, before the printer had finished work on the booklet, dear Rev. Butler was taken seriously ill and died.

Bill had been so supportive in recent years, and I felt his loss terribly, but now that the booklet had been completed I made another appointment for a sitting with Mrs. Olive Orde in the hope that the Spirit of Light would speak to me again. He did, but to my surprise he made it clear that the little 'book' I had been working on was NOT the one spirit were anxious for me to produce, saying:

'The MESSAGE TO MANKIND is an excellent little book, and since the content came to you direct from spirit, it could not be otherwise, and it will help many people. However the book we wish your help with was written many years ago, but needs reviving, and bringing to the attention of modern readers. When the time comes for you to locate the book, you will meet three men dressed all in black whose names will be George, Arthur and Frank, and one of these men will point you in the direction you should go.'

It all sounded rather mysterious. For the last year various mediums had been asking me, 'What is this book that spirit are so anxious for you to write?' while others said 'Why do I see you surrounded by piles of books, it looks as though you have a lot of writing to do in the future.'

But to return to the current little booklet, THE MESSAGE TO MANKIND: When finally work on the booklets had been completed I attempted to put an advertisement in PSYCHIC NEWS, then Spiritualism's most widely read newspaper, but to my utter dismay it was rejected, their advertising manager explaining that the booklet contained 'some statements which were rather questionable.' I wrote to the newspaper's editor to ask if he would revoke his advertising manager's decision, but this he would not do.

Despite this initial setback spiritualist churches in Hertford, Harlow and Welwyn Garden City were all eager to distribute quantities or my little booklet, and Mrs. Olive Orde requested I send her two hundred for distribution in Barbados when she went out there to do a clairvoyance tour and broadcast.

To further promote it locally, I hired the largest public hall in Hertford, and gave a lecture to stimulate interest. Only about forty people turned up to listen to me, but their number included the chairman of the local spiritualist church who invited me to fill a vacant seat on his church committee, which I was pleased to do.

My duties included taking charge of a church service every sixth Sunday, and giving healing to members of the congregation each week. Later when the church librarian had to relinquish her post, I took this job over too. In no time at all my ideas for displaying the books had increased interest in the library so much, that the number of books being loaned out trebled and the church voted me cash to buy more.

During the years 1979 and 1980 the church was to take up an ever-increasing amount of my time. There was always a demand, especially amongst younger members of the congregation to establish more 'circles' to promote knowledge of clairvoyance and healing, so I decided to hold a circle in my own home every second week.

Normally one did not invite more than six people to join a group, but because of the demand I allowed ten into mine. I say 'mine' but in truth it was the church chairman who wanted to take charge, indeed he insisted on it, saying that, 'someone of experience' was needed, which was true, but it had already become apparent that 'length of service in years' did not always add to one's spiritual wisdom or understanding of it.

At all my circles the chairman would go into trance and speak in a variety of voices. But since all these entities seemed to say very much the same thing with little or nothing of any real spiritual value, I began to grow increasingly dissatisfied, as did other members of the group. Finally towards the end of 1980 I found an excuse to wind the group up.

I felt it was important to hold regular 'Question & Answers' sessions at the church - something the younger members were always pressing for, but the chairmen would only allow one such evening per YEAR! I felt this was quite ridiculous although I knew the reason, his inability to answer many of the questions likely to be asked. I argued that orthodox churches were criticised for withholding spiritual knowledge, yet here we were doing the same thing!

Spurred on by an ever increasing discontent amongst the more progressive members of the church, I was determined once and for all to make the chairman and the committee face up to their responsibilities. I wanted to see less time spent on 'survival' messages, as comforting as these might be to some, and more emphasis on philosophical studies and the teaching of spiritual awareness.

Eventually I decided to take the plunge and do something about it regardless of the consequences, and I felt the best time to do it would be the next occasion it was my turn to 'chair' a service.

It took a lot of courage to take the plunge, and at the last moment I wondered if I could go through with it. For several weeks I had planned what I would say, now as the moment drew near, I began to feel sick inside, but suddenly it was as though a small voice inside me was saying, 'Courage, Ron, if you are to be true to yourself and all you honestly believe in, then you MUST speak out.' And somehow I felt a little calmer.

Soon all the congregation was assembled and I was facing them, our two guest speakers sitting one on either side of me. The service started with hymns and prayers in the usual manner, then I introduced the first of our guests to give an address. This over, we sang another hymn, I read out the church notices, then it was time for me to speak my mind.

Loud and clear I heard myself saying all those things I knew would damn me forever in the eyes of the chairman and most of the committee (two of whom were his relatives). As I spoke I glanced at the chairman but could only see the top of his head, for with elbows on his knees he was holding his head in his hands. I glanced at various members of the committee, a couple were smiling in agreement, but the rest sat frozen-faced.

I spoke for about twenty minutes ending with, 'There are those who want harmony at any price, but harmony is something you have to strive for, but not at the cost of truth. Did gentle Jesus keep silent in the temple when he saw how his Father's house was being misused? No, he overturned the tables, took the cord from his waist, and using it as a lash drove out the offenders! John The Baptist too could hardly be described as a passive man and if we do not take action when it IS necessary, then

170

not only do we betray our fellow men and women, not only do we betray ourselves, we betray God also.'

As soon as the service was over a couple of people came over and praised me for being so outspoken, but the chairman's brother-in-law remarked, 'You have done it now! I don't know WHAT will happen!' A few moments later he returned to inform me that a 'special' meeting of the committee was being called for the following evening.

Guessing that this meeting was to remove me from the committee, I was determined that they should not have the satisfaction, and so the next night when we had all come together, before anything could be said I announced that I was resigning.

A broad smile of relief spread across the chairman's face, although one old lady (our secretary), remarked, 'Oh Ron, you must not leave the church. You have done so much good work since you joined us.'

I replied that I was not leaving the church, only the committee, and the library too, just as soon as soon as someone else could be found to take over my duties.

The following Sunday the congregation had dropped to half its normal size - but it WAS a Bank Holiday weekend, and I heard the chairman say to his brother-in-law, 'Ron Wright is to blame for this. He has turned the people away.'

Feeling terribly isolated and sick in the pit of my stomach I sat in my usual seat, and, closing my eyes I prayed earnestly to God, 'Dear Lord, I sought only to do what I thought was best. I had no wish to drive people away from this church.' I said what I did in the best interests of my fellow men and women. 'If however I HAVE done wrong, dear Lord, then punish me as I deserve. If however I have NOT done wrong, then PLEASE find some way to tell me so. For I cannot bear the terrible torment my mind is going through at this moment, thinking what damage I have done to this church which I have tried so hard to support in the past.'

I felt so upset, so full of remorse as the chairman took up his position at the head of the church, it being his turn to take charge that particular week. Keeping my head low, I felt hot tears of sorrow trickling down my cheeks, and wished the earth would open and swallow me up.

Then something remarkable happened. We had reached that part of the service where a demonstration of clairvoyance was to be given, and the chairman introduced Mrs. Peggy Goodwin, not a local person, she was completely unaware of all that had taken place the previous week.

The lady rose to her feet and turning slightly to her left, in my direction, she put her hands together as if in prayer, and bowing very low (something I had never seen a medium do before), she pointed to me and said, 'A very bright being from the highest spheres has just entered this building with a message which I am asked to give to you. I am to tell you that you have no need to take yourself to task. Everything you said in this church recently was true. YOU know the pathway of truth. You have been given knowledge and understanding of spirit beyond many others, and must go ever forward ignoring all those who would stand between you and truth.

'You must be as steady as a rock in a raging stream, and a rock of strength you must remain for others, disregarding all those who would criticise you. They count for naught. You have much work to do in the future, and you are surrounded and protected by many spirit beings eager to help you in this work. You are to bring light where there is darkness and knowledge where there is ignorance. Be strong and fear no one my brother, for God is always with you.'

Having conveyed her message, Mrs. Goodwin once again placed her hands together in an attitude of prayer took another deep bow in my direction, then taking several minutes to regain her composure, she said to the congregation, 'What a wonderful experience that was. I have been a medium for many, many years, but never before have I been lifted to such a high state of spirit. You must therefore forgive me if it takes me a little time to get back to the normal level of spirit I am accustomed to working on. After being in the presence of such an exalted being, this is not easy. If I appear to falter or make few mistakes in the next half hour or so, please forgive me.' Then Mrs. Goodwin went on to give the usual kind of messages that the congregation expected to receive.

At the end of her demonstration the lady again repeated her apology for a possible erratic delivery of spirit messages, and once again she remarked how privileged she felt to have been the bearer of a message from such an exalted spirit, and turning towards me she thanked me for giving her the opportunity to enjoy such a wonderful experience. Indeed she gave the impression that it was I who had bestowed some kind of honour upon her, adding that it would be a memory she would cherish for the rest of her life.

Can you imagine how I felt? I was deliriously happy. I had prayed that I might be given some sign that I had done the right thing, and my prayer had been answered in the most dramatic way.

Such a message and the source it had come from should have shaken the chairman rigid, and caused him once and for all to see how truly lacking in spiritual awareness he really was. Unfortunately, it fell on deaf ears, and in the weeks that followed I was made to feel so uncomfortable that I stopped attending the church altogether, deciding that in future I would do all my praying at home in private, just as Jesus himself had suggested we should do, for he too had little time for organised religion.

My decision was to upset a lot of church regulars, and in the weeks that followed, no less than fifteen of them called at my home and pleaded with me not to cut myself off like this. One elderly man actually burst into tears. All said that were I to start a new church, they would support me, but as grateful as I was for their loyalty I told them I had no wish to split the church. I had followed my conscience, they must follow their's. When the time was right, I would return.

# Hafed, a Prince of Persia

It was at the end of 1980 while making one of my daily lunch hour visits to the church of St. Bartholomew the Great at Smithfield, that I fell into conversation with the church's elderly verger and learned to my surprise that he was interested in Spiritualism. When I mentioned my little booklet A MESSAGE TO MANKIND he asked if he might have a copy.

After that particular visit to the church I became so involved with our Christmas trade at the office that I was not able to go back again until early in the New Year. When I did, I could not find the old man anywhere, then suddenly I was approached by a tall unfamiliar figure dressed in black vestments. A young man, he asked if he could be of any assistance to me.

I explained the reason for my visit, and was told that the old verger had recently retired to an old people's home. He said he would gladly pass on my booklet and suggested that I follow him into the vestry where I could write a little note to go with it if I wished. There I found myself confronted with two more men wearing long black robes, both of whom looked extremely old and kindly. The instant my eyes alighted on them I was to remember something the Spirit or Light had predicted, 'One day you will meet three men dressed in black whose names will be George, Arthur and Frank, and one of these men will point you in the direction you are to go.'

No Sooner had the memory flashed through my mind than the younger man was saying, 'Let me introduce you to my friends George and Arthur.' Before he could say more, I blurted out, 'And is YOUR name Frank?'

Looking somewhat surprised the young man answered, 'Yes, but how did you know that?'

I replied, 'I am afraid it would take too long to explain.'

The young man handed me an envelope, pen, and piece of notepaper, and I quickly wrote a few lines to the old verger. While I was doing this, one of the elderly men remarked, 'That looks a very interesting little booklet you have there.' I replied that since the contents were basically concerned with Spiritualism, I feared his orthodox background would hardly allow him to approve of it.

To my surprise the old man said, 'You would be amazed if you knew just how many of us ARE interested in the subject, although it is something we have to keep quiet about. I will tell you a little secret, I have a friend who is a Papal Legate and he informs me that the POPE sits regularly with a medium in the Vatican!'

Then the old man said, 'Since YOU are so interested in the subject, there is a certain book that you really should read, a truly wonderful book called HAFED, A PRINCE OF PERSIA. I first read it many, many years ago when a young man, and I imagine you would have great difficulty trying to find a copy today since it was published well over a hundred years ago. I suppose the best place to start your search would be among the many second-hand bookshops that surround the British Museum.'

I thanked the old gentleman for the information, shook hands with all three of them, and made my way back to my city office, marvelling that the Spirit of Light's prediction had come to pass.

It was about 2.15pm when I sat down at my desk again, and no sooner had I done so than the telephone rang and a familiar voice at the other end said, 'Hello Ron, this is Norman.' My caller was an old friend who had once been a lecturer of law at Liverpool University.

Now retired, he lived on the Isle of Man, and I presumed that was where he was speaking from, but he said, 'I am down in London for the weekend. It is so long since I last saw you, I was wondering if we could meet up somewhere tomorrow for a meal and a chat?'

I said I would love to see him again, and willingly agreed to his suggestion. Then Norman said, 'While I'm in London I would like to buy a few gay magazines. Where is the best place to buy them?'.

I asked where he was staying and when he said the Vernon Hotel close by Tottenham Court Road Underground Station, I told him to meet me outside the station at 4pm and we would take the Central Line to Notting Hill Gate where I knew of an excellent shop he would get all he wanted.

Next day, promptly at 4pm I stood waiting, Norman arrived twenty minutes late apologising and exchanging a few pleasantries he shook my hand. Then to my surprise instead or walking into the station, he started to walk away from it. Thinking that perhaps he wanted to purchase something before we set off on our journey, I said nothing but simply followed him.

Having turned the corner and gone some distance down Charing Cross Road we suddenly halted outside of Foyles famous bookstore, and turning to Norman I said, 'Do you want to buy something here then?'

Looking at me somewhat puzzled, he replied, 'No. I thought the intention was to go to Notting Hill Gate. I simply followed you, thinking YOU wished to go somewhere else first!'

'But I was following YOU!' We looked at each other in amused astonishment.

'Oh well, since we ARE outside Foyles,' I remarked, 'would you have any objection to my popping up to their rare books department? There is a certain book I would like to enquire about.'

Norman said he did not mind so long as it left enough time to get the gay magazines he was so anxious to take home with him.

Unfortunately, by now I had forgotten the title of the book I sought, all I could recall was that it concerned a certain Persian Prince, and that it had been published about a century ago.

With so little information, the assistant I spoke to had no idea what I might be looking for, but suggested I might try Zimmers Bookshop just across the street. I did, but they too were at a loss to know what I was looking for. They suggested I try a fusty old second-hand bookshop next door. There I found myself confronted by an equally fusty-looking old man.

When I tried to explain what I was looking for, he said, 'Oh yes, I think I know the book you mean, I cannot remember its title now, but it went out of print many, many years ago and you will find it difficult to locate a copy today. Really I think the best place for you to search would be among the second- hand bookshops around the British Museum.'

I told him that had already been suggested to me, but since I happened to be in Charing Cross Road that day- a street famous for its bookshops, I thought I would try here first.

By now it was 4.40pm and poor Norman was getting a bit upset, because it was too late to go to Notting Hill Gate. However he cheered up when I told him I knew of another equally good sex magazine shop not far away which would have all he could possibly desire. If he would bear with me just a little longer, I would take him there.

Norman heaved a sigh of relief and seemed content to let me try all the other bookshops which lined the street, some dozen in all. But none of them had the faintest idea what I was looking for, and finally I resigned myself to continuing the search another day when I could spare the time to go to Bloomsbury.

We turned into Cecil Court where the gay bookstore was situated, and although this small side street is also lined with bookshops, unlike those in Charing Cross Road, these were all closed with the exception of the one Norman was so keen to visit, and another specialising in very old books, called Watkins.

Norman was delighted with his selection of magazines, and once he had paid for them we left the shop and made our way back into Charing Cross Road once more. Only then did I remember the other bookshop which had been open, Watkins, and blurted out 'Norman, now that you have got the magazines you wanted, I must just dash back to Watkins before they close to see if they know the book I am searching for.'

'You run ahead,' said Norman, 'Otherwise they WILL be shut. I will follow at my own pace and wait for you outside.'

In the shop I found a middle-aged woman sitting behind the till knitting, while several customers browsed amongst the shelves and book-laden tables. Like everyone else, she had no idea what book I was looking for, but as I was about to leave she called out, 'Just a moment. My husband is in the next room and knows more about books than I do. Have a word with him, perhaps he will be able to help you.'

In the adjoining room I found a man kneeling in the centre of the floor, surrounded by books which he appeared to be sorting out. More clients were looking at the bookshelves which lined the walls.

Stooping down I asked the man if he knew of a book published about a hundred years ago that concerned a Persian Prince? He asked, 'What is its title?' I told him I had forgotten. 'Well, who was the author?' he asked. Again I had to say I did not know. Looking a bit exasperated he then asked, 'Well, who published it?' Yet again I had to admit that I had no idea. 'You don't seem to have much information to go on, do you!' he retorted.

The next moment to my utter astonishment I heard myself declare, 'It's about the missing years in the life of Christ.'

What on earth could have induced me to say such a thing! I had no idea WHAT the book was really about!

My remark immediately triggered the man into action, and rising to his feet he said, 'Ah yes. Just a minute? I think I may have what you want,' and disappearing down a flight of stairs into a basement, he returned a few minutes later carrying a very battered looking old book in his hand.

'That's not IT?' I cried excitedly.

'I think it might be, it's called HAFED, A PRINCE OF PERSIA. The funny thing is it did not register with me until you mentioned the missing years in the life of Christ.'

Handing it to me, the man continued, 'It is very strange. I have worked with books all my life, but had never heard of his one until a few minutes ago when a man walked into the shop and sold it to me saying, "It's about the missing years in the life of Christ"- the very SAME WORDS you said! Isn't that astonishing? I have not had time to look at it properly, or price it, but you can have it for eight pounds. Incidentally the man who sold it to me has not left the shop yet, that's him standing over there,' and he pointed to an elderly man with a beard who as I looked at him turned away from the book he was browsing through, to look directly at me and give a knowing smile.

Norman was waiting patiently for me outside the shop. 'I can see by the joy on your face that you found the book you were looking for,' he said.

As we walked to a nearby restaurant for a meal, I observed that it must have been spirit who diverted us away from our intended trip to Notting Hill Gate, and sent us instead walking down Charing Cross Road. But this being so, why had they wasted time in sending me into all the wrong bookshops?

With his customary logic Norman replied, 'I would have thought the answer to that was obvious. Clearly you WERE intended to have the book, but had you been directed to that particular shop sooner, you would have arrived BEFORE the book. And in consequence still been without it. Spirit delayed you just long enough to make sure that it WAS there when you arrived. In fact the timing was perfect!'

Poor Norman, I am afraid for the next hour I was not very good company, so anxious was I to start reading the book. Realising this, he kindly suggested we cut short our evening, and after the meal I headed for the railway station and home, reading the book as I went.

It was certainly the most beautiful and rewarding book I had ever read. It was a big book, well over six hundred pages in length, and first published in 1876. It had apparently first come into being as the result if six men meeting regularly in the city of Glasgow for the purposes of psychic research. Their instrument at these séances, a well-known local direct-voice medium named Mr. David Duguid, a cabinet maker by trade, and a man of poor education.

One evening this little band of truth-seekers was delighted when a spirit came through and announced that he was a Persian Prince who had lived on earth two thousand years ago. He gave is name as Hafed (Hafiz), and the excitement of the group increased when they discovered that this man was in fact one of the legendary Three Magi who had followed the bright star to Bethlehem and paid homage to the newly born Saviour of Mankind.

Incidentally, no names are given to the Three Magi in the Bible, and the names Balthazar, Melchior and Casper, by which they are commonly known, are in fact purely mythological.

Naturally relating all that Hafed wished to convey to the assembled group could not be accomplished in a single evening. And so over the next four years Hafed was to speak to the group no less than one hundred times. Notes were carefully made of all he said and these were later published in the form of a book, the book I now held in my hands.

In telling his story, Hafed was to reveal much about the early life of Jesus not disclosed in the Bible. In fact the childhood and youth of Jesus have always been a complete mystery. From he time Joseph and Mary fled into Egypt with their family, until Jesus begins his ministry some thirty years later, the Bible makes only a single reference to his childhood, this being when at the age of about twelve he visits the temple in Jerusalem and amazes the scholars and teachers with his knowledge and wisdom which far outshines them all.

The mystery of what DID happen during those 'missing years' must have intrigued millions of people throughout the centuries, particularly since the birth of Jesus and the years of his ministry were so well documented. It was almost as if such information had been deliberately withheld, and the more I discovered for myself, the more I am inclined to think this was the case. However the facts, the light, the REAL truth cannot be withheld from mankind forever, and it was not intended that it should be.

Having described his own early life in great detail, Hafed had been a much travelled man, the picture he paints of the ancient world and its customs is both clear and knowledgeable, he then proceeds to give a detailed account or his existence in the spirit world after his 'death' which is truly fascinating and ends speculation on so many things.

To add to my considerable excitement as I read the book, I discovered that the Spirit of Light who a few years earlier (through Mrs.

Orde) had told me that I was to 'One day help in the writing (rewriting) of an important book', was none other than the SAME spirit who had commanded Hafed and his two companions to pay homage to the newly born Saviour! That same voice speaking to me some two thousand years later!

Without a shadow of doubt I knew now that this must be the book I was to work on. In its nineteenth century form it was certainly much too long and wordy for modern readers. It would require editing and abridging, and so in the weeks and months that followed I diligently set to work on the task.

Having started the revised version of the book, I decided to visit Olive Orde again at Belgrave Square to see if perhaps the Spirit of Light had anything more to say to me. He had, and here from a taped recording I made at the time is what was said:

'I bring greetings to you my brother. Once more we speak to you. We are aware of what has taken place, and the reasons why you have come, but we must be brief, we must be quick. You have come this day for confirmation and enlightenment, and we are anxious in the very short space of time to give you the answers you need.

Now you feel a little disappointed regarding the disposal of your earlier writing (my MESSAGE TO MANKIND), but not to worry, it will go in the right places at the right time, it was not wasted, although of course as we said before, it was not THE work you had to do when told to write. We are not saying it is not good, because it has come as direct enlightenment from spirit, and it will open the eyes of many people yet, make no mistake about that. And even though from a financial point you may not benefit from it, we will see that the material things are taken care of for you. It is important that it gets through to the people, the message that is there for them, and so it will go out in different directions.

Now. We thank you for heeding and following the guidance you have had through various channels, and yourself, and have had the courage and conviction to activate this, because when it comes to it, many people are given guidance and instruction, but when it comes to activating, ah, they are afraid. Then it is seen whether you can prove your faith, belief, and your trust in what you are receiving, and of course you realise that you have got to dissect from time to time the various things you receive from various channels, as well you know. And so, in this respect my brother, we are very, very proud that you have answered the directions given to you, step by step, as we told you it would come step by step. You could not organise it yourself. It had to come through the directions and guidance of spirit.

Now at your disposal comes the very essence of light and enlightenment (the book HAFED, A PRINCE OF PERSIA). It is for you to reproduce it so that it is understandable and acceptable to man. It is in the 'finishing off' of the book you also have to help. It was started, but you are recreating it, and so in the completion you will find that there is a company who will accept and publish for you. It will be a company with TWO names, and it will reach out to the people.

Now you have started on the journey of life. The real journey of life when the spirits of the physical unite in harmony and they find the real ONENESS OF BEING, and in the oneness of being they live, and they give, and you will never regret taking this first step. We will always place at your disposal all the various instruments who will be necessary from time to time, to give further guidance and directions on which path next to take.

And now we are going a step further, and this WILL astound you. Later on in life you will have your own temple of light to activate and work from, and this is as it should be, freedom of expression, freedom to activate spiritual truths in the enlightenment that is given to you, and you will heal, and you will speak.

You will give guidance and instruction to the people, and they will come to your abode, and the symbol of light emblazoned around the STAR OF DAVID will be your symbol. You will be at the helm, and you will gather people around you. As the Nazarene gathered his disciples, you will gather people around you who will work with you, and who will follow the pathway of light that you will be able to guide them into.

We told you at the beginning, that there was a great work for you to do, you are merely on the threshold. THIS is the beginning, but it has got to expand. This is the time for preparation, when you are working with people, when you are getting known, when the quality of your work is getting better, in preparation for the time when you will have your own temple. It does not matter if it is humble, if it is a place of enlightenment that is all that is necessary. And so remember this, because this is yours.

We are very, very proud to know that we have been able to bring you into the company of people who have been important in your spiritual adventure, and you will be brought into the companionship even yet of others who will help in establishing the spiritual fulfilment that is for you.

Loved with everlasting love. Made by grace that loved to know. Spirit Divine descending with power and glory, YOU ARE A MESSENGER, you have got to prepare the ground for others to follow, and there will be new avenues placed at your disposal.

Unfortunately my brother we are being made aware of earthly time, but the message that was important to you, we have given, and we know that you will accept, and you will follow, as you are guided, guarded, and instructed, step by step.

The Light, and the power of Light, God Creator of all that is, and ever shall be, descend upon you and enfold you in grace, purity, and strength.'

Whilst on the subject of Hafed's autobiography, I should just mention yet another remarkable thing that happened. For more than a year before the book came into my hands, several mediums when giving me personal messages would remark, 'Ned and Nellie send you their love.' This had always puzzled me, because as far as I could discover we had no relatives with those names on either side of the family.

With the purchase of Hafed's book however, the mystery was finally solved, for inside the front cover were the hand written words, 'With best wishes from Ned & Nellie, 25th September, 1925.'

Yet another truly amazing thing that in fact had happened before I resigned from the Spiritualist church in Hertford, but after I had discovered Hafed's book, happened one Sunday when it had been my turn to 'chair' a service at the church.

I had spent most of the previous day preparing the sermon I intended to give, and at the actual service as I was about to read from my notes, a voice inside my head said, 'Put those down, that is NOT what I want the congregation to hear.'

Putting the notes down as told, I wondered what on earth I WAS supposed to speak about, but the next moment spirit took over my tongue, and I just stood there astonished as I heard myself giving the most wonderful sermon I had ever listened to, yet I had no idea WHO was actually giving it!

However when I went to sit down, our visiting medium for that Sunday, turned to me and said, 'Do you have a Persian Guide?'

When I asked why, the medium replied, 'Well when you were speaking just now, your beard grew longer and turned white, a beautiful blue turban appeared on your head, and you were clothed in a long white dazzling robe.'

Then I knew who HAD just given the sermon - Hafed! For in his autobiography there was one sentence which read, 'And as I grew older and my beard turned WHITE, it became my custom to always wear a BLUE TURBAN AND A WHITE ROBE.'

When I eventually found a publisher (Regency Press) for my revised version of Hafed's book, yet another prophecy was to be fulfilled when I discovered that the publisher, had a sister company who did their actual printing, called Buckland Press, and so it WAS a 'company with two names.'

One thing the company did persuade me to do because they considered the book was too long, was to split it in half, part one to deal with Hafed's earthly life and to retain its original title, and part two, dealing with his life in the spirit world, to be called HAFED & HERMES. Part one was published in 1987, part two in 1989. Both books were to become bestsellers in the psychic world, and indeed copies are still selling to this day.

Later I went on to write three popular books of my own: WHAT DID GOD SAY?, JESUS - THE WHOLE STORY, and INVISIBLE REALITIES.

As my reputation as a writer began to grow, so more and more members of the public wrote to me seeking help or advise on spiritual or psychic matters. I also found myself being invited to address public meetings, which I always enjoyed.

# Extracts from Patients' Letters

Throughout the 1970s and the 1980s I continued to do more and more healing, seeing patients in our little sitting room at home, and spending a couple of hours every evening to send out vibrations (absent healing) to those who lived too far away to visit me.

Although I was of the opinion that a healer should not charge for his or her services, my practical mother pointed out that, having given up a great deal of one's personal leisure time to benefit others, healers should not be expected to be out of pocket financially as well. The additional heating, lighting, and stationary bills being quite considerable. For this reason I gratefully accepted small donations from 'contact' patients, and also requested those seeking 'absent' healing to kindly provide a stamp and addressed envelopes if writing inside the UK, or international reply coupons if writing from abroad.

Since I had no wish to raise false hopes among people, I always explained that for various reasons complete or even partial cures could never be guaranteed. There might be karmic reasons why I was unsuccessful, at other times a patient might put up a barrier of doubt and disbelief so strong that no healing vibrations could penetrate it. On the whole however, my success rate was very good indeed, especially where animals were concerned, and incidentally I feel these dear creatures offer the best prove of all that healing CAN work. How could I for example influence the thought pattern of someone's pet cat or dog?

The one big disappointment for me, was the fact that I could do nothing to relieve the awful agonies my own dear mother suffered from arthritis. She had undergone every kind of hospital treatment, taken every type of drug, but all to no avail, and although I might be allowed to do so much for others, my own dear mother just had to go on suffering, and this broke my heart.

Just how much I WAS able to accomplish as an instrument of spirit, you can judge from the following letter extracts, the originals of which I keep on file so that anyone wishing to inspect their authenticity may do so if they wish:

Mrs. AC (Welwyn Garden City): One evening, on closing my eyes I saw hundreds of blue and purple sparkling stars like a wonderful firework display. LATER - Am beginning to feel much better, this week very little pain in the neck and shoulders. LATER STILL- Woke suddenly at 10.30pm, my bedroom was full of purple sparkling stars which gradually bunched together and faded away. My neck is unbelievably mobile, and at the moment no pain. Now isn't that good news? I think I shall call you and your spirit helpers my 'star makers.' (Lady had received severe neck and wrist injuries in a car accident)

Mrs. LF (Stuaton, USA): Good news again this month. There is only one lump remaining in my breast. The lumps must have spread through the chest area, because now there is no restriction felt in the chest, the feeling before was as if something attached. One other good item, I am sleeping much better than before. I was so worried before, and that made me restless. LATER- Am happy to report that every day I show more improvement. The breast no longer pulls, it seems to be free - in fact it feels as if the lump has dissolved from under the breastbone. LATER STILL- The healing is all but complete, and in the beginning I feared cancer. Spirit healing is truly wonderful. (The lady's doctor had said the lumps - four of them 'can only be removed by surgery')

Mrs. KM (London): Amber's eye condition (she was blind in one eye) has improved to the extent that she can now read a book. It's amazing because our doctor and two hospitals said there was no hope of her regaining her sight. They said the back or the eye was like a battlefield, so many scars. (The same lady wrote about the sudden disappearance of a year-old verruca on her daughter's foot, which she had been told would have to be cut out in hospital, since it was so deeply ingrained)

Miss MG (Huddersfield): Wrote to say that her kitten was going blind and her vet had told her that nothing could be done for it. Later, after I had sent out healing vibrations to the kitten, she wrote, 'Dana is not blind, I have tested her, she followed a piece of string.'

Mr. TL (Ipswich): Asked for help concerning his girlfriend who suffered from frequent epileptic fits. LATER HE WROTE- My girlfriend has felt much better these last few days. She tells me it is the first time she has been free of pain for some time, and she felt like going to a party. LATER HE REPORTED - Progress still continues. Headache-free thank God and hopefully lessening the chances of any more fits occurring.

Mrs. AC (Wembley): Writing about her father - One ulcer literally seemed to clear up overnight and the others my mother tells me are appearing to heal. He sounds much stronger in voice and is more confident.

Mrs. CS (Slough): I feel able to relax very quickly and get strong vibrations through my arms down to my fingertips. Sometimes Topaz (her cat) sits on my lap, she also relaxes, her fur has stopped dropping out, her eyes are much wider and brighter, she is a much happier cat.
LATER- I wonder if you have any idea why the vibrations are so much stronger on a Tuesday night? So much so that my upper arm and a section of the lower arm ache so much I don't know what to do, and feel almost as if an electric current were shooting through my fingers. Another

strange thing, my husband says my hands are red hot to touch afterwards, but to me they feel cold.

Mrs. HC (London): Pet dog had chronic arthritis in the hip. Vet was to operate, taking out femur bone and replacing it with a plastic joint, but after one week of healing the lady wrote - Walking nicely and seems rather more frisky. LATER- Joey has made good progress and seems very happy, his leg seems to be better. LATER STILL- At the moment he can walk faster than I can! We are so grateful to you when we see him enjoying life. Please feel you have been a great help to me too, somehow you have enabled me to feel more serene end able to cope with myself calmly, and I cannot thank you enough.

Mr. WH (Hoddesdon): Your healing did my back a power of good last year. I have had no trouble with it since.

Mrs. AC (Wembley) writing about her cat: I know you sent healing to her, as her eye seemed to get better almost the day after I wrote to you. It looks completely normal now. I am so pleased. It was taking so long to heal before.

Mrs. SK (Reading): Lucy's progress is dramatic in that she seems to be generally so much more energetic than she's been for months, and her eyes look brighter. (Cat had chronic bronchitis and tracheitis)

Miss KB (Enfield): It is good to be able to walk almost normal again, also manage stairs a bit better. The swelling had gone completely from my body. LATER SHE WROTE - I am pleased to report that my legs are now much improved and I am now back to running for the bus once more, my knees are certainly normal, and the calfs softer than they were before.

Mr. GF (Birmingham): The spirit friends are very active around me - I keep seeing blue and white lights flickering around me. I am full of vitality which I was not before I started healing with you. Thank you for all you are doing to help me. I couldn't afford to pay in money all that you are doing to help me. Will always be in debt to you.


One of the most striking cases of spirit healing I can recall occurred as a result of my meeting a neighbour in the street one day, and asking how her husband was - some eighteen months earlier he had undergone surgery for cancer in the stomach, the lady told me he was deeply depressed, because he was having to travel to St. Bartholomew's hospital in London three times a week to have his dressings changed, the wound simply refusing to heal, even eighteen months later. I promised to say a few prayers for her husband and send out healing vibrations to him.

A few weeks later when I chanced to meet the lady again, and enquired how her husband was, she replied, 'Well, it is amazing really, but the day after I last saw you, my husband went up to London again to have his dressings changed, and when they removed the dressing they found the wound had suddenly healed so well that no further dressings would be needed, and no more trips to the hospital were necessary. The hospital staff were stunned by the sudden healing, and so was my husband, although I dare not tell him it might have been as a result of your healing prayers. You see, my husband is a staunch Roman Catholic and does not believe in that sort of thing.'

Perhaps even more intriguing in a way, was the case of little Nicholas. His grandmother, Stella, lived at Cheshunt in Hertfordshire, and had originally written to me seeking help for her dog. This having been successfully dealt with, she wrote to me again, this time asking if I could help her six-year-old grandson Nicky who lived in Ware. Stella informed me that the child suffered acutely from asthma, which caused both her and the child's parents great anxiety at times. She also told me that she was writing without the knowledge of her daughter or her son-in-law, since they did not approve of spiritual healing. Could I help?

I told Stella I would pray for little Nicky and send out healing vibrations to him, and I emphasised that she could help too by linking with me in thought and prayer at a given time.

The following day Stella telephoned me at my office and said, 'Mr Wright, I just HAD to ring you. This morning my daughter telephoned me in great excitement and said, "Mum, the most strange and wonderful thing has happened. Last night shortly after I had gone to bed, I felt a desperate need to go into Nicky's room just to check that he was all right. When I opened his door and looked into the room, what do you think I saw? Floating through the open window was a stream of GREEN BUBBLES! At first I could not believe my eyes. The bubbles were drifting across the room to Nicky's bed where they formed a kind of little cloud over him. I was absolutely stunned. I just stood there for a moment or two in astonishment. Then I went I went over to see if Nicky was all right. He was sleeping peacefully, so I crept out of his room and went back to bed again. But those BUBBLES! I dare not wake his father and tell him, he would have thought I was mad. The best of it is that this morning Nicky is so much better. His breathing is quite normal and at breakfast this morning his appetite had improved, too. In fact, he seemed to be a much happier little boy altogether. I just don't know what to make of it all".'

Well, Stella expressed her own delight at little Nicky's sudden change for the better, although she did not tell her daughter that she had been in touch with me about the child, but thanking me for my help, she asked, 'But why the green bubbles, Mr. Wright?'

I suggested that perhaps bubbles would delight a child more than stars or bright lights which other people sometimes saw, had he suddenly woken up, and green was the generally accepted colour for healing as a whole, although there were different colour vibrations for different conditions.

The final case I will mention concerns a beautiful dog whose owner Mrs. GL of London W2 wrote to me as follows:

'We have a lovely young Saluki, six months old, female, that we acquired just a month ago, and even in that short time, we have become very attached to her. Last Tuesday evening, my husband took the dog on the London Underground (for the first time), and there was a serious accident involving both him and the dog on the escalator at Holborn Tube Station. Apparently, the dog's right foot got jammed in the escalator at the step-off at the top, and my husband tried to free it, but unsuccessfully, the dog biting him in the process.

Finally, an LRT employee came and turned off the escalator, and they managed to free the dog and called the RSPCA. Sara (the dog) was taken in an RSPCA van to their hospital in N7 where she still remains (my husband was treated at a local hospital, and was released, none the worse for wear, but badly shaken.)

We telephoned the hospital yesterday and learned that Sara's paw is badly damaged, with a lot of stitches and they had to amputate one of her toes. This news distressed us deeply, as you can imagine, and we are very concerned about her recovering and being able to walk, and run, normally again. I thought (not immediately, being in a state of shock myself, but later, i.e. today) about asking a spiritual healer for help.

I do not know if you are familiar with Salukis as a breed, but to them running (even more than other breeds) is of the utmost importance. I would even go so far as to say that their personality is built around their running ability, they are the fastest dogs known (except whippets and greyhounds, on a short stretch), and truly feel that Sara would lose the will to live, if she realised that she could not run again. Running is their whole life.

Above and beyond that are the memories I have of our beautiful Sara running like the wind, so very happy, and I cannot bear to think of her as a cripple at her young age.

I wonder if you would be willing to try to direct some healing power to her, in the days to come. She is now recovering from surgery at the animal hospital, and is expected to remain there another five days.

With many thanks for your kind assistance,
Sincerely, GL'

ONE WEEK LATER I received the following letter from the same lady:

'Dear Ronald Wright,
Just a note to let you know that Sara has completely recovered from her foot (paw) injury. Thanks in great part, I am sure, to your healing energy. She is amazingly running about just as she did before (at 30 mph!) and I

think you can consider it another "miracle cure"!

Again, all my thanks for all you have done for her, and Sara too, I am sure, says thank you - from the bottom of our hearts.

Sincerely, GL'

*My books on Spiritualism*

*Book-signing in Bournemouth, 1989*

# The Extraordinary Mrs. Holiday

Something I found very gratifying was the number or times various mediums told me that the famous Victorian surgeon Lord Joseph Lister was using me as his instrument, and whenever I think about Lister, I am reminded of a lady named Mrs. Audrey Holiday who came from Welwyn Garden City.

A bright, very cheerful woman in her late forties, Audrey first came to see me because she was experiencing severe pain in her back and legs. Sitting her down I took her hands in mine and proceeded to go into trance, but hardly had I begun to do so than she started having some sort of convulsions. Jerking back her arms and shoulders violently, she said loudly to someone quite unseen to me, 'I CAN'T get them back any further!' Astonished, I asked who she was speaking to? She replied, 'An elderly gentleman standing next to me wearing funny old-fashioned clothes.'

As I sat there in amazement, so the lady continued to go through a series of exercises which she claimed she was being instructed to do by the 'old gentleman', and at one point when she wanted to bring her shoulders forward, she found she was quite unable to because HE was pulling them back! What to make of this I did not know. Was the woman a nut-case, or was she a genuine clairvoyant herself without perhaps being aware of it? Before leaving she made another appointment to visit me the following week.

The day following her visit to me, Mrs. Holiday telephoned and made a most extraordinary statement. She claimed that when attempting to rise from her bed that morning, she had been unable to do so, at least not until she had first been (involuntarily) put through a series of violent exercises as she lay in her bed! She stated that her legs had performed the movements as though having a life of their own, quite independent of her mind. These exercises had lasted for half an hour, and although at the end of them she had felt quite exhausted, she claimed that once she was allowed to get to her feet, she felt like a new woman.

Mrs. Holiday asked if this was typical of the kind of thing all my patients usually experienced and I had to admit that I had never known such a thing happen before. More and more I began to wonder if perhaps the woman was hypersensitive and it was all a product of her own imagination.

On her second visit to my home Mrs. Holiday again declared that the 'old gentleman' was in attendance, assisted this time by a little old lady dressed in what appeared to be a very old fashioned nursing uniform. Suddenly Mrs Holiday said, 'Good heavens, the old lady is putting a small cauldron by my feet, there seems to be something soaking in it that looks like a piece of cloth.'

Saying that the old lady was now lifting some of the wet material out of the cauldron, Mrs. Holiday suddenly let out a loud cry, 'Ugh. She has slapped it on my back and I can feel the water running all down my spine,' she wailed. By the time Mrs. Holiday was ready to leave my healing room, she reported that her back was feeling fine.

When the lady made her third visit to me - although she now seemed quite fit she continued to visit me because she declared, 'The only time I ever see spirit is when I am in your healing room.' Her clairvoyance seemed to grow decidedly more interesting and convincing, for apart from seeing the usual old gentlemen and having a CONVERSATION WITH HIM, she suddenly said, 'Oh, a coach and horses has just pulled up outside your house, and a most beautiful lady is getting out of it. She is wearing lovely clothes- a dress that is all kind of ruched up in the front and gathered into a kind of lump at the back.'

'I think you are referring to a bustle,' I remarked.

Next Mrs. Holiday told me that the elegant lady, who was also wearing a little flowered hat, was talking to the old gentleman, and listening to their conversation Mrs. Holiday suddenly said, 'That's funny, the lady says her name is Alexander - that's a funny name for a woman, isn't it?'

Almost immediately Mrs. Holiday was saying, 'Oh dear!'

'What is the matter?' I asked her.

Looking a little surprised she announced, 'The lady has just told me off! She said, "My name is NOT Alexander. It is ALEXANDRA- DRA! DRA!"...'

In fact I had already guessed the identity of Dr Lister's visitor myself, but was anxious not to give Mrs. Holiday any clues. I waited to see what else she might say. Almost at once Mrs. Holiday was saying, 'That's odd. An arch of WILD ROSES has suddenly appeared over the head of the lady.' Then after a slight pause she added, 'Well that's even funnier. Now I can see a hand holding a charity collection tin, just a hand and the tin, no arm or person... Whatever can it mean?'

Having listened in fascination to all that Mrs. Holiday had said, I explained, 'The lovely lady you can see must be Queen Alexandra. The appearance of both the "Alexandra" roses and and the collection tin are confirmation of this. I also remember reading somewhere that people often mistakenly called the Queen "Alexander" and when this happened she would angrily correct them saying, "My name is Alexandra, dra! dra! Since Lister was also surgeon to her husband, King Edward VII, the Queen would certainly have known him.'

Then Audrey said, 'The lady is preparing to leave now. She is going outside and I see her climbing into her coach, and my goodness! There is a little old white-haired lady waiting for her in the coach, and do you know who I think it is?'

'Yes,' I replied. 'Her mother-in-law, Queen Victoria, who was another of Lister's patients.'

On another occasion when Audrey came to see me an old uncle

had suddenly appeared to her, an uncle still living. Eerily she also saw a skeleton standing beside him, and both stood before an open grave.

'I do not, like the sound of that at all,' I said to Audrey.

'Is your uncle seriously ill at the moment?'

'I don't know. He lives in Yorkshire and we rarely write to each other,' she replied.

Next day Audrey received a telephone call from relatives in Yorkshire to say that her uncle had died the previous night at exactly the time she had seen him in my home!

Yet another occurrence that happened one evening when Audrey came to see me, was when she arrived suffering from an extremely bad throat. So husky and croaky that indeed she could only speak with great difficulty.

As she sat opposite me, she had come for healing on this occasion, she saw Dr. Lister enter the room carrying a large bottle and a spoon. She informed me that he had started to pour a green liquid into the spoon and was instructing her to open her mouth so that she might swallow it. Obediently, she opened her mouth and gulped down the 'medicine' as told. Quite miraculously when she opened her mouth to speak again, her voice was perfectly normal, no trace of hoarseness, and she remarked that the soreness she had been experiencing was completely better now also.

Before leaving the fascinating subject of Audrey and her extraordinary ability to 'see' spirit with such clarity, I must relate just one other remarkable happening which occurred around about the time she paid visits to me, although this particular case had nothing whatever to do with her.

The story came in the form of a letter from a friend who lived in Ramsgate, Kent. His name was Bramwell Cook, and he was an ambulance driver for the Thanet area of Kent. Bram was also at that time a member of the Salvation Army, and while not believing in Spiritualism himself, he respected my own views and convictions.

The strange story Bram had to tell went as follows: A friend named David, who also lived in Ramsgate but worked some distance away in Canterbury, was driving home from work one evening in his car along a very quiet stretch of road near Reculver, when suddenly walking along the grass verge ahead or him he saw a young friend named Paul. Since Paul was a motorbike enthusiast, David thought it strange that he should be walking along the roadside on foot like this. Pulling up beside the lad, he asked Paul if he would like a lift? To his surprise the young man replied, 'No thank you. I need the exercise, I will walk.'

Reaching home David prepared himself a meal and was just about to sit down and eat it, when the telephone rang. It was Paul's mother on the line, and between tears the poor lady told him that her son had been killed that afternoon riding his motorbike along a lonely stretch of the road near Reculver! Stunned, David asked Paul's mother at what time the accident had occurred. She replied, 'About 3pm.'

'But that is quite impossible,' David had gasped, 'I saw and spoke to Paul on that part of the road around 6pm!'.

Bram, as mystified as David, and unable to offer any explanation himself, had written to me to see if I could throw any light on the matter. It was the fact that David had not only SEEN young Paul, but SPOKEN to him some three hours after his fatal accident that puzzled him so.

# Some Dramatic Changes

The late 1980s brought dramatic changes to my business, social and home life, and things would never be the same again. In the spring of 1986 our hamper company moved office from Central London to the small market town of Hoddesdon, only seven miles from my home. This suited me fine, the short journey by country bus being far more pleasant than the daily scramble into the city on crowded trains and tubes.

The following year saw a sudden decline in my mother's health, and she had to go into hospital for several weeks. I was told she could only be released if given constant care and attention, and so that she could receive this while I was at my work, mother moved to my sister's bungalow on the other side of town. Soon after, it was discovered that she had faulty heart valves and would never again be able to climb stairs. Since our bedrooms were on the third floor, we were faced with quite a problem. The doctor insisted that until a stair-lift was installed, mother could not return home again. Our landlady refused to allow this, and suggested I apply to the local council to rehouse us in a bungalow or ground-floor apartment, clearly unaware that we might have to wait many months or even years for such accommodation to become available.

When I told mother the news, she became deeply distressed. Having already spent some fifty years in our present home, she was very reluctant to drag up her roots. The doctor, social welfare people and even the council supported our request for the installation or the stair-lift, and eventually after many months of wrangling the landlady capitulated and mother was able to return home once more.

It was good to have her back again, although her doctor made it quite clear that mother must not be left alone for long periods. This meant I would either have to start working on a part-time basis, or pay someone to come in and look after her while I was at the office.

By now it was May, 1986, and quite unexpectedly my problem was solved for me. Without any warning whatsoever my brother-in-law arrived at our home just as I was preparing to leave for the office and said, 'Sorry, you are now redundant. We sold the company yesterday!'. I just stood there in shock unable to speak, as he continued, 'I'm taking you to the office, but not to do any work, just to collect your redundancy cheque, and so that my partners can thank you for your past years of service.'

Nearly eighteen years of service being brought to such an abrupt end was staggering. Both mother and I could not understand why both my brother-in-law and sister had been so secretive about it all. They must have known for weeks, even months, what was being planned.

Later we discovered that my sister and her husband were anxious to start a business venture in their enormous garden, a cattery, and had pressured the hamper company's other directors to sell up. I felt I had been stabbed in the back.

At least now I would be at home to attend to mother myself. We would have to live on a tighter budget now, but we were no worse off than thousands of other people, and luckily I have always been a very domesticated person, and so the new role I was being called upon to play came as no hardship to me.

What leisure time I had, I spent writing this autobiography, I had actually begun it years earlier when I had been in prison! When finished, I found myself a good agent who felt it would do well. Published in the summer of 1990, with the title FLESH - THE GREAT ILLUSION, as might be expected, it immediately attracted the attention of THE NEWS OF THE WORLD who printed a large article with the heading, 'BIZARRE ORGY SECRETS OF THE GAY PSYCHIC' and illustrated it with the two photos I had chosen to go one the front cover of the book. My agent was delighted, and said the publicity, 'Was worth thousands!'. I hoped she was right.

Sadly, about a year later, after a lot of suffering, my mother finally died on June 2nd, 1991. Six weeks later I was invited to give a public talk about my 'HAFED, A PRINCE OF PERSIA' book at Castle Hall, Hertford, where a Psychic Fair was being held.

In my audience at the Fair was Katarina, 39 year-old divorced wife of a wealthy publisher, who lived locally. After my talk Katarina came up and asked a few questions about my past spiritual experiences, and as we talked she happened to remark what a nice suntan I had. On learning that I was in fact a nudist who liked an all-over tan, but my garden was too over-looked by my neighbours to strip completely naked, she immediately offered me the use of her own very secluded garden, and I was pleased to accept.

The following afternoon when I took up her offer, I arrived at her lovely detached house and found two sun-loungers already in place, side by side on the terrace at the back of the property.

It was a beautiful, hot sunny day, and I had arrived in just shorts and short-sleeved shirt, which I quickly removed before lying down on one of the loungers. Katarina, a tall, very slim girl, with the most amazing head of long blond hair I had ever seen, had opened the front door to me wearing a pretty summer dress, but after bringing two glasses of lemonade out onto the terrace, and placing them on a small table, she disappeared into the house again, returning a few minutes later wearing a blue, one-piece swim-suit.

No sooner had she laid down on her own lounger, than she began to peel the top of her swimsuit down to waist level, as I imagine she had already anticipated, I immediately started to get an erection, and smiling she reached out with one hand saying, 'My, we must do something about THAT!' and gripping my cock tightly she literally pulled me to my feet, and keeping a firm grip all the time, led me through the open French windows, up a flight of stairs to her bedroom, then after pushing me backwards onto the bed, dropped her swim-suit and pounced on me!

She clearly enjoyed uninhibited sex as much as I did, and by the time she had to go and collect her little six-year old son from school, we had enjoyed rampant sex three times, twice on the bed and once in the shower.

Our relationship lasted nine years until February 15th, the day AFTER St. Valentine's Day, 2000, and during that time I endeavoured to be a good step-father to her two children, there was also an eight-year-old daughter. The children saw very little of their father, who lived in North London spent most of his time on business trips to New York and Frankfurt. He seemed to be under the impression that money could replace affection, and both Katarina and particularly her son, seemed starved of love.

Soon Jamie was worshipping the very ground I walked on, and I was regarding him as the son I had never had. Becki, his sister, was different, she seemed at times to resent my presence in her mother's house, and we did not always get on too well together, but it was not for the want of trying on my part. I also got on well with Katarina's mother, only a year older than me! There was a twenty-four year age-gap between Kate and myself, but because I looked twenty years younger than my age (63), we looked the same age, and everyone thought we WERE.

I slept with Katarina about four nights in every seven, and we enjoyed several 'family' holidays together in the Greek Islands, Zantos or Rhodes, and while her mother looked after the children, Katarina and I celebrated her 40th Birthday with a long, romantic weekend in Amsterdam. Not that we saw much OF Amsterdam, as we spent most or the time having sex in bed, or in the shower. We were like rabbits - fucking at every opportunity.

Everything went well until 1998 when I started having disputes with my landlady, and I moved to a small but lovely little semi-detached bungalow in Watton-at-Stone which had a large garden my two cats adored. However my move from Hertford, five miles away, did NOT please Katarina. She had been used to seeing me every single day, now we would only be able to see each other a few times a week, and she was very dissatisfied. She had a car, I didn't, and had never wanted one. I much preferred public transport.

Perhaps now feeling a little neglected, Katarina began to look elsewhere for 'comfort', and found it in several other relationships with men, although none of them seemed to last any length of time. We finally split in 2000 as I have already said, although we have remained good friends ever since. Eventually I am pleased to say Katarina DID settle down with a very nice guy she has remained with for about twelve years now.

Before leaving the subject of Katarina, I should just mention that during the first few years we spent together, we quite regularly attended the Hertford Spiritualist church, all the people I had previously known there had now been replaced by others. One Sunday we had met a visiting medium from Harlow named Duggie Arnold, and when Duggie became aware that it was I who had revised and republished HAFED, A PRINCE OF PERSIA, he invited us to join his weekly clairvoyance circle in Harlow, saying that Hafed had been using HIM as an instrument since a youth, and STILL spoke through him regularly to his circle.

The circle had twelve members, all Harlow people, and Katarina and I attended regularly each week until Duggie died just two years later. Hafed DID regularly speak to us through Duggie, and imparted most valuable wisdom and information about the future, much of which has come to pass in recent years.

Hafed had also begun dictating YET ANOTHER BOOK - this time a book of wisdom entitled, A NEW SET OF VALUES - something he said this world was badly in need of at this time. Hafed had completed dictating the book before Duggie died, and Hafed gave me the responsibility of getting it published, just as I had his previous work. This I did, and it finally appeared in bookshops in 1998, the year I moved away from Hertford.


Not long after my arrival in Watton-at-Stone I interrupted two young men attempting a burglary - in my home! It was late at night and I was watching television in the dark. Suddenly I was aware of a loud 'banging' and thought it was someone slamming a car door outside, but when the banging continued, I got up to look out of the window to see what was causing the noise, but could see nothing. In fact the noise was coming from the BACK of the bungalow, but I did not realise this at the time.

After a few minutes I noticed through the fanlight above my door to the hall, that the hall light was switched on, and I was certain I had switched it OFF earlier in the evening. Going into the hall, I then saw that my bedroom door was open and the light switched on in there also.

Knowing that I HAD shut my bedroom door, I went to investigate, and as I pushed the door open still further, saw a young man in the process of searching through my chest of drawers.

As he turned to look at me, another young man appeared from behind the bedroom door, and to my question, 'What the hell are you two doing in my home?' the older one said, 'Well isn't this Tina's place?'

'Tina's place?' I repeated. 'Do you usually search through HER private belongings then? You know damn well this is not Tina's place! Now get out of my home before I call the police,' I shouted at them in a furious temper.

To my surprise they both meekly followed me to my front door, and stepped outside when I opened it and shouted 'Now get out!'

For a moment, after closing the door, I just stood there in shock. Then I realised I ought to get their car's license-plate number, if they had a car, and so opening the door again I ran up the path towards the road.

However by the time I did get to the gate, their vehicle, an old van, was already speeding away in the distance.

Back in my bedroom, I checked to see if anything was missing, and luckily I had interrupted them before they had got to the drawer that contained both jewellery and a large amount of cash. I had been extremely lucky.

I then telephoned the police, who arrived just ten minutes later, and explained what had happened. When I remarked how obediently they had followed me out into the hall, one of the policemen said I had been unwise to turn my back on them - that was a moment they might have hit me over the head with something. I laughed and said I thought they had been more scared or ME in a temper, than I had been of them!

While I was talking to one police officer, his partner was searching to see how the two lads had gained entry, and it was found that they must have used an iron bar to break the lock on my bathroom window at the BACK of the bungalow, this is what had caused all the 'banging' I had heard earlier.

Since that night, I have taken the precaution of putting heavy steel chains across all my windows - perhaps not very sightly, but at least they are secure.

*Katarina and me, 1992*

*Drawing of Georgina Starr as Cleopatra for THEDA*

# A New Dawn Breaks

In June, 2006, Katarina's daughter Becki, then a world travelling fashion model, introduced me to Georgina Starr, the young creative and experimental artist well known in international art circles. They had first met in Tokyo, Japan, when Becki was on a fashion shoot, and Georgina was attending her latest art show.

Georgina had mentioned to Becki that she was going to make a black and white art film about the silent screen legend Theda Bara. Theda had been the first Hollywood actress to portray Cleopatra, Salome and other famous characters on the silver screen between 1915 and 1920.

When Becki had mentioned that I had met and sketched quite a few Hollywood stars, Georgina asked if she could be introduced to me, might I be willing to supply some drawings for her movie? Georgina was planning to star in the film as well as direct it herself. A very versatile young woman, she was not yet forty.

Having met Georgina (she looked about twenty), I agreed to do five portraits of her in the various roles she intended to create in the film, and I attended it's premier in London on November 14th, 2006, at the Prince Charles cinema off Leicester Square. Imagine my surprise when watching the film, to see not only my drawings on screen, but Georgina doing an impersonation of a portrait artist called RONALDO WRIGHT!

Faithful to the 1920s, not only was the movie silent, it had a musical accompaniment to provide an environment for the images on screen. In the old days this was usually provided by a person playing piano, however for THEDA Georgina had actually engaged a seventeen-piece experimental orchestra, each individual musician playing their own interpretation of what they saw on screen. The result can only be described as incredible.

As a result of my work for THEDA, my life would never be the same again. Georgina was not only fascinated by my association with film folk of the past, she wanted to know all about my psychic experiences, my life as London's top life model, and my work as an artist and editor for gay magazines in the 1950s and 60s, for she was also embarking on a series of recordings focusing on people's unusual experiences. The next couple of years we spent a lot of time working together both in Watton-at-Stone and in London.

Not only did I get to know Georgina, but her famous artist partner Paul Noble, whose own drawings, huge in scale, were a great source of wonder and inspiration to me. Quite quickly I also got to know their wide circle of very interesting friends from the worlds of art, fashion and music, all half my age, but when in their company I felt as young as they were. They in their turn found it difficult to believe that I was as old as I was.

Instead of being buried away in the Hertfordshire countryside, I now found myself making regular trips to London to attend a wide variety of shows and exhibitions, and it gave me a new lease of life which I was very grateful for.

At the beginning of 2007, the British Library created an archive of my gay artwork from the 1950s and 60s, which were housed at the London School of Economics in Portugal Street, off Kingsway, along side the Hall Carpenter archives of gay art and photography. Georgina and I visited the LSE to make an 'on the spot' recording of me talking about my work, and this was later released as one or Georgina's popular monthly audio podcasts for GRRRRRRRADIO (yes, seven R's). The covers of the recording were illustrated with numerous nudes of me and my artwork and entitled 'Looking at Ron.'

That same year, 2007, Dinah Sheridan's fourth husband died in California, and on September 17th (her 87th Birthday), she returned to live in London so as to be near to her family.

That very same day I was on a plane flying in the opposite direction, to New York. I was attending both the American premier of Georgina's movie THEDA, and the launch of Paul Noble's latest art show at the Gagosian Gallery. Katarina's daughter Becki attended both functions as she was living in New York now, and it was so nice to see her again.

There was a champagne reception after the showing of THEDA, and a dinner party for about thirty special guests after Paul's new art show, given by the owner of the gallery at a nearby restaurant. It was all great fun and I loved every minute of it. Everyone was now calling me 'Ronaldo' because of the character in THEDA based on myself, and the name has stuck ever since amongst our own close circle of friends.


Two friends I had sadly lost touch with over the years had been Ray and Ian, the two 'young' men who had first introduced me into the world of gay London back in the 1950s. We sent each other Christmas cards, but that's about all. Then one day I received a telephone call from Ray, now living in Harlow, Essex, who informed me that Ian had been very ill with prostate cancer, and that as he made regular trips to visit him, do his shopping, and take him out for hair-cuts etc., would I care to accompany him one day to see Ian who had been living in Tolworth, Surrey, for many years. I said I would love to see them BOTH after so many years, and our reunion became a regular occurrence until Ian got worse and entered hospital, where he eventually died.

Ian had asked that Ray take his ashes to the place where he was born and grew up as a child, the Isle of Rassay, off the West coast of Scotland, and there scatter them on his grandma's hill-top grave. I went with Ray, collecting one of his sisters from Newcastle on our drive north, and although our mission was a sad one, it WAS one of the most enjoyable and memorable visits to Scotland I can recall.

We had to take a ferry from the Isle of Skye to Rassay, and a short drive took as to the tiny village of Inverarish, where we stayed in a traditional stone cottage, next to the one that Ian had been born in. We were only there for three days, but it was an unforgettable experience. Open coal fires, walks through the wooded hills in all kinds of weather, sunshine, rain and snow.

The cottage was just a stone's throw away from the pebble beach, and a mountain stream that rushed past the bottom of our garden and flowed into the sea. The island had just one general store, and no pubs. Sheep seemed to outnumber the population, and the icing on the cake was to drive down one of the narrow roads one evening with a beautiful stag trotting along the road in front of us for quite a distance.

Socially 2008 turned out to be a most enjoyable and interesting year. In January Georgina celebrated her 40th Birthday with a big party held in the large studios she and Paul occupied on the third floor of a large Hackney warehouse. There was a disco and a cabaret, plus Paul jumping out of a large cardboard Birthday cake, wheeled into the middle of the dancefloor by four pretty dancers dressed in pink and blue! Once out of the 'cake', Paul then joined them in dancing to 'Dream of You' to everyone's delight.

In April, in company with Georgina and Paul I attended the East London Film Festival (documentaries), in the Rio cinema at Dalston, where our friends Rayna Nadeem and Stuart Bamforth had an entry. Stuart regularly travelled the world making documentary films for the 'Save the Children' charity.

In September, to mark the centenary of the London Underground Railways iconic logo, 100 artists were invited to submit 100 works of art to an exhibition at the Rochelle gallery in Shoreditch, opened by the Mayor of London. The pictures were reproduced as posters and auctioned off at the end of the three-week long exhibition. The posters were also displayed at various underground stations all over the network.

Among the pictures was a portrait I had done of Georgina. This depicted her wearing a single long earring, on the end of which dangled a miniature copy of the famous logo. A photo of the drawing appeared in the INDEPENDENT newspaper a few days later.

Then in October I attended the GSK Contemporary Art Show at the Royal Academy in Burlington Gardens, where Georgina had been invited to 'perform', symbolically smashing some antique statues she had created specially for the show, a sort of 'out with the old, in with the new' kind of demonstration.

She had about five to smash, lifting them above her head, then throwing them onto the marble floor. Since this had to happen without warning, while a hundred or so people stood around sipping champagne, you can imagine the shock it caused for a moment. Paul and I were both aware of what was to happen, plus a couple of newspaper photographers, but not the public.

The GUARDIAN newspaper had a wonderful shot of her holding one statue above her head ready to smash it - all in full colour too!

In November I was attending an art show entitled YARNS & TALES. The yarns referring to the fact that all the exhibits were tapestries, recreated from the paintings or drawings of fifteen of the country's top modern artists. Paul's contribution was huge in size, and spectacular in conception. WALLPAPER magazine later devoted three pages to Paul and his work.

Also in November, our friend Rayna was showing another of her documentaries, called DEADLIFE, at the cinema in Stratford, and all our circle of friends met up for drinks in a bar afterwards.

I was also introduced to yet another of Georgina's artist friends I had not met before, Tariq Alvi.

The year ended on a sad note for me however when I discovered that as a result of diabetes, Dinah Sheridan who had previously had some toes amputated on both feet, now had to have one of her legs amputated as well.

Georgina Starr & Paul Noble
present

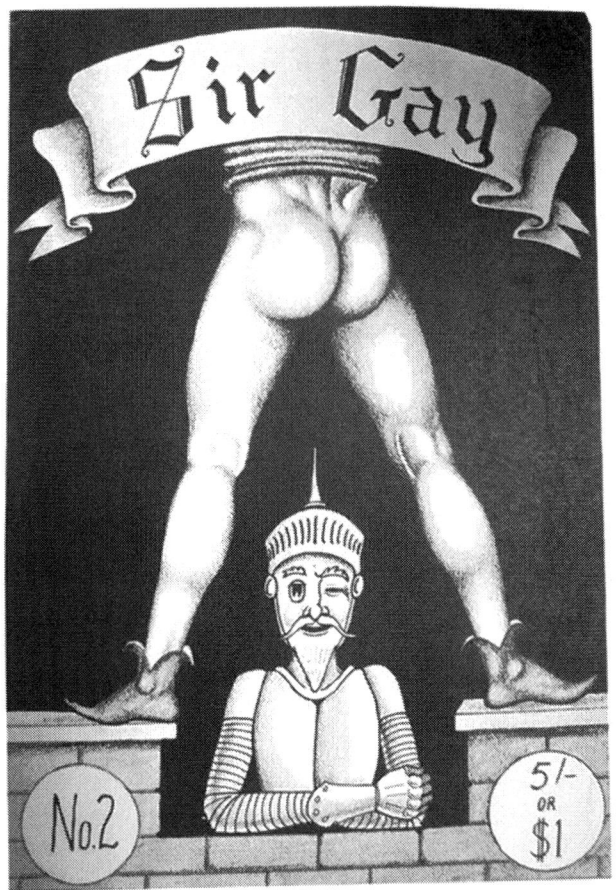

The Life and Work of
# RONALD WRIGHT
Schwartz Gallery
3rd to 27th June 2010
Preview : 2nd June 6·10pm

The exhibition is supported by The Elephant Trust.

# My 'Circle' Expands

2009 started quietly and in June I went to the Greek island of Kos for a short holiday. I had in fact been the previous summer, and liked Kos town so much, I felt I must go back for a repeat visit.

I had a lovely relaxed time, however on the very last day I was knocked down by a car as I was crossing a street in the town. In fact the car had backed into me from a stationary position, as I was passing behind it.

People rushed to pick me up, sat me down in a nearby shop, and someone gave me a glass of water, asking if I wanted an ambulance, but as it was my last few hours on the island, I didn't want to spend them in a hospital, and so told everyone I was OK.

The driver was particularly upset, but relieved when he saw I was not going to press any charges, and a few minutes later, not much the worse for wear, I continued on my way, but at my age it was a bit of a shock, and although I suffered no broken bones, I had some nasty grazing to my left arm and leg, and a big black bruise on my hip.

Not long after I got back from Kos, Georgina and Paul brought some new friends down to Watton to see me, and among them was American artist and musician Fritz Welch. Fritz was originally from New York, but at present was living with his artist wife, Rachel in Glasgow.

Fritz was part of an American trio of musicians called PSI who specialised in unusual sounds, and having just recorded a new LP he asked me if I would like to provide artwork for the record covers. I said I would be delighted to. The record was called 'Pestilence and Joy' and he said he wanted a cover that was both 'shocking and arresting'.

When my artwork was eventually taken to the printers, they were indeed SO shocked, they refused to handle it, and Fritz had to find someone else to do the work for him. Anyway, Fritz loved my pictures, and it was generally agreed that probably people would be more inclined to buy the vinyl for my artwork than for the music!

In July the popular London magazine TIME OUT, describing Georgina as 'a visual artist', invited her along with six other experts to voice their opinions on the new movie ANTICHRIST, which had recently shocked and wowed audiences at the annual Cannes Film Festival.

Then in August our friend Verena Paloma Jabs opened up a fashion boutique called Coco Career's Boutique, and among the items on offer were tee-shirts with one of my most popular gay drawings from the 1950s on the front, plus prints to hang on the wall. Georgina and Paul had also provided artwork for tee-shirts, and we all went along to the launch party.

After that Paul had a couple of drawings on show at the Tate Britain, and Georgina flew off to Toronto for the Canadian premiere of THEDA, although both were back in time to attend Tariq Alvi's latest show at the Chisenhale Gallery in East London. I attended too of course, and because these functions usually went on until a late hour, I usually stayed overnight at the Imperial Hotel in Russell Square, or the Bedford in Southampton Row. On rare occasions I had stayed at Georgina and Paul's lovely apartment at Hackney Wick, overlooking the river Lea. In November we were all attending Verena Paloma's latest show held at Tatty Devine's in Brick Lane, a now fashionable area of the East End. The show called 'Diamond Tears' was a collection of mixed media collages and animation. The place was packed out, and we all had a great evening. By now Verena was offering my 'gay' tee-shirts and prints on the internet.

2010 was to be a very special year for me, although I did not realise it at the time. It started early in February when I attended the 40th Birthday party of Andy Lewis the musician and singer. Andy had done several world tours with pop star Paul Weller as supporting guitarist, although Andy had his own band and label, Acid Jazz.

A week later I was attending the launch of Rupert Smith's latest gay novel, MAN'S WORLD at the Royal Festival Hall on London's South Bank. Rupert had been to interview me at home the previous summer, bringing a recorder with him to tape my memories of what life was like in London for gay men in the 1950s and 60s, and many of them he had included in his new book.

Later Rupert sent me a letter telling me that he had just been named 'writer of the year' at the Stonewall Awards, and added, 'I really couldn't have written the book without the help of you and a handful of others.' Certainly a lot of the book was describing my own experiences.

Also in February, I was interviewed by the popular glossy gay magazine ATTITUDE, who wanted my views on how I cope with old age! The following month under the heading 'Grand Old Age' and a very large photograph of me sitting in my rather 'grand' sitting room, my views were published.

In March I and more than a dozen of Georgina's close friends all flew down to Poitiers in South West France, where a month long exhibition of her vinyl LP's and recordings were on show at Le Contort Moderne. Georgina and Paul were staying for a week, but the 'group' were there for just three days.

On show were several of the recordings she had made with me, and a selection of my movie star portraits, gay drawings, and frontal nude photos of myself. THEDA was also being screened in a separate room.

Large crowds attended the opening, and I was flattered when several very young French people recognised me from the photos on display, and asked me to pose for photographs with them, and also sign autographs.

After the opening, we all went along to a nearby wine-bar, where

Georgina had organised a disco and cabaret with pop singer Momus. While we were there, a well-known journalist, Marie Lechner from the Paris newspaper LIBERATION, interviewed both Georgina and myself. A very nice review was reported in the newspaper the following week.

Poitiers is such a very beautiful and historical old city, and I explored as much of it as I was able in the short time I was there. It also gave me a good opportunity to get to know some of the 'group' a bit better, especially Andy, and his lovely artist wife, Liz Ridley.

Someone else I got to know on that trip who I had not really spoken to before, was Rachel Ortas, who had been a well known pop star in the 1980s. She, her partner and family now spent most of their time in London.

The following month, April, I was surprised and honoured to discover that the Hertford museum had created a book called HERTFORD FACES. In this was described the town's eighty best known faces in the past one hundred years. They included not only mayors, but Alfred Russel Wallace (Naturalist & Scientist), W.E. Johns (Creator of the 'Biggles' books), Shirley Williams (MP), Rupert Grint & Brian Wilde (Actors)... and ME!

Also in April, it was Stuart Bamforth's turn to throw a 40th Birthday party. Everyone seemed to he half MY age.

Then in May, Andy Lewis invited several of us to watch him in concert at the Royal Albert Hall, where he was supporting Paul Weller for a week-long show.

Along with Georgina, Rayna and myself were Liz and her lovely parents. We all had a meal at a nearby restaurant before going to the concert, and afterwards Andy came and escorted us to the VIP lounge for a few drinks. Georgina and Rayna then left us to go home, while Andy took the rest of us along to Paul Weller's dressing-room. All the band and their girlfriends were there drinking and talking, Andy introduced me to Paul, and as we were chatting, a clock suddenly struck midnight, whereupon someone shouted, 'Paul, it's your Birthday!' (his 52nd), and we all sang 'Happy Birthday to you'.

We left half an hour later, and as we came out of the stage door, there was still a large number of fans waiting to get the autographs of Paul and other members of the band. Andy obliged, then we jumped in a taxi and headed off towards the West End. Andy kindly dropped me off at the Bedford, then he and his family headed off to their home near the Barbican in the City.

I love eating out, especially in London, and on those rare occasions when Georgina had some spare time on her hands we would meet up for a meal in town. Over the years I had got used to people pointing me out in the restaurants, bars, streets and airports etc., saying, 'Look, there's Rolf

Harris!' I had even had people shout to me from passing cars, 'Hello Rolf'.

On one occasion when I had invited Georgina and Paul to dine with me at the Sorostas in Drury Lane, Covent Garden, our meal was interrupted by a lady who wanted Rolf's autograph, and when I tried to tell her I wasn't him, she was sure I WAS, but wanted to remain 'incognito', and so asked me if I would pose with her for a photograph instead. Seeing it was useless to argue with her, I obliged.

By now everybody in the restaurant was sure I was Harris, and when I went to the loo half way through the meal, I found it it packed out with guys all saying, 'We think you're great Rolf,' and I made them all laugh by saying, 'Well, if you think I'm going to show you my diggareedoo, you are all wrong!'

At the end of the evening and we were about to leave, as I passed two tables at which were seated about sixteen men, perhaps football supporters, or a stag party, they all insisted I have photographs taken with them.

Both Georgina and I HAVE met Rolf Harris, but neither of us think I really look like him. Indeed I think he really looks more like ME!


The previous Christmas Georgina and Paul had bought me a lot of artist materials in the hope they could encourage me to start working again, and so as not to disappoint them I did indeed industriously produce a dozen or more new works - portraits, male nudes, and quite a number of abstracts. One particular drawing which I called 'Sextotem', Paul was so smitten with he wanted to buy it. I had priced the drawing at £1,500 but gave it to him as a gift, I had grown so fond of him. Both he and Georgina had come to mean a great deal to me since I had first come to know them, and I knew they had grown quite fond of me too.

For some months they had been saying that I deserved a retrospect exhibition, and secretly they set to work making arrangements to stage one. When they finally told me that I was to have a one-man show opening on 2nd of June for a month at the Schwartz Gallery, I was over the moon with excitement AND gratitude.

The gallery occupied the whole ground floor of the huge warehouse in which Georgina and Paul had their studios, which was also very convenient. I had read in one newspaper that there were now more art galleries in London's East End, than in any other part of the world.

Georgina and Paul worked SO hard to make the exhibition a success. They wanted to show every facet of my working life over the last sixty-odd years, and to show the environment I lived in, they actually recreated my sitting room in one corner of the gallery, which meant transporting the entire contents of my living room from Watton to London. For five weeks at home I had to make do with a set of garden furniture in my sitting room. Neighbours seeing all my furniture etc. being loaded onto a van, thought I was leaving the village!

The London School of Economics, author Rupert Smith, and photographer John McKay, all kindly loaned material from their archives, and two handsome lads, Robbie and Alex, personal friends of Georgina, agreed to man the champagne bar and provide music on an accordion for the preview evening.

I spent most of the opening night chatting to people and signing scores of publicity photos that had been placed on the bar, and posing for photographs with people. When the gallery closed around 10.30pm, Georgina, Paul and I, walked round the corner to a late-night cafe to get a cup of coffee. The place was packed with people who had just come from the gallery, and to my delight and Georgina's amusement, as we walked through the door, everyone stood up and began to clap their hands. It made me feel quite tearful. I felt it was Georgina and Paul who deserved all the applause- for all the weeks of hard work they had put in.

The success of the show can be judged by the reviews it received. The DAILY MIRROR declared 'This is an amazing and unforgettable show.' ATTITUDE magazine said, 'It is a triumph and shows a sense of spirit and gay abandon that we don't much see in these times. We're hoping that the exhibition is taken around the UK and even the world. Everyone should get a chance to see it.' Indeed we did get a request from an interested gallery-owner to take the show to Hollywood, but transporting everything half-way round the world would have proved a problem.

TIME OUT enthused over the show and awarded it four out or five 'stars', which both Georgina and I found highly amusing, as the magazine had only awarded THREE stars to the latest show at the TATE, which included some of Paul's work!

Halfway through the run of my show, I gave a public talk at the gallery, and we were so pleased when Marie Lechner came over from Paris for the day, so that she could hear me speak and also interview me for her newspaper. She had hired a London photographer to take pictures, and when her report was finally published, I found myself sharing the front page of LIBERATION with both the French President Sarkozy and model Naomi Campbell. Three pages of their colour supplement had been devoted to my work, including a whole-page photo of me on the front page of this too. All I needed was a translator to tell me what Marie had said about me!

*View of the SIR GAY exhibition, 2010*

*My 'living room' in the exhibition, 2010*

*Sir Gay exhibition details, 2010*

*Georgina Starr and me, at the premiere of her film THEDA, 2006*

*Paul Noble and me, in his studio, 2010*

*With Amy Lamé at the RVT, 2010*

*With BBC Radio 4 presenter Fy Glover, 2010*

**Libération**

Libération

[EXCENTRIQUES]
«Libération» part
à la rencontre
de personnalités
hors normes.
Aujourd'hui:
Ronald Wright,
un dessinateur
homo-érotique
avant-gardiste.

Par **MARIE LECHNER**
Photos **MICHAEL GRIEVE**

# Bien en chair

Ronald Wright

Q uel est le lien entre la star hollywoodienne Marlene Dietrich, le gangster Roy Gardner, le dandy de la photographie homo-érotique Royale, le danseur étoile Noureïev, les Rolling Stones... Tout cela ne formerait-il pas un certain arthritique ? Toutes ces personnalités ont en commun d'avoir croisé à un moment le destin rocambolesque de Ronald Wright. A 83 ans, le charmant petit monsieur aux lunettes d'écaille et aux cheveux de neige impeccablement coiffés, au langage châtié et aux manières exquises, a vécu plusieurs vies, plus extravagantes les unes que les autres. Tout à son aise parmi la faune jeune et branchée qui s'était retrouvée en mars au Confort moderne à Poitiers pour l'exposition de Georgina Starr, le fringant octogénaire, embaqué et parfumé, papillonnait autour de la young british artist atypique et de son boyfriend Paul Noble, autre grand nom de la scène contemporaine britannique. «Je vous présente mon ami Ronald Wright», dit l'espiègle rousse qui raconte s'être vouée homme alors qu'elle travaillait sur la diva oubliée du muet, Theda Bara. ● ● ●

216

L'artiste dans son salon reconstitué lors de l'exposition «Flesh: the Great Illusion» célébrant sa vie et son œuvre à la Schwartz Gallery de Londres.

*** «Je cherchais quelqu'un pour faire le portrait de la vamp hollywoodienne et une connaissance m'a parlé de Ronaldo, et de ses étonnants dessins.» Gina vit... visite le chaleureux retraité à la Carogne..., dans son petit bung alow de Hart... ford (nord de Londres) où il a passé la plus grande partie de sa vie en compagnie de sa mère. «Je m'amusais avec m... croyable collection de portraits dédicacés tout en me racontant ses rencontres avec les stars des années 50-60 avec passion et force détails! A l'époque je ne connaissais rien d'autre de sa vie.»

Tandis qu'elle se lie d'amitié avec ce singulier vieillard, elle va de surprise en surprise au point de consacrer en juin dernier une exposition baptisée «A la vie et l'œuvre de Ronald Wright» à la Schwartz Gallery à Hackney, quartier en vogue de Londres. L'occasion pour le visiteur éberlué d'un périple à la mise le siècle dessins sur les traces d'un personnage attachant, transgressant l'image lui, confronté aux normes socio politiques de son temps.

## Mourir de honte

Né le 20 avril 1928, dans le comté val... lonné d'East Hertfordshire, Ronald s'énamoure dès sa prime jeunesse des stars du grand écran qu'il fréquente assidûment. Il réalise ses premières esquisses à 14 ans à partir de photos de magazines mais c'est durant sa conscription à Manchester en 1946 que son supérieur lui propose de croquer les vedettes de passage dans la ville en chair et en os. En mari d'une actrice,

Dessins de stars hollywoodiennes par Ronald Wright.

Les nus photographiques de l'artiste à la Schwartz Gallery.

le colonel H.I. Buckmaster avait conservé ses connexions avec le show-biz et voilà le jeune homme tenant dans la loge de Vivien Leigh, «pâle et défraîchie, toujours habillée de noir, avec son chat Mr. John». Face à la légendaire Mae West, venue dans une limousine blanche: «Même quand elle n'était pas en représentation, elle laissait tourner le moteur.» Ronald dessinera aussi quatre portraits de la «fabuleuse Marlene Dietrich».

En feuilletant ses portfolios, Georgina alors découvre que Ronald Wright a mis son coup de crayon au service d'un autre genre de dessin avec le même mérite, devenant entre les 2 mondes du dessin homo-érotique, «après Tom of Finland» d'après ses propres dires. «A la fin des années 50 et 60, Ronald Wright était l'un des plus grands artistes gays en Grande-Bretagne, écrit le magazine International for Men, il officiait dans des revues calteriennes, magazines gays qui ne disaient pas leur nom.

Le jeune Ronald a découvert entre-temps qu'il n'est pas tant attiré par les filles que par leurs copaines. Il s'essaye au sexe entre hommes en partageant le lit de Roy Gardner, l'amant brutal d'une amie de sa sœur – qui deviendra accessoirement une figure de la pègre londonienne inoubliée d'une film des plus grands à alice de coca aine de l'histoire britannique. Ronald a ouvile à l'époque dans une boutique de vêtements pour hommes, où il rencontre Royet son ami lock qui, contrairement au prude de museux, assument pleinement leur homosexualité. Les deux tourbillon s'em... mènent en virée dans les bars

217

Some months earlier, in the spring, Robin Witemore, a young man associated with London Gay Pride marches and the celebrations that follow, had come down to Watton to interview me for a small book he was writing called GROSS INDECENCY. This was to contain twelve accounts of what life was like for gay people in the 1960s. Now, at the end of July, Robin had invited me to attend the big annual gay disco and cabaret at Camden Town Hall, where his booklets were to be given out free of charge to revellers.

It was a great event with hundreds of guys and girls all wearing fashions from the 1960s. I saw Dame Edna Everidge staggering about the dance floor wearing a gorgeous black lace dress that had so many layers of net underskirt, it stood out like a ballerina's. He had the usual elaborate wig, and of course the large gem-studded spectacles, plus high heeled shoes. I must say he DOES have very good legs. Almost tripping over his own feet, he raised his glass of wine to me, and winked an eye.

Bette Bourne (male, despite the name), was also there. He had been to see my show at the Schwartz some weeks earlier. Bette has been well known in gay circles for many years as both an entertainer and a serious actor on both the West End and New York stages. Actually he has a striking resemblance to 'Dame Edna', but when I mentioned this to him, he did not seem very pleased. At the party he had come dressed as Al Capone.

The bubbly and lovely Amy Lamé, a presenter for LBC Radio, was hostess for the stage show, and only a week later I was to meet her again when she was hosting a 1960s Talk Show at the famous RVT (Royal Vauxhall Tavern), London's only real theatre-pub. Paul O'Grady had made his first appearance there.

I was one of four people (three men and one woman), to speak on stage about gay life in London in the 1960s. A bunch of friends had all accompanied me to the RVT, including Georgina. The interviews went well, and we got a good round or applause from the packed audience, several of whom wanted to buy me drinks when I came off stage.

Three weeks later, in August, Georgina and John McKay, were my guests at the RVT again. This time it was an evening of music, song and dance, called 'Cocktails and Performance'. One of the performers, a young woman, walked slowly stark naked through the audience to get to the stage, wearing nothing but a feathered headdress and a pair of red high-heeled shoes. Amy Lamé was again the show's hostess, and seeing me, came across to our table to give me a kiss and say hello.


September 9th saw me flying to Berlin where Georgina's movie THEDA was to be screened at the Delphi cinema as part or the 'Erstes International Caligari Festival'. Georgina and Paul had flown out three days earlier, but I only went for 24 hours. Nevertheless it was amazing how much I managed to pack into that brief visit. I loved Berlin. It was so much greener than I had expected, and so friendly.

Unlike previous screenings of THEDA, instead or using an orchestra to supply the music, Georgina had decided to engage the well-known German singer Sigune von Osten, noted for her most unusual voice range, and for providing her own music on a variety of string instruments, cymbals and temple bells. The general impression was amazing.

Later in the month, September 25th, I gave yet another interview. This time to Fy Glover at Broadcasting House, for her regular Saturday morning show, 'Saturday Live' on BBC's Radio 4.

At the end of October, Paul had a six-month long exhibition starting at the Laing Gallery in Newcastle and I went up for the preview. Georgina was there too of course, and she had her parents from Scarborough with her. I had met them several times before in London. I also met Paul's parents and brother for the first time.

After the preview we all had a meal at a nearby restaurant, then went on to a party at a private house in the city centre. The following day Georgina went home with her parents for a few days rest, and I travelled by train with Paul to London.

Next it was the turn of Liz to put on a show. She had for some months been working on a humorous adult comic called THE FERALS, and now all her friends were attending the launch party at a venue in Shoreditch. As well as the comic book, Liz was also selling a new range of tee-shirts bearing her special 'feral' motifs.

In December Georgina and Paul invited both Liz and myself to dinner at the plush Cecconi's restaurant in Mayfair. We all had a wonderful evening, and it was hoped we would be meeting up again just before Christmas. However the weather turned nasty, and for once we really DID have A White Christmas, which meant we didn't meet again until 2011.

# What Now?

In the New Year 2011 I attended one of Andy's gigs at a music venue called The Bowery in London's New Oxford Street, where with his band he was playing a selection of songs from his latest mini album called 41. Andy writes all his own songs, words and music, and I have become a real fan. I particularly like is earlier CD, 'Are you trying to be lonely?.' Paul Weller also sings on this 4-track CD, and Liz designed the cover.

Unfortunately at the gig I caught a severe cold, which kept me at home for six weeks. Paul had yet another exhibition in March, this time at the Cooper Gallery in Dundee, Scotland, and I felt it too far for me to go in my condition.

In June, both Georgina and Paul had exhibitions in Venice, and while there decided to stay for a short holiday. Also in June, Martin Perry, creative and editorial director of the glossy gay culture magazine OUT THERE, came to visit me in Watton with photographer David Edwards, accompanied by Georgina. I posed for numerous photos, and shots were also taken of my home and artwork. When published at the end of the year, I was thrilled to see that no less than six pages had been devoted to me, and Georgina had written a wonderful article to go with the pictures.

In the summer I held a small garden party at home, and most of my London friends were able to attend. Andy kindly brought me a copy of his latest recording, 'Good soul and good times' to go with my growing collection of his work.

During the summer Liz and Andy had also agreed to look after a most beautiful white fluffy pedigree cat called Barney while his owner was away for a couple of months. Knowing my love of cats (there had been a time when my mother and I owned eight cats of our own, and daily fed thirty-two feral cats who had made their home in a nearby timber yard) I was invited to meet Barney, who was not only gorgeous, but had one green eye, and one blue.

Liz and Andy were so sad when the time came to hand him back to his owner, but as a tribute to him Andy wrote a piece of music called Barney's Theme, and Liz made an animated short-film featuring drawings of Barney, as well as hiring three very attractive young female dancers who did a routine that expressed Barney's feline qualities perfectly. A really delightful little DVD.

October 8th saw Georgina screening THEDA in the theatre on the end of Bournemouth Pier, as part of the town's very first Arts Festival. Sigune von Osten flew over from Germany to sing and provide the musical accompaniment again and the show was an enormous success. THEDA being set in the 1920s, we were amused to see that a number of the audience had turned up in appropriate attire.

Following the screening or the film, everyone moved to the beautiful ballroom and bar next door where they were served a light supper, and we could spend the rest of the evening dancing to music played by two young DJs. I stayed until 1am, dancing, drinking and chatting, then made my way back to my hotel for a good night's sleep.

In November I attended Paul's latest exhibition at the London Gagosian Gallery. It was very impressive, and got wonderful reviews in several of the nation's leading newspapers.

Throughout the summer Georgina had been working on a series of large paintings, she had also been making recordings, and learned to tap-dance! A most versatile young lady. The combined result of all her hard work was revealed in her latest exhibition which was launched at the Pink Summer gallery, Genoa, Italy, on 20th January, 2012. A wonderful start to her New Year. I had hoped to attend the exhibition's launch, but unfortunately at the last moment there was a problem with the travel arrangements and I had to drop out. Later, in March, Georgina was invited to give a screening of THEDA in Stockholm, Sweden. That film certainly does get around, and I am so pleased that I had some small part to play in its creation.

As I write this closing chapter in May, the national newspapers have just announced that Paul is one of the four artists nominated for the prestigious Turner Prize this year. The work of all four artists is to be displayed in London's Tate Britain gallery in October, and the winner will be announced on December 3rd. I am so excited for him.

As for my own activities recently: my little 1976 'art appreciation' book comprising of drawings I did, and photographs I posed for in the 1950s, 1960s, and 70s, has just been republished, and a limited edition of two hundred copies gone on sale.

I have also been working on the republication of my 1990 autobiography, bringing it up to date, and hopefully you are holding a copy of it in your hands at this very moment.

As I approach my 85th year there still remain so many things I still want to do, and this summer Martin Perry is hoping to shoot a documentary film about my life and work.

Is there one thing more than any other that I would like to be remembered for? Yes, the Spiritualist books I have written, and bringing Prince Hafed's knowledge and wisdom to public attention once more. His more recently published book A NEW SET OF VALUES is something this world of ours is badly in need of as humanity faces the greatest crisis in its very existence.

Unless we quickly learn to respect Mother Nature, the animal kingdom, and each other, we have no future. The facts are as simple as that.

I am sorry to end this book on such a sombre note, however I would be failing in my duty as a MESSENGER FOR SPIRIT if I did not point out the dangers mankind is facing.

As Prince Hafed prophesied, a new age is dawning, and like a woman giving birth to new life, this cannot take place without a great deal of suffering taking place in the process.

This is the time for a new AWAKENING, not through any one spiritual leader who will suddenly appear, but by a spark of awareness, enlightenment, call it what you will, that needs to be triggered-off in each and every one of us individually.

The Christ (light) must return through US and IN us, and our attempts to establish a new order, a new way, a NEW SET OF VALUES.

We do not need science and technology in order to make the most astounding discoveries, if we would only function as the Great Creator intended that we should... By using those spiritual gifts and abilities which we all have deep within us, abilities that sadly in the vast majority of people lie dormant and untapped all their earthly lives.

Religious bigotry and fear are born of ignorance, and the more materialistic we become in our outlook, the further we leave behind the simple, lovely, spiritual truths. Truly spiritual people know none of the boundaries which MEN establish, be they religious, racial, or political.

Spiritual knowledge can bring about an awareness of the natural laws which allow one to perceive beyond the limitations our brothers suffer from. Allegiance should not be to a Creed, a Book, a Church, but to the Great Spirit of Life and His eternal natural laws.

The grave does NOT end life, life is deathless. When Jesus said the 'dead' would rise from their graves, he simply meant the SPIRITUALLY dead would rise from their ignorant minds which had so long been closed to truth.

Every single person on this planet is a child of God. We are all brothers and sisters. Only religions divide us through ignorance. We are each responsible for our sins, and God measures each person's worth by the service they give to others.

True spiritual knowledge points the way for individuals to achieve a fuller development of their nature, physically, mentally, as well as spiritually. It brings an awareness of the purpose that our earthly life has in the universal scheme of things, and thus enables us to fulfil ourselves as the natural law intends we should do. Our temporary sojourn here on earth should be a preparation for the greater life which is inevitable for us all.

Just think what man might have accomplished by now, had his psychic faculties not been suppressed by the Church since the days of Jesus. Viewed correctly, the miracles of Jesus and others in the Bible demonstrate a perfect manipulation of the natural laws of the universe. They were not supernatural - but SUPERNORMAL.

222

This is not the end!

For more visual material, interviews and news please visit:

**www.ronaldwright.co.uk**

Originally published in 1976, this "fanzine" looking at the world of Physique
Magazines, consisting of 48 pages (including a special fold-out poster) of many of
Ronald Wright's original drawings and photographs of him with Hollywood stars,
has been reprinted as a limited edition and is now available from:

**www.ronaldwright.co.uk**

Made in the USA
Charleston, SC
25 November 2013